MW00570565

WITHDRAWN
From Toronto Public Library

MONEY TO BURN

TRUDEAU, MULRONEY, AND THE BANKRUPTCY OF CANADA

D'ARCY JENISH

Copyright © 1996 by D'Arcy Jenish

All rights reserved. No part of this publication may be reproduced or transmitted in any form or by any means, electronic or mechanical, including photocopying, recording, or any information storage and retrieval system, without permission in writing from the publisher.

Published in 1996 by
Stoddart Publishing Co. Limited
34 Lesmill Road
Toronto, Canada
M3B 2T6
Tel. (416) 445-3333
Fax (416) 445-5967

Stoddart Books are available for bulk purchase for sales promotions, premiums, fundraising, and seminars. For details, contact the Special Sales Department at the above address.

Canadian Cataloguing in Publication Data

Jenish, D'Arcy, 1952–
Money to burn: Trudeau, Mulroney,
and the bankruptcy of Canada

Includes index.
ISBN 0-7737-2942-9

1. Debts, Public – Canada. 2. Deficit financing – Canada.
3. Government spending policy – Canada. 4. Fiscal policy – Canada.
I. Title.

HJ8033.C3J45 1996   336.3'4'0971   C95-933294-4

Credits: pages 52–53, the excerpt from *How Ottawa Spends 1993–94*
(ISBN 0-88629-201-8) is reprinted with permission of the publisher,
Carleton University Press, on behalf of the authors, James Rice and Michael Prince;
page 162, from *Shooting the Hippo* by Linda McQuaig. Copyright © Linda McQuaig,
1995. Reprinted by permission of Penguin Books Canada Limited; pages 46–47,
from *The Northern Magus* by Richard Gwyn. Used by permission of the
Canadian Publishers, McClelland & Stewart, Toronto; page 53, from *The
Microphone Wars* by Knowlton Nash. Used by permission of the Canadian Publishers,
McClelland & Stewart, Toronto; page 57, from *Where I Stand* by Brian Mulroney.
Used by permission of the Canadian Publishers, McClelland & Stewart, Toronto.
Stoddart Publishing will gladly receive information that will help rectify any
inadvertent errors or omissions in subsequent editions.

Cover Design: Bill Douglas at The Bang
Text Design: Tannice Goddard
Cover Photo: Eric Pearle

Printed and bound in Canada

Contents

Acknowledgements   *v*

1 The Storm at Our Door   *1*

2 A Rose and a Worm   *26*

3 The Trouble with Brian   *51*

4 Chrétien's Crafty Liberals   *75*

5 Who Is Riding the Gravy Train?   *99*

6 Who Is Pulling the Strings?   *123*

7 Squirming on the Left   *146*

8 The Shenanigans in Ontario   *171*

9 Ralph's Revolution   *195*

10 If We Fail   *219*

Epilogue: Selling Sacrifice   *240*

Index   *245*

Acknowledgements

Today, we have a full-blown fiscal crisis on our hands, with federal deficits exceeding $30 billion annually, the debt surging toward $600 billion, and interest charges of $40 billion a year. Those are huge numbers, and so is the story behind them. This book could not have been written without guidance and assistance from many individuals. I am indebted to John Turner, Gordon Osbaldeston, Charles McMillan, David Slater, and Gordon Robertson for their invaluable insights. I would like to thank Donald Savoie, Jeff Moore, Robin Richardson, and Tom Courchene, all of whom assisted me at various points. I will always be grateful to the following friends and associates for their many pertinent observations and suggestions: Steve Hopkins, Geoff Ellwand, Ric Dolphin, Tom Fennel, Fred Grady, and my brother Greg.

I owe a special thanks to Jack Stoddart for giving me the opportunity to pursue this project and to Don Bastian, whose enthusiasm and support ensured that a rough proposal became a finished manuscript. I would like to thank my children, Jesse, Isabel, and Patrick, for their patience and understanding. Finally, I would like to express my deep appreciation for my wife, Helene, who supported me in countless ways from start to finish.

O Rose, thou art sick.
The invisible worm
That flies in the night,
In the howling storm,

Has found out thy bed
Of crimson joy,
And his dark secret love
Does thy life destroy.

— WILLIAM BLAKE,
"The Sick Rose"

I

THE STORM
AT OUR DOOR

We are living in a period of high anxiety and diminished expectations. An era of open borders and global competition, dwindling resources and economic uncertainty. A time of irony and contradiction. We tame inflation, but interest rates take off, and the dollar darts up and down like mercury. The economy rebounds, exports swell, and profits soar. But most people are merely hanging in rather than getting ahead. This is the jobless recovery, a boom in which the last recession is still fresh in the memory and the next one may be just around the corner. Change is relentless, unpredictable, and globally interconnected. Money traders dump the Canadian dollar in New York and Tokyo, and mortgages cost more in Moose Jaw and Medicine Hat. A corporate merger in London puts executives on the street in Toronto. A manufacturer restructures in Ohio and a plant closes in Ontario.

We have become a nation of skeptics. We suffer from a glut of information and a dearth of wisdom. The Internet is here, the information highway is close, the 500-channel universe looms. We demand speed, efficiency, convenience. We are going fast, but where are we going? Progress has become frightening, technology baffling. What is a chip? How much is a megabyte? We question everything: family, the schools, the professions, our institutions, our leaders. Doubt is in, belief is out.

Our political loyalties are as fickle as the weather. We hand our leaders big majorities and crushing defeats. Our faith in the usefulness and efficacy of government is slipping. But how could it be otherwise? Government costs more but governments at all levels deliver less. Health care is free but services are rationed. Beds close, wards close, doctors go south. We wait in Emergency. We line up for surgery. We recover at home. If you can't leave hospital on your feet, you leave in a wheelchair. Governments give today and take tomorrow. Child tax benefit cheques still arrive in the mail monthly, but Ottawa claws back most of the money at income-tax time.

The best of intentions produce the worst of results. Unemployment insurance creates unemployment. Welfare begets dependency. The social safety net becomes a trap.

Everywhere we look the state is in retreat. Post offices close. Passenger trains fade away. Tuition fees rise and user fees go up. Class sizes grow. Teachers can't find jobs. Civil servants, long coddled and tenured, face layoffs and salary freezes.

And the citizen pays. Higher income taxes. Higher payroll taxes. Higher UI premiums. Higher Canada Pension Plan premiums. A federal sales tax. Provincial sales taxes. Property tax. Gasoline tax. Alcohol tax. Tobacco tax. Taxes on telephone calls, auto insurance, cable television. A tax when selling the family home. The average Canadian must work until about mid-July each year before earning enough to cover the total annual tax bill, according to the Fraser Institute, a Vancouver-based think tank. The reality is that there is no such thing as after-tax in Canada anymore. We start paying taxes when we wake up New Year's Day and we are still paying when we go to bed, 365 days later, on New Year's Eve.

We grumble about less service and higher taxes. Anti-tax rallies draw big crowds. The underground economy flourishes. People scurry to avoid the hand of government. There is talk of the decline and deterioration of public programs and institutions. We fear that the future will bring more of the same: high unemployment, fewer services, and less disposable income. We sense that our national life is threatened.

The unity of the country is in jeopardy. The economy is sliding rather than advancing. And even as we wrestle with these political and economic problems, we must also come to terms with a grave fiscal crisis. What threatens the health of the country today, besides Quebec's separatists and persistently high unemployment, is public-sector debt.

The build-up of that debt will stand alongside official bilingualism, the Charter of Rights and Freedoms, the Canada-U.S. Free Trade Agreement, and the rise of Quebec separatism as one of the defining political developments of the last quarter of the twentieth century. Like these landmarks, the debt will shape the country we pass on to our children. It will cast a long shadow forward well into the twenty-first century. And its impact is evident all around us today. Debt is hobbling our governments and handcuffing our politicians. Interest payments are cannibalizing our budgets federally and provincially. Debt is the scourge of our day, just as inflation, depression, and war were the curses of former governments and previous generations of Canadians.

The debt of the federal government, accumulated almost entirely since the mid-1970s due to overspending and frequently reckless tax policies, is approaching $600 billion and growing steadily. Throw in the $200 billion or so that the provinces owe, and Canada is $800 billion in debt. But our liabilities do not end there. The Fraser Institute contends that the country's total government debt is closer to $2 trillion when we consider the unfunded commitments made under the Canada and Quebec Pension Plans, the unfunded obligations of provincial worker compensation boards, as well as the debts of hospitals and local governments. The problem with all these figures is that they are essentially meaningless to us. We have no points of reference for judging numbers of that magnitude, no way to grasp their scale and proportion. A debt of $2 trillion is certainly worse than a debt of $800 billion, but how much worse? We may as well be looking at the night sky and trying to comprehend how many stars are out there.

Somebody is always trying to bring the issue down to a level that makes sense. And occasionally they succeed. Here's how Edward Newell, chief executive officer of Calgary-based NOVA Corporation, put it in a speech to the Investment Dealers Association of Canada in Toronto in September 1994: "When my father retired in 1964, our national debt was about $17 billion. Given our population at the time, that represented about $900 per Canadian. Of course, we had to pay interest on that debt. The cost of that interest — spread among Canadians — was less than $40 per person per year. Since then, however, government debt has grown alarmingly. When my daughter presented us with our first grandchild in 1982, his share of the combined federal and provincial debt was about $6,400. Today, at the ripe old age of 12, my grandson's share of the total government debt has skyrocketed to over $26,000. At the turn of the century, my grandson's generation will be leaving high school. By then, per capita debt will likely be more than $30,000."

Size is merely one dimension of the problem. The rate at which the debt is growing is equally disturbing, a point graphically illustrated in Finance Minister Paul Martin's economic and fiscal update of October 1994. "The debt statistics are beyond real comprehension and have probably lost their power to shock," the document says. "A figure more at human scale is that interest on the federal debt is now accumulating at $85,000 a minute, 24 hours a day." Now, most people can relate to a sum like $85,000. That's two good annual salaries, or one modest three-bedroom bungalow in a small town or medium-sized city. It is the rate that leaves the mind reeling. Eighty-five thousand dollars a minute means that the country's debt meter is running faster than the speed of sound but not quite as fast as the speed of light.

It means that interest on the federal debt is growing by $5.1 million an hour, or $122 million a day. Common sense suggests that this is an undesirable, perhaps dangerous, state of affairs. Some would say that it is a symptom of the vicious circle of debt, a terrible predicament created by twenty years of excess. In the mid-1970s, the annual federal deficit began to grow and our national debt began to climb. Like cancerous cells in the human body, the deficit and debt expanded quickly, without causing any discernible damage or raising any alarm among the populace. Each deficit was added to the debt, and a bigger debt one year meant the government was paying more interest the next. The growth in interest charges led to larger deficits, more borrowing, and more debt. When the three components of the problem — the deficit, the debt, and the interest payments — began feeding each other, the vicious circle was complete.

In the early 1980s, our deficits exploded due to a deep recession. By the end of that decade, we had, through our propensity for overspending, jeopardized the integrity of the country's finances. The deficit-debt-interest circle had achieved enough momentum to become a genuine menace to our collective well-being. And as in the case of cancer, by the time the problem became apparent, almost any solution resembled radical and painful intervention, the political equivalent of chemotherapy. Future historians will no doubt be perplexed by this crisis. They will be astounded when they realize that an entire generation of Canadians did nothing to stop the problem until it was almost too late. We can almost anticipate their incredulity as they ask, how on earth did this happen?

After all, as most Canadian historians know, Canada has always been an importer of capital. Borrowing money was a fact of life in a huge country that was resource-rich but sparsely populated. We lacked the local markets and domestic savings that could generate the wealth required to develop and exploit our resources. So our entrepreneurs, and sometimes our governments, borrowed from abroad, largely in London and New York, and the money was invested in canals and railways, mills and mines, and numerous other productive assets that increased the wealth and enhanced the well-being of the country. Over the past twenty-five years, however, we have witnessed a historic change in our borrowing patterns. Governments, rather than the private sector, have become the major consumers of capital. And they have used the money to finance consumption — initially programs and services but more recently interest payments — rather than putting the money into wealth-producing assets or infrastructure.

In this respect, Canada has behaved like most other Western industrialized nations. Government deficits, debts, and interest payments have risen in most European countries, as well as in the United States, Australia, and New Zealand. But where most dug a hole, we tumbled into a chasm. Canada has achieved the dubious distinction of becoming one of the most indebted countries in the developed world. Interest payments on the national debt are now the largest single item in the federal budget, consuming about one-third of all federal revenues. Coming out of the recession of the early 1990s, we had the second highest deficit in relation to gross domestic product (GDP) among the G-7 nations. Only Italy was worse. Similarly, our combined federal-provincial debt was approaching 100 percent of GDP, second only to Italy's. Our total public-sector spending stood at slightly over 50 percent of GDP, whereas the G-7 average was around 43 percent and in the U.S. it was about 39 percent.

On one crucial measure of fiscal weakness, foreign indebtedness, we are in a class of our own. At the end of 1993, we owed foreign lenders $313 billion, a figure equivalent to 44 percent of our GDP, while Italy was second among G-7 countries at 12 percent. In his fiscal and economic update of October 1994, Martin noted that Ottawa and the provinces have had to borrow abroad because the supply of savings in the country is not large enough to meet the financial requirements of both business and government: "Canadian savings chronically fall short of the amount needed to finance domestic investment and annual government deficits. In 1993, for example, Canada's private savings, by households and businesses, totalled $131 billion, enough to fund total private investment of $109 billion, with about $22 billion to spare. But the borrowing requirements arising from federal and provincial deficits were $50 billion. This was more than the remaining domestic savings could cover. So the difference of $28 billion had to be borrowed abroad."

The direct cost of foreign borrowing is easy to calculate but hard to swallow. We are sending over $30 billion out of the country every year to cover the cost of our borrowing. The indirect costs cannot be calculated with any precision. But they are steep and daunting. We are forced to offer higher interest rates on our government bonds to keep the lenders in New York and Tokyo and London onside. This makes money more costly at home. We all pay more for mortgage money, car loans, and financing for business ventures. And the most serious consequence is this: We have thrown away our economic sovereignty because we now depend upon the patience and goodwill of foreign lenders to finance the operations of our governments.

The numbers reveal everything we need to know about the dimensions of the problem and almost nothing about the nature of the problem. They are merely the end result of thousands of decisions made and actions taken throughout the course of a given fiscal year by everyone from politicians to civil servants to consumers. They do not tell us how we got into such a mess, or how we can get out. We can only arrive at a deeper understanding of Canada's fiscal crisis by examining ourselves and questioning our political attitudes, values, and practices. We should be asking ourselves some hard questions. Do we demand too much of government? Do we rely too heavily on government? What is the proper role of government? Where do the obligations of the state end and the duties of the citizen begin?

We should also scrutinize our leaders. Those who achieve high office are entrusted with many responsibilities. Jean Chrétien has said that "The first responsibility of the Prime Minister of Canada is to ensure the unity of the country." And he is correct. Beyond that, nothing a prime minister does is more fundamental or vital to the interests of his constituents than the management of the nation's finances. Curiously, this aspect of our leaders' performances has often been overlooked altogether. This is particularly true in the case of Pierre Trudeau. Historians, biographers, and other commentators have repeatedly concentrated on his achievements such as the introduction of official bilingualism, the creation of the Charter of Rights and Freedoms, his victories over Quebec separatists, and his battles with the premiers. We can anticipate that the histories and commentaries on Brian Mulroney may eventually focus on free trade, the failed constitutional accords, and the imposition of the goods and services tax, once our preoccupation with the scandals and the man's many perceived shortcomings begins to fade.

But given the magnitude of the country's fiscal mess, our interests have been misdirected. The deficit-debt crisis is a story of failure at the highest level of our political system. And the plot is as simple as this: Pierre Trudeau lit a fire; Brian Mulroney wouldn't put it out; so the problem has landed on Jean Chrétien's desk.

Canada's fiscal crisis also raises deep and perplexing questions about the ability of our elected representatives to control and manage contemporary governments. For half a century, our governments have been in an expansionary mood and, all too often, parliamentarians were merely along for the ride. For a civil servant, the surest way to climb the ladder and advance professionally was to build an empire. Year after year, bureaucrats recommended new programs, bigger staffs, and increased budgets, and cabinet ministers almost always approved. Ministers were wont to fall in love with their departments, regardless of how brief their tenures were. Our governments came to resemble freight trains without brakes, and legislatures did nothing to stop them. Government backbenchers, opposition members, and legislative committees had neither the time nor the resources to examine spending estimates. And even if they did scrutinize them, they usually lacked the authority to alter or reject them.

Despite this powerful institutional bias toward growth and spending, our leaders must ultimately be held responsible for Canada's fiscal crisis, and judged accordingly. Trudeau's many achievements and triumphs notwithstanding, he was a careless and profligate politician who mismanaged Canada's finances and put us on the road to bankruptcy. And despite his reputation as a radical dismantler of all that we hold dear in this country, Mulroney was a timid leader who set modest deficit-reduction goals and consistently failed to meet them.

The Conservative prime minister and his government ignited a raucous public debate over the impact of government deficits and debt. Unfortunately for the average voter, the debate often resembled high-speed table tennis. Arguments and counterarguments were batted back and forth on the floor of the House of Commons, in the daily scrums following Question Period, in television panel discussions, and on the editorial pages of the country's newspapers. Facts and figures, rhetoric and insults, flew to and fro fast enough to cause motion sickness.

Nobody won these debates and nobody lost, because no one ever conceded defeat. The objective was simply to take shots, to unleash verbal spikes, to score points. Brand your opponents as extremists. Paint them as uncaring, uncompassionate friends of the rich, or reckless free spenders, depending on your perspective. We were not muddling toward a consensus. Instead, the country sank further and further into a financial quagmire with each passing day, and the real loser was the average taxpayer.

The conflict was invariably portrayed as left against right. This was done by politicians for partisan purposes, by special interest groups motivated by self-interest, and by the media to simplify the story. But this characterization was both foolish and misleading. As our debts and interest payments skyrocketed and our public finances visibly and substantively deteriorated, the issue transcended political labels and the left-right dynamic of the public debate. Debt is now driving our governments and shaping our nation.

In the mid-1990s, every senior government in Canada, whether left, centre, or right, whether New Democrat, Liberal, or Conservative, has been forced to deal with the problem. But leadership has come from the eight smaller provinces. As recently as fiscal 1993–94, their collective deficits surpassed the $4-billion mark, and all eight wound up in the red. Twelve months later, they had cut their combined shortfall to about $800 million, and their budgets for 1995–96 projected a total deficit of $400 million. During that two-year period, seven of the eight provinces, Prince Edward Island, New Brunswick, and Newfoundland, as well as all four Western provinces, have produced balanced budgets or projected small surpluses. Meanwhile, Nova Scotia's Liberal government has declared that it intends to eliminate its deficit by 1997–98.

These developments, while encouraging, were no cause for celebration or complacency. For one thing, Ontario and Quebec, which account for about two-thirds of provincial spending, were several years behind their smaller counterparts. They were expected to ring up combined deficits in the neighbourhood of $13 billion in fiscal 1995–96. With the election of Mike Harris's Conservatives in June 1995, Ontario finally had a government that was committed to eliminating its deficit. Unfortunately, under the leadership of Jacques Parizeau, the Parti Québécois spent the first year of its mandate zealously pursuing its separatist agenda at the expense of dealing with the province's deteriorating finances.

Nevertheless, public-sector debt has done something that few problems have ever done in this large, diverse, and often fractious country. It has created ideological gridlock. And that in turn has caused considerable dismay among those who cling to left-wing, social democratic principles. In a column that appeared in the *Globe and Mail* in the spring of 1994, writer Rick Salutin commented, with obvious exasperation, on this phenomenon. "It no longer seems to matter what Bob Rae, John Savage or Jean Chrétien say they'll do before they're elected," he wrote. "Once in office, they turn to the same policies as Brian Mulroney had. For that matter, they more and more often say the same things too. In this situation, why vote?" Salutin barely mentioned the words deficit or debt. Yet he had captured in a nutshell the tyrannical quality of our debt problem.

The dead weight of too much debt has even brought the Chrétien Liberals down to earth, although they were belated and reluctant converts to the cause of fiscal realism. They romped through the October 1993 election campaign promising to create jobs, jobs, and more jobs, and as a government they did create short-term employment for several thousand Canadians through their $6-billion infrastructure program. A key plank in the Liberal platform, the program was a classic case of good politics and bad economics. Ottawa, the provinces, and hundreds of municipalities borrowed money and spent it on high-priced frivolities like enclosed bocce courts at an Italian community centre in Toronto and renovations to the Calgary Saddledome. The program led to a flurry of press releases, photo opportunities, and cheque presentations rather than the creation of new wealth or real jobs. It and other prime ministerial initiatives, like the trade mission to China, allowed Chrétien to keep banging the drums about jobs and growth while his ministers concentrated on ratcheting down the deficit.

In the fall of 1994, after a year of internal study, review, and debate, the Liberals released four major discussion papers, all slugged Agenda: Jobs and Growth. First there was then Human

Resources Minister Lloyd Axworthy's green paper entitled "Improving Social Security in Canada." Next, Finance Minister Martin released a purple paper called "A New Framework for Economic Policy" and a grey paper entitled "Creating a Healthy Fiscal Climate." Finally, Industry Minister John Manley unveiled an orange paper bearing the title "Building a More Innovative Economy." Each of these documents opened with the same remark from a speech the prime minister delivered to the Quebec City Chamber of Commerce in September that year. "A strong economy is the essence of a strong society," Chrétien had said. "My government will focus on a jobs and growth agenda."

But for all the bold talk about building, creating, and improving, the Liberals were essentially stuck with the job of attacking the deficit. In their first budget, introduced in February 1994, they tried to take a balanced approach that emphasized job creation, social policy reform, and deficit reduction, in that order. More importantly, that budget left the status quo intact by allowing for marginal increases in program spending in each of the following two years. However, rising interest rates and growing international pressure for change demolished the deficit-cutting plan in the 1994 budget. The same forces also killed any illusions that Liberal cabinet ministers may have had about being able to pursue their own agenda on their own terms. The result of this awakening was Martin's 1995 budget, a political watershed that inflicted the first actual cuts to program spending and posed the first real challenge to the status quo in half a century.

The Liberals had arrived in office with their celebrated campaign Red Book, formally entitled *Creating Opportunity*, which contained plans to carry out moderate reforms of the government and the economy. It dealt with the deficit but scarcely mentioned the grim business of cutting government services, programs, and benefits. At the time, however, the country was perilously close to a financial meltdown. Over the past twenty years, we had spent too much, taxed too much, and borrowed too much. We hit the spending wall under Trudeau, meaning that subsequent governments could not contemplate major new social programs. We hit the tax wall under Mulroney, meaning that the public resents new or increased levies imposed by federal, provincial, or municipal politicians. We have not hit the borrowing wall yet because domestic and foreign lenders continue to buy our federal bonds, which keeps our national government afloat.

However, the fear of hitting that wall haunts the Chrétien administration, shapes its thinking, colours its planning. Hitting the wall would be a calamity for the country and a fatal blow for the government. Here is how a senior Liberal put it to *Toronto Star* columnist Richard Gwyn during a conversation in the summer of 1994: "There's only one way we can lose the next election or the Quebec referendum. That's if a financial crisis happens. So count on us to do enough about the deficit to prevent a financial crisis." Liberals are gambling that cutting the deficit to $25 billion, or 3 percent of GDP, as they promised to do during the 1993 election campaign, will be enough to keep the lenders in line and avoid the wall. They intend to reach that goal by March 31, 1997, the end of the 1996–97 fiscal year, and just in time for the next election. Meeting that target has become the central objective of this government.

For many Liberals, this is a politically necessary but distasteful task. Their party and their leaders, starting with Mackenzie King in the 1940s and concluding with Trudeau in the 1970s, created Canada's social safety net. They were the architects of the era of universal entitlements. They conceived, designed, and built some of the most comprehensive and progressive social security programs in the world. The Canadian welfare state was a response to the hardship and deprivation of the Great Depression and World War Two. It ended the age of laissez-faire capitalism that had guided our governments in the last half of the nineteenth century and first half of the twentieth century. The Liberals instilled in our culture the notion that the wealth of the nation should be shared equitably.

They changed our way of thinking about poverty, unemployment, and the personal misfortune of others. They made compassion one of our core political values. They enlarged the role of the state in the economy, raised our expectations of government, and redrew the line between the obligations of the state and the responsibilities of the citizen.

—◄○►—

By almost any measure, the challenges facing the Liberals and the country today are equal to or greater than those of the immediate post-war era when the welfare state was being erected. We have entered an era of "zero-sum politics," according to University of Toronto political scientist and law professor Richard Simeon. "The age-old question — who gets what — becomes the modern question, who loses what," as Simeon put it in a 1994 Benefactors Lecture sponsored by the C. D. Howe Institute. "The politics of restraint and restructuring is very different from the politics of growth."

For one thing, our economy and our society are utterly dependent upon borrowed money. We are hooked, to put it succinctly. In the early 1990s, our federal and provincial governments collectively were running annual deficits approaching or exceeding $60 billion, and borrowing to cover the shortfalls. And what they borrowed they spent, on everything from interest on past debt to major social programs like health care to cultural institutions like the CBC and right down to tiny grants of a few hundred or a few thousand dollars to community groups.

The extent to which public money permeates our economy and shapes our society can become apparent in unusual ways and in unlikely places. Toronto author and writer Bronwyn Drainie discovered this while touring the country in the fall of 1994 to promote her book *My Jerusalem: Secular Adventures in the Holy City,* and she wrote a couple of perceptive columns about it in the *Globe and Mail.* On one occasion, a seniors group in Etobicoke, Ontario, asked her to speak at a world events forum and paid her a $125 honorarium. "I thought my money was coming from the $2 they were collecting at the door," Drainie wrote. "But it turned out they were being funded by a grant from Health and Welfare Canada. At times like these, I realize what a sticky web the whole structure of public funding for culture is in this country."

During a stop in Thunder Bay, she was struck by the amenities — a university, a community college, public libraries, a symphony orchestra, an art gallery, a professional theatre company, and a crafts council — that give this small, isolated city on the north shore of Lake Superior an unexpected sophistication. "What you also realize, though, as you marvel at these cultural riches in such an improbable setting, is that they have mostly come into being because of public funding at the national, provincial and local levels, and that communities like Thunder Bay are very hard hit when those funds start to dry up," she wrote. "As Thunder Bay goes, so go many small to medium-sized Canadian cities, all struggling to keep up the quality of life of their citizens while staggering under enormous present and future debt loads."

Drainie eloquently presented the upside of government largesse: social, educational, and cultural organizations that enhance our communities. At the other end of the spectrum, three backbench MPs, John Bryden, George Baker, and Randy White, exposed flagrant abuses of federal spending programs. Bryden, a Liberal who represents a Hamilton, Ontario, riding, studied forty charitable and nonprofit organizations which are among the thousands that receive grants and financial contributions from the federal government totalling an estimated $7 billion annually. He compiled his findings in a report entitled simply "Special Interest Group Funding," which he released in November 1994.

"The practice of using general tax revenues to finance groups with particular axes to grind has created a multi-billion dollar system of bureaucratic patronage that operates with little accountability to ministers, members of parliament, the media or to taxpayers," he concluded. "It has created a government-dependent industry where misrepresentation is a common business practice, where semantics and twisted definitions enable the spirit of laws to be ignored, where individuals award themselves huge salaries, hire professional lobbyists to get more money, and attack critics with name-calling and noisy demonstrations. It is an industry of the one-room office — a desk, a telephone, and some letterhead — that taps into government money year after year."

One striking case, in which some of the problems surfaced, involved the Canadian Labour Congress (CLC) and its president, Bob White, according to Bryden. He said that in the fiscal year commencing April 1, 1994, the CLC received a grant of $2.83 million from the Department of Human Resources Development. The size of the grant was determined on a per capita basis: $1.21 for each of the 2.3 million people who belong to unions affiliated with the CLC. Bryden charged that White supplied the minister, Lloyd Axworthy, with the 2.3 million membership figure in a letter written in late January, 1994. But the CLC's annual report for the year ending December 31, 1994, states that the membership of affiliated unions was only 1.9 million. "This is a serious discrepancy," Bryden noted, "for if the payout were based on this number (1.9 million) instead of the one supplied by Mr. White, it would only be $2.34 million, a difference of $482,992."

Bryden also found organizations that routinely indulged in what might be called double-dipping — obtaining more than one grant a year by applying to different departments. Vancouver-based MediaWatch, which monitors the portrayal of women and minorities in newspapers and magazines, on television, and in other modes of communication, received Secretary of State grants ranging from $170,000 to $214,000 annually over a nine-year period ending in 1993–94. The organization collected smaller grants annually ranging from $37,400 to $75,600 from the former Department of Employment and Immigration. "This situation raises questions about the accountability of the grant-giving bureaucracy," Bryden concluded. "A ministry printout of funding to a particular group does not always indicate that the group is receiving funding from another ministry. Thus unless one is prepared to query every relevant ministry, multiple funding of a group may escape unnoticed during a routine check."

Along with Bryden's stories of special interest featherbedding and double-dipping, there were George Baker's revelations about millionaires on pogey. Baker, a Newfoundland Liberal, scrutinized previously unpublished Revenue Canada statistics on the 2,340 Canadians who reported income of over $1 million in 1992. He discovered that fourteen of these people, with incomes averaging $1.6 million, had collected unemployment insurance that year. Another 500 had received old age security, and were able to keep it all because their net incomes were less than $55,000, and several hundred members of this select group had paid no income tax. Baker was attempting to embarrass his caucus colleague, Finance Minister Martin, and force him to eliminate inequities in the tax system as a means of reducing the deficit.

And B.C. Reformer Randy White was on a similar mission to embarrass the government into action. His chosen target was the Atlantic Canada Opportunities Agency (ACOA), a creation of the Mulroney Tories which distributes about $375 million a year in regional development grants. On the day that Government Services Minister David Dingwall announced plans to convert ACOA grants to repayable loans, White released a list of very questionable handouts from the 1992–93 fiscal year. A Nova Scotia company called Canadian Hybrid Farms had received almost $100,000 to develop genetically altered hamsters. A local industrial commission on Prince Edward Island got $31,000 for its I Want To Be A Millionaire Program. Another $80,000 went to Acadia University for a program to introduce students to the fundamentals of entrepreneurship. But for White, the epitome of folly was the $22,300 awarded to the University of Moncton for "a study to develop blueberry jelly."

As the three backbenchers independently demonstrated, many

government programs are wasteful, frivolous, or unnecessary. But, it is equally true, as Drainie noted, that government spending has raised our standard of living and improved the quality of our lives. The problem is that our governments have committed us, often indiscriminately, to worthy and unworthy endeavours, and artificially inflated both through the use of borrowed money. Had we been living within our means for the past twenty years, we would have had far fewer universities, community colleges, public libraries, art galleries, symphony orchestras, theatre companies, and craft councils sprinkled across the country. We would have supported fewer special interest groups. We would have cut off the millionaires on pogey. And we would have spent much less on regional development.

But we have not been living within our means. We have borrowed over half a trillion dollars. In the early 1990s, our provincial and federal governments were overspending by about $60 billion a year, which represented 8 to 10 percent of the economy. That portion of our economy is not real. It is artificial because it is based on other people's money rather than income earned through legitimate economic output. Take the borrowed dollars out of our economy, as we must do, and the results are stark but simple: we must start making some real choices about which programs survive and which die. And some of those choices inevitably will affect our quality of life. So it should come as no surprise that many federal Liberals have been reluctant to cut spending.

But at the same time that the sorry state of our national finances threatens our collective well-being, cash-strapped governments are facing formidable new challenges due to international trends such as the globalization of trade and commerce, along with the rise of the new information technologies. Simeon captured the impact of these forces on Canada in his Benefactors Lecture: "On the one hand is the pressure to enhance international competitiveness and promote restructuring, which means policies to free up labor markets, reduce labor costs, rein in the size of government [and] trim the costs of the welfare state. On the other hand, the restructuring caused by the information economy, new technologies and globalization is inherently disruptive and destabilizing, increasing the vulnerability and insecurity of workers, and creating new winners and losers. Thus, governments are increasingly called on to manage change-induced social tensions, to mitigate increasing inequalities, and to compensate those left behind. Ironically, the global capitalist system throws new burdens onto governments, and limits their ability to respond to them."

Under these circumstances, the government that simply does enough to avoid a fiscal crisis is not doing enough. We need the same kind of far-reaching and fundamental reforms that the Liberals introduced in the post-war era. We need leadership that can put forward bold new ideas and convince the public to embrace them. We need a prime minister who aspires to be an architect rather than a carpenter, a leader who can unite a highly diverse and increasingly divided society. In the absence of a powerful and compelling voice from the top, there is a good chance that any reforms, no matter how well designed or well intentioned, will be impaled on the fixed positions of the myriad special interests who never cease to assert their rights, defend their positions, and demand their due from the public purse. In his C. D. Howe paper, Simeon describes contemporary Canada as "a society well designed to express differences and conflict, less well designed to build consensus or to make effective compromises among competing groups."

In most of the major debates of the past decade, whether it was free trade, privatization, deregulation, or downsizing of government, these competing groups have pushed what Simeon calls the agendas of social justice and economic success. And, they have often behaved like two hostile solitudes, shouting at each other from opposite sides of an ideological breach as broad as the Gulf of St. Lawrence. "On the one hand are those who talk tough about

deficit reduction, economic restructuring and competitiveness,"
Simeon says. "On the other hand are those who focus on equality
and social justice. The proponents of one see the fundamental
responsibility of the state as ensuring that the economy and society
adapt to the inexorable logic of global capitalism, and they judge
governments in terms of their ability to make the necessary tough
decisions and impose losses on the groups that will be affected. The
advocates of the other see the primary role of the state as protecting and shielding its citizens from these very pressures while
responding to the new needs and demands arising from a changing
society. They evaluate governments in terms of their success in
preserving and enhancing the welfare state."

The advocates of social justice and the proponents of economic
success clearly and forcefully argued their cases during two sets of
public hearings leading up to the February 1995 budget. These
hearings, before the Commons human resources and the Commons
finance committees, were a microcosm of the debate that alternately has simmered and raged for the past decade over the role of
government and the future of Canada's social programs. The MPs
on the committees presided over parallel processes. They never
crossed paths, and rarely was there ever a meeting of minds among
the competing groups that testified before the committees. The
adversaries in this debate did what they have grown accustomed to
doing: they retreated to the comfort and safety of their fixed positions. All the fissures and fractures in our diverse and divided
society became evident. The public was frequently treated to
unwholesome displays of acrimony, animosity, and self-interest
rather than the wisdom, generosity, and breadth of vision necessary
for effective compromises or productive consensus.

The human resources committee travelled to twenty-two cities
across the country, hearing from close to 650 organizations in
response to Axworthy's proposed social policy reforms. Many
articulate voices and bright minds — leaders of the labour movement, the women's movement, the arts community, social justice

organizations, and senior citizens' groups — argued that our deficits and debts remain manageable. For many of them, Canada's fiscal crisis exists largely in the minds of neurotic conservatives and greedy businessmen. The government, they believe, can eliminate the deficit in three easy steps: close the tax loopholes that benefit the rich; impose effective rates of taxation on the big corporations; and order the Bank of Canada to lower interest rates. Along with these arguments, most of them demanded that the country's social programs be preserved or improved. They offered few, if any, creative solutions to the country's problems.

Theirs were the voices of reaction, and the rigidity of their positions was evident in the headlines above newspaper stories about the hearings. Indeed, the headlines served as a simple but effective barometer for tracking the tone and tenor of the debate. Advocates for poor assail social reforms, said one. Proposed UI reforms condemned, said another. Use profits to battle debts, unions urge. Big Quebec unions oppose proposed social program cuts. Women challenge Axworthy. Axworthy deaf to views on social safety net, Bob White says. Seniors demand Ottawa end cuts. Cost cuts go too deep, U of T head says. Acrimony rises on all sides over social reforms. Mob crashes hearings on Axworthy reforms. And, finally, from the University of Ottawa *Fulcrum*, a student newspaper, this war cry: "Look out Lloyd Axworthy. We're not going to take it."

Meanwhile, on the other side of the breach, the business community and its allies made their views known to the finance committee, which heard directly from over 450 witnesses while another 186 groups and individuals submitted position papers. The testimony usually contained dire warnings and exhortations to cut now and cut deep. Each morning, we are playing Russian roulette with the Canadian economy, one witness told the committee. The deficit is a terrifying vice that is jeopardizing Canada's long-term survival, another said. The deficit is like using our MasterCard to pay off our Visa bill. The deficit is simply stealing from our kids. Many of the presentations ended with a familiar refrain: "Don't touch our benefits." After several days of testimony, finance committee chairman Jim Peterson bemoaned the dearth of fresh ideas, and near total absence of a spirit of altruism. "Most of the witnesses are very self-serving in terms of protecting their own programs," Peterson observed. "The very rare witness is the one who says I have something to put on the table."

The parliamentary committee hearings were a rerun of the sterile debate between the proponents of economic success and social justice, the adversaries who had locked horns again and again over the previous decade. What broke the deadlock between them was pressure for meaningful social and fiscal reform from two constituencies the government could not afford to ignore: international financial watchdogs and the Canadian public.

From the earliest days of its mandate, the government has been under subtle but mounting pressure from the international community. According to a story that appeared in the *Globe and Mail* in November 1994, officials from the Washington-based International Monetary Fund (IMF) visited Ottawa shortly after the Liberal election victory and conducted a detailed review of the country's finances. "Not only did discussions with the Department of Finance and old and new Bank of Canada governors John Crow and Gordon Thiessen last longer than usual," the newspaper reported, "but they were resumed for one day in March [1994], after Mr. Martin's budget of Feb. 22. The discussions were unusual in that for the first time they involved the IMF's highest-ranking official for the Americas, Sterie Beza. In a further departure from previous talks, the roster of Canadian participants was broadened to involve more government departments. Canada has suffered a significant credibility gap in its relations with the IMF in recent years by repeatedly coming in with higher deficits than forecast in annual budget speeches."

On the basis of its review, the IMF prepared a confidential report, dated March 31, 1994, in which it reached the following conclusion: "It would be appropriate to plan on the basis of a more ambitious medium-term target in the 1995–96 budget, with a view to accelerating fiscal consolidation in the next few years." In plain English, the organization was telling the Chrétien government to develop a more ambitious deficit-reduction plan, and to set a more stringent deadline for completing it.

The IMF review was just the beginning of the pressure. There were also negative commentaries in two of the world's most prestigious English-language business newspapers, *The Financial Times* of London and the *Wall Street Journal*. The New York–based *Journal* caught the attention of Canadians across the entire country with an inflammatory editorial entitled "Bankrupt Canada?" Published in mid-January, 1995, the editorial declared that our debt was so unmanageable that we were headed for third-world status. However, rising interest rates through mid- to late 1994, more than anything else, jolted the Liberals into action. "If you see interest rates increasing by one percent, do you know what is the cost to the taxpayers?" an incredulous Chrétien asked one interviewer following the 1995 budget. "One percent of interest is $1.7 billion."

Public opinion polls also sent the Liberals a message: Canadians were looking for substantial changes in the way the government did business. An Angus Reid survey, commissioned by Axworthy's department and conducted in June 1994, revealed that 78 percent of the participants supported the government's general objective of reforming social programs. That figure jumped to 96 percent in Decima Research polling done in early November that year. The polls also revealed a hardening of attitudes toward perceived abuses and weaknesses in the programs. Decima found that 75 percent of Canadians supported a two-tiered system of unemployment insurance in which frequent claimants would be forced to work longer and receive lower benefits than those who make only a few claims in a lifetime. Another Toronto-based polling firm, Compas Inc., disclosed that 81 percent believed that certain types of welfare recipients should be required to do community work or take training courses, a concept known as workfare.

A large and detailed survey conducted in 1994 by Ekos Research Associates of Ottawa for several government departments confirmed a public thirst for change. "People's expectations of government are diminishing," Ekos president Frank Graves wrote. "This decline is produced by growing recognition of a deficit crisis, disillusionment with the efficacy of government and a consensus that citizens cannot rely solely on government to solve the range of problems that government was expected to solve in the past. There is, however, considerable ambivalence in the public's surface resolve to shrink government in order to manage the public debt. Despite a somewhat unrealistic belief that eliminating inefficiency and waste would go a long way to solving fiscal problems, there is no consensus to withdraw the big ticket items which could truly reduce deficit problems."

Ekos also found what it described as "profound differences" among Canadians of different socioeconomic status: "There are sharp divisions over the future role of government as an agent of social justice and wealth distribution. The secure classes are increasingly loathe to see further expenditures in this direction as a function of tax fatigue and deficit concerns. The economically distressed feel increasingly abandoned and see themselves losing touch with the economic standards of average Canadians. The growing economic bifurcation of Canada will pose the greatest challenge to governments as we approach the year 2000."

In this type of polarized environment, we need leadership that can build a bridge across this socioeconomic breach. The prime minister and his lieutenants must be credible and persuasive enough to convince the general public and the competing elites to support and contribute to fundamental reforms of our fiscal affairs. But the Chrétien administration can achieve this only if it possesses the wisdom and vision that allowed an earlier generation of Liberals to create the welfare state.

"The post-war welfare state represented an accommodation of values," according to Simeon, "bridging the gap between efficiency and equity, between economic growth and social justice. Business was provided with a secure, educated workforce and a stable economy, leaving it free to generate jobs and profits. This, in turn, generated the financial resources with which to finance the stronger social safety net. Growth and equality could go hand in hand, each re-inforcing the other. Thus the welfare state might be described as a broad social contract, a policy blueprint, a wide consensus across party and regional lines."

What we need now is a similar contract or blueprint that will serve us in an era of retrenchment and restructuring. We face a long, arduous trek back to solvency. It may take twenty years. It will require sacrifice. We need to balance our budgets, a monumental undertaking given the size of our deficits and the number of governments involved. Our governments must generate surpluses for a number of years in order to pay down our debts and reduce our annual interest payments. We need co-operation and conciliation where we now have hostility and mistrust. We must remain a compassionate society, committed to providing for the poor, the sick, and the elderly. But compassion alone will not sustain us.

We must also rediscover the values that carried this country for a century and allowed us to build railways, fight two world wars, populate the West, and create a prosperous, vibrant nation. Those values — resourcefulness, ingenuity, and fiscal prudence, a belief in balanced budgets and a reluctance to borrow money or raise taxes — must be restored to their proper place at the core of our political culture. The practices of the 1970s and 1980s, which were based on the premise that we could live beyond our means in perpetuity, must be recognized for what they were: historical aberrations that were neither realistic nor sustainable.

2

A ROSE
AND A WORM

For nearly three years after leaving office, Pierre Elliott Trudeau
held his tongue and remained aloof even as his monuments fell.
He said nothing publicly when Brian Mulroney dismantled the
National Energy Program (NEP), nothing when Mulroney gutted
the Foreign Investment Review Agency, nothing when Mulroney
mocked his legacy and challenged his accomplishments. Then, in
May 1987, Trudeau spoke. And his words landed like rain in a
desert. He attacked Mulroney's Meech Lake Accord, bluntly and
forcefully, and triggered a flash flood of dissent and discord.

His subsequent utterances, though less unexpected, were equally
devastating to Mulroney. Trudeau appeared before the Senate in
Ottawa in March 1988 to renew his attack on the Meech Lake
Accord, and his opposition helped derail the prime minister's
cherished constitutional reconciliation with Quebec. Trudeau was
also implacably hostile to the Charlottetown Accord, Mulroney's
second constitutional deal. In October 1992, a few weeks before a

national referendum on the agreement, Trudeau delivered a scathing attack before a crowd of 400 people who packed a Montreal Chinese restaurant called La Maison Egg Roll. "This mess deserves a big No," he concluded. And most Canadians agreed.

In the decade after he left office, Trudeau's stature grew remarkably. Time enhanced his mystique among members of the Liberal party, the public, and the press. But time alone has not made Canadians grow fonder of the man they repeatedly elected and rejected. Biographers, film makers, historians, and former colleagues have all been busy burnishing his image as a great prime minister. First, there were Stephen Clarkson and Christina McCall, whose 1990 book, *Trudeau and Our Times*, began with the succinct and compelling opening sentence: "He haunts us still."

That same year, Trudeau himself began to participate directly in this image-enhancement exercise. He and his former principal secretary, Thomas Axworthy, coedited a collection of essays entitled *Towards a Just Society: The Trudeau Years*. It was an unabashed defence of the former prime minister written primarily by men who had worked with and for him. And it put a publicist's gloss on many of the events and initiatives of the Trudeau era. The book boasts of major triumphs, sweeping changes, noble efforts, exhilarating years, the boldest moves, the most extensive programs, and the true visionary nature of the Trudeau government.

In the fall of 1993, we were offered his memoirs, compiled by a team of writers but edited, amended, and approved by Trudeau. In early 1994, CBC television broadcast a six-part series about Trudeau's life, produced with the full co-operation and participation of the former prime minister. Finally, the prominent University of Toronto historian Michael Bliss declared, in his 1994 book, *Right Honorable Men*, that Trudeau was our Abe Lincoln. The cumulative effect has been to transform the Trudeau years from history into myth, and the man himself from politician into saint.

Trudeau was a winner, at the polls and in the political trenches. He was as tough as they come. "Trudeau became the most formidable political warrior in Canadian history," Bliss writes. "He confronted separatists, terrorists, provincial premiers, Conservatives, anyone who disagreed with him, and he almost always won. In Lyndon Johnson and Ronald Reagan, the Americans had a real cowboy and a Hollywood cowboy in the White House during the Trudeau years. But it was the Canadian prime minister, alone and exposed on the stage and television screen, jacket off, tie loosened, fingers hooked in his belt — the gunslinger on Main Street — who most resembled Clint Eastwood."

There were a few battles that Trudeau did not win during his years in power. But the losses were not for lack of effort. Inflation burned like a brush fire despite every effort by Trudeau and his ministers to control it. Unemployment refused to retreat despite stimulative budgets, regional development policies, and job creation schemes. Interest rates soared to record levels in the early 1980s, with disastrous consequences for homeowners who had to renew mortgages or businessmen and women who had to borrow money.

Yet even a cursory examination of the recent literature on the Trudeau years reveals curious lack of attention to economic issues, and a near silence on fiscal matters. These are significant omissions. As a manager of the economy, Trudeau's performance ranks somewhere between dismal and abysmal. Fiscally, he led the country into a swamp. He inherited the strongest federal finances of any post-war prime minister. Canada had an eminently manageable national debt of $18 billion in April 1968 when Trudeau captured the leadership of the Liberal Party and became prime minister. By the end of his years in office, the debt was headed for $210 billion, more than a tenfold increase. There is only one conclusion to draw from these numbers: Trudeau was the father of the monstrous federal debt that looms over our national affairs like the shadow of some brooding, menacing Brobdingnagian and possesses the size and mass to crush us as if we were a nation of Lilliputians.

But in his few public utterances on the subject since leaving office, the former prime minister has simply dodged the issue.

Toward the end of *Memoirs*, Trudeau compares his record — $180 billion in new debt in sixteen years — with that of the Mulroney Tories, who added close to $300 billion in nine years. In any event, he writes, a government's economic legacy should not be judged solely on the basis of debt. "It should be assessed on the health of the economy in general," he concludes. "From the point of view of economic growth, job growth, unemployment, and so on, we had a healthy record. I look back on such accomplishments without shame."

◄○►

Trudeau became prime minister at a time when Canadians were still captivated by the euphoria of Centennial year. We were proud of the country's past, and optimistic about its future. In the course of 100 years, we had transformed a fragile and improbable Confederation, comprising four far-flung colonies, into a bustling dominion that stretched from sea to sea to sea. We built two transcontinental railways. We populated a vast Western hinterland and turned millions of acres of Prairie wilderness into productive farmland. We fought for the British Empire in South Africa. We displayed remarkable courage and tenacity in the trenches of World War One, and through our performance on the battlefield became a completely sovereign nation. We endured the hardship and deprivation of the Great Depression. We gave our lives to defeat Nazi Germany and we stood by Great Britain in her darkest hour.

The post-war years brought peace and prosperity like the world had never seen. Medical advances eradicated killer diseases, increased life expectancies, and reduced infant mortality rates. Industry filled our homes with new appliances and wonderful gadgets. Governments provided us with a social safety net that stretched from the cradle to the grave. No wonder Canadians were in a euphoric mood in 1967. We had a century of dazzling accomplishments to celebrate. We had built a country, a stable and flourishing democracy, a robust and growing economy. A diligent and deferential citizenry and their prudent, frugal governments had performed a miracle.

But even more remarkable was the simple fact that we had achieved all this and still lived within our means. Canada in 1967 was a financially solid country. At the end of World War Two, the national debt was equivalent to 108 percent of the country's gross domestic product, the total output of the economy in a single year. Over the next twenty years, successive federal administrations whittled away at the debt while the economy grew at a remarkable rate. By Centennial year, the debt stood at 26 percent of the economy and it would continue to fall in relation to GDP, reaching a low of 18 percent in 1975. Finance ministers throughout the postwar era had brought the debt down by adhering to political values that had served the country since its formation.

From the days of Confederation until the celebration of our Centennial, Canadian political leaders disliked borrowing and avoided raising taxes. They borrowed to finance great national projects like the railways and the St. Lawrence Seaway or to cover the cost of the war efforts. But they paid for government operations, programs, and services — in other words, consumption — out of current tax dollars. The finance minister of the day invariably aimed to balance the budget, or produce a surplus. In times of peace and prosperity, the minister tried to pay down the national debt.

One aging Liberal who remembers how things used to be done is Jack Pickersgill, a cabinet minister in the St. Laurent and Pearson governments. "We thought the debt should be paid off," said Pickersgill, who at age 90 was living in Ottawa's Rockcliffe Park. "Both Doug Abbott and Walter Harris, who were Liberal finance ministers, paid substantial chunks of it off. Even the year we had the election, in 1957, Harris had an $800-million surplus and he insisted on using half of it to pay part of the national debt, and the other half was applied to some small tax reductions, but mainly to increasing the old age pensions and the family allowances. There never was any borrowing outside Canada by the government of

Canada. We were worried about having to pay off a debt or even pay interest in other people's currency."

Then along came Pierre Elliott Trudeau. He was young, handsome, and daring. He was unlike any national leader in living memory. He sparkled when compared to the bumbling Pearson, the pompous Diefenbaker, the courtly St. Laurent, the cunning King, or the baronial Bennett. Canadians were in a giddy, celebratory mood, ripe for a charismatic, visionary leader. We were unperturbed by the fact that Trudeau was a dilettante who had never had to worry about personal finances or balance a budget or meet a payroll. We hadn't begun to question the cost of our social programs or the size of our governments or the roles they played in society. Nor did we become alarmed when the federal government, under Trudeau, began piling up larger and larger annual deficits and by the mid-1970s began borrowing to cover the cost of routine, day-to-day operations.

In keeping with his Liberal predecessors — Pearson, St. Laurent, and King — Trudeau was determined to enrich our social programs and expand the role of the state, and he approached both tasks with energy and enthusiasm. His ministers, most of whom shared his passion, refused to be deterred by senior civil servants who attempted to apply the brakes, however gently. "I can remember a meeting I was present at," says Gordon Robertson, who served as secretary to the cabinet from 1963 until 1975. "It was a cabinet finance committee meeting in which Bob Bryce, who was deputy minister of finance, was arguing quite strenuously with some of the ministers. I remember his words. He said they could do everything they wanted to do but they couldn't do them all at once without adverse results. The problem was that year after year revenues were up and after awhile it seemed like it was possible to do everything at once."

Trudeau and his free-spending ministers needed money, and they discovered that vast sums were available through the domestic and, to a lesser extent, foreign bond markets. They also realized that borrowing was painless. By tapping the markets, they could increase expenditures without raising taxes, arousing the wrath of the voters, or creating political trouble for themselves. From the point of view of the lenders, both individual and institutional, Government of Canada bonds were a great investment, largely due to the sound management of previous administrations. "The government balance sheet was very strong," says Ted Carmichael, an economist and senior executive with the Toronto-based brokerage firm J. P. Morgan Canada. "We were a low debt country. Our governments were low debt governments. There was a lot of room for borrowing. The fact that money was accessible and there to be borrowed seems to have dulled the old sense of duty that governments, over a period of years, ought to try to balance the books."

Ironically, the Trudeau Liberals came into office preaching fiscal prudence. During the 1968 election campaign, Trudeau had promised to balance the federal budget. In the Speech from the Throne in September of that year, the new government declared, "Just as incomes cannot increase faster than productivity if price increases are to be restrained, so government spending by all levels of government cannot increase faster than productivity if we wish to restrain the increase in levels of taxation. These two realities are among the most important that Canadians and their leaders must bear in mind during the months and years ahead."

Unfortunately, the prime minister and his colleagues quickly forgot their campaign promise and what the throne speech called important realities. The Trudeau government produced a surplus of $371 million during the 1969–70 fiscal year, its first full year in office. But that was the last time federal revenues exceeded expenditures. The following year, 1970–71, the government ended up $638 million in the red, and in 1971–72 the deficit doubled to $1.3 billion. From that point on, the Trudeau government never regained control over the nation's finances and the shortfalls began to explode. By 1975–76, the deficit had surpassed $5 billion. Two years later, it eclipsed the $10-billion mark. By the start of the 1980s, the country was approaching another threshold, a

$15-billion annual deficit. In 1982–83, at least partly due to a deep recession, the shortfall surged to almost $26 billion, another landmark. And when Trudeau left office in June 1984, the federal government was headed for a $38.5-billion deficit.

The Trudeau administrations not only ran deficits on a scale that was previously unthinkable in peacetime, they also broke with a long-established political practice. Earlier governments had borrowed primarily to finance lasting projects and enterprises such as railways, canals, and airlines. Trudeau and his ministers, however, borrowed to pay for social programs and the day-to-day operations of government. The former prime minister, along with his admirers and apologists, have justified these actions on the grounds that the overriding objective was the pursuit of a just society. "Without a doubt," Trudeau wrote in the concluding chapter of *Towards a Just Society*, "the two main facets of the policy lay in equality of opportunity for all Canadians regardless of the economic region in which they lived, and regardless of the language they spoke — French or English." However, Trudeau has never publicly acknowledged that the spending habits and borrowing practices of his governments created a mountain of debt and a huge injustice for future taxpayers, most of them now children or young adults. They will be forced to pay the bills for services consumed and benefits received by their parents or grandparents.

During the first seven or eight years that he occupied the prime minister's office, Trudeau allowed spending of every sort to grow at rates which, by current standards, seem incomprehensible. In the first half of the 1970s, social spending increased at an average annual rate of 19 percent, according to Hideo Mimoto and Philip Cross, two senior policy analysts with Statistics Canada, who in 1991 undertook a comprehensive study of the growth of the federal debt. Federal expenditures in other areas, such as industrial development, environmental regulation, and regional planning, roared ahead at an astonishing rate of 18.5 percent yearly. Mimoto and Cross, as well as many other commentators, argue that

33

Trudeau and his ministers sobered up in the mid-1970s and began to curtail the rate of growth of government. They note that spending was increasing at about the same rate as the economy was growing. Nevertheless, by the time Trudeau retired, federal spending represented 26 percent of the country's economy, compared with 17 percent when he became prime minister.

As startling as these numbers are, they tell only part of the story. The rapid increases in expenditures, and the corresponding growth in the size of the government, reflected the political values of the Trudeau Liberals, values which were, according to some observers, prevalent throughout the Western industrial democracies. "Governments around the world undertook to be everything to everybody," says Gordon Osbaldeston, who spent thirty-two years in the federal civil service, including fourteen as a deputy minister and three as clerk of the Privy Council. "People thought they could do everything. There was no end to growth. You couldn't lose. It wasn't just Canada. In England, the United States, France and Italy, never mind Scandinavia, central governments overreached. It was also the era of the mega-corporation. There were sprawling conglomerates all over the place. The business community was as affected by the same disease as were governments. It was a societal condition."

By almost any yardstick, Trudeau and his ministers caught a bad case of this disease. They built museums and bought oil companies, created departments and spawned crown corporations. They established a bewildering array of new boards, agencies, and councils, as Osbaldeston notes in his 1992 book, *Organizing to Govern*, which traces the growth of our federal government since 1940. He lists 114 new administrative and regulatory entities that came into existence between 1968 and 1984. There were advisory councils on aging, the status of women, and fisheries and ocean research. There were advisory committees on veterinary drugs, the saltfish industry, and mining and metallurgical resources. In some cases, the oil and gas industry for example, Ottawa acted as referee, scorekeeper, and player. The federal government controlled exports through the National Energy Board, scrutinized production and prices through the Petroleum Monitoring Agency, and competed in the industry through Petro-Canada.

The Trudeau Liberals established seven new government departments: environment; communications; employment and immigration; fisheries and oceans; supply and services; industry, trade and commerce; and regional economic expansion. They also borrowed a position — the minister of state — from the British. Ministers of state were supposed to serve as assistants to overworked cabinet ministers or they were expected to manage specific departmental functions. Over the years, Trudeau created ministries of state for economic development, science and technology, social development, and urban affairs. "They were thought of as temporary positions, created to solve problems," says Osbaldeston. "Originally, there were only three or four of them, but we ended up with seventeen or eighteen. We let these people become full-fledged departments with their own budgets and staff. They became new centres of government growth and spending, and the competition was on. It was a case of 'What can I say in tomorrow's press release?'"

The creation of new departments and ministries of state ultimately led to bloated and unwieldy cabinets. According to Osbaldeston, Canada was governed by fourteen ministers in 1867 and twenty in 1950. Thirty years later, we had thirty-nine ministers. He also compares Canada with eleven other democratic countries and shows that in the early 1980s our government had almost twice as many cabinet ministers as most of the others. The British government came closest to Canada with twenty-five ministers, while Switzerland managed with just seven. The president of the United States, meanwhile, ran the world's largest economy with just twenty ministers. We had achieved the dubious distinction of becoming one of the world's most overgoverned democracies.

New ministers meant new projects and demands for bigger budgets. "We used to say that if there were thirty people in cabinet, there's one anti-spender, the minister of finance, who had to have the support of the prime minister, and twenty-eight spenders whose main purpose in life was to get more money," recalls David Slater, a former chairman of the Economic Council of Canada and a senior official in the finance department from 1973 to 1978. "Sometimes, the contingency reserve for the following year was totally committed before the year even began. I recall an occasion when a minister went out to his region and announced projects which he knew were not in the budget or approved by Treasury Board. Some of these guys would get out there and they'd promise things that weren't even in the spending estimates. It was just incredible."

This may have been bad news for the average taxpayer, who was expected to foot the bill for all this growth, but it meant opportunity and excitement for anyone in the civil service. The Trudeau administrations, particularly in the late 1960s and early 1970s, encouraged innovation, welcomed growth, and rarely questioned the cost, according to those who served in the bureaucracy. Managers were expected to come up with new projects and programs. Requests for additional employees were often approved within forty-eight hours. Frugality could be detrimental to a manager's career prospects. Empire building often led to promotions. "The more you spent, the better your assessments," recalls a retired civil servant who was moving up the ladder at the time. "They were bubbly times. It was a free-for-all. I can't think of one self-respecting manager who wasn't priming the pump, and nobody gave a damn."

◄o►

The odd man out in this environment was the minister of finance, the man who was supposed to be the anti-spender, and in his time, Trudeau had six. The first, Kingston, Ontario, accountant Edgar Benson, lasted three years before giving way to John Turner, who took over in January 1972 and brought in five budgets before quitting the cabinet, for reasons which he has never publicly disclosed, in September 1975. Nearly two decades later, from his law office in downtown Toronto, Turner still vividly remembered the mentality that prevailed within the Trudeau cabinet. "I'll tell you, I went to the washroom during a cabinet meeting one day and, by the time I got back, they'd approved new spending of $250 million," he says. "I managed to get it rolled back but that showed you how people were thinking. Canada was a bounteous country. We had unlimited resources, great opportunities, every year was going to be better."

Turner contends that he and deputy minister Simon Reisman, who resigned in April 1975, maintained tight control of federal finance. Their deficits, he says, averaged $750 million a year. From his perspective, the problems began after he and Reisman left. Following Turner's departure, Trudeau went through four finance ministers in his last nine years in office: Donald Macdonald, Jean Chrétien, Allan MacEachen, and Marc Lalonde. Finance became a revolving door. The politicians who held the portfolio made little or no effort to halt the growth of the deficit, and none lasted long enough to reverse the decline of the nation's finances.

Federal budgets of the Trudeau era often resembled grab bags of goodies, with tax cuts and spending increases on the same page, write-offs for manufacturers on one page, investment credits for small business on the next. Despite the apparent lack of coherence, Liberal finance ministers pursued two overriding objectives for most of the 1970s and into the 1980s: they tried to control inflation and, at the same time, stimulate economic growth. In his November 1974 budget, Turner added another item to the cluttered Liberal agenda — controlling government spending — even though his budgets, and those of his successors, invariably contained measures that would increase federal expenses. "We must do all we can to restrain the growth of governmental expenditures," he told the House of Commons. "We have sought and shall continue to seek to cut waste, to place limits on the growth of the public service and to approve only the most essential new programs."

By the time Turner made that commitment, the Liberals had already made major changes to unemployment insurance and old age pensions. They had enriched and expanded a social safety net that was essentially complete when Trudeau became prime minister. Previous governments, most of them Liberal, had set up a welfare system, unemployment insurance, old age security, public pension plans, the family allowance, and universal health care. Nevertheless, in 1971, Labour Minister Bryce Mackasey completely overhauled the UI program, partly as a response to stubbornly high rates of unemployment, partly to correct perceived inadequacies in the prevailing system.

Under the old rules, about 65 percent of the labour force were eligible for benefits. The new rules extended coverage to 90 percent of all workers. Mackasey raised the maximum weekly benefits to $107, more than double the old ceiling. He made it simpler to apply and qualify, lengthened the eligibility periods, and provided for extended benefits in regions of high unemployment. He also drastically underestimated the costs. In 1972, Ottawa paid out almost $1.9 billion in benefits, more than twice what it handed out a year earlier. By 1977, payments doubled again to hit $3.8 billion.

Almost from the time they took office, the Trudeau Liberals were saddled with another social scourge — persistently high inflation — which eroded incomes, corroded confidence, and undermined the economic well-being of Canadians. The Liberals made two high-profile attempts to halt the relentless rise of prices and wages by controlling the behaviour of Canadians. In 1975, they established the Anti-Inflation Board, and in 1982 they introduced a two-year program aimed at limiting annual pay increases for Members of Parliament, Senators, and civil servants to 6 percent and 5 percent. They also attempted to shield Canadians from the impact of inflation, just as earlier administrations had created a panoply of social programs to minimize the effects of poverty, joblessness, old age, and disease. The Liberals' antidote to rising prices was called indexation, and it eventually played a major role in expanding the federal deficit and building up the national debt.

Turner announced in his budget of May 1972 that Old Age Security payments and the Guaranteed Income Supplement, a program for low-income seniors, would be fully indexed, and in a subsequent budget the Liberals indexed Family Allowance payments. Indexation meant that benefits paid to individuals under these programs rose automatically at the same rate as the consumer price index, whereas with previous governments such payments were raised only when it was deemed necessary. These changes, along with a more extensive and much more generous unemployment insurance program, were at least partly responsible for driving up the cost of transfer payments to individuals. In 1971, the year before full indexing was introduced, the federal government spent $2.1 billion on pensions for the elderly. Within five years, the figure had doubled to $4.2 billion, and by 1981 it had doubled again.

Despite such sharp increases in costs, many economists and fiscal policy analysts contend that the Trudeau Liberals cannot be accused of excessive social spending. In their study of the growth of the federal deficit, for example, Mimoto and Cross point out that from 1972 until 1982, when a major recession occurred, social spending grew at roughly the same rate as the economy and so remained stable at about 9.5 percent of GDP. Many of those same commentators argue that the real damage occurred on the revenue side of the balance sheet.

The Liberals, they note, increased government spending by indexing social programs and cut revenues by indexing personal exemptions and tax brackets. Historically, federal governments had welcomed a moderate amount of inflation because as incomes rose people automatically moved into higher tax brackets and therefore contributed more money to the federal treasury. Economists referred to this phenomenon as "the inflation dividend."

But in his budget of February 1973, Turner eliminated the so-called dividend on the grounds that it was unfair to individual wage earners. He also argued that the government had to provide average taxpayers with some protection against inflation.

This was achieved by indexing the basic personal exemption, the marital exemption, two exemptions for dependents, and exemptions for the elderly, the blind, and the disabled. If, for example, the annual rate of inflation was 10 percent, all of these exemptions would increase by that same amount. Turner also indexed tax brackets so that they rose at the same rate as inflation. In concluding his remarks on indexing, the minister of finance told the House of Commons, "I suggest that this new system will be recognized everywhere as a bold and sensitive response to a fundamental tax problem. With the introduction of this change, Canada will join a very select group of countries which have eliminated the hidden revenues accruing to governments through the effect of inflation on a progressive tax system."

Indexing the tax system was undoubtedly an innovative idea. It was also very expensive. But the cost was not immediately obvious for three reasons. The Liberals were not spending money directly. Instead, they were collecting less revenue through the tax system. And they made no attempt until 1980 to calculate how much indexation was costing the federal treasury in forgone revenue. Coincidentally, in that year, the finance department published an economic analysis entitled "A Perspective on the Decade," which estimated the price of indexing at $6.0 billion between 1973 and 1979. The same document also listed seventeen other Liberal measures, a veritable smorgasbord of tax cuts, breaks, and exemptions. They were introduced primarily by Turner to stimulate the economy but ended up costing the government another $8.0 billion in forgone revenue over that six-year period.

A more damning picture of Liberal tax policy emerges in a 1984 report from the Economic Council of Canada entitled "Steering the Course." The council compiled a list of selected tax breaks and exemptions and estimated their cost, in terms of lost revenue, between 1976 and 1982. Some fifteen measures introduced by the Trudeau governments cost the treasury $22 billion in that five-year time span. Another twenty-five initiatives, conceived by previous governments but continued under Trudeau, cost $38 billion. The total estimated price: $60 billion. "Our research thus shows that much of the fiscal plight of governments today is of their own making," the council concluded, "since they have forgone, in various ways, revenues that in earlier days they were able to levy effectively."

The business community was a big beneficiary. The Liberals granted lower tax rates for small business and manufacturers. There were tax write-offs for research and development spending, write-offs for Canadian oil and gas developments, tax credits for investments in farming and fishing, and tax exemptions on purchases of transportation equipment. The Liberals were equally generous with individuals. They forgave the sales tax on clothing and footwear, as well as home heating fuels and electricity. They made the first $1,000 of pension income tax free and gave younger Canadians a break through the Registered Home Ownership Savings Plan.

"I was a bit astounded at how far the government was prepared to go with tax shelters for things like rental housing and condominiums, or tax shelters for scientific research," recalls Slater. "You ask yourself, why is it that the corporate tax system produces so little revenue, and these incentives and tax shelters were a significant factor. It became possible for profitable companies to buy unprofitable companies and use the takeover target's accumulated tax deductions for their own benefit. These ideas came from all over the place. Other departments were always pushing finance for ways to get their things done. They came from business lobbies, from tax accountants and tax lawyers. They had endless ideas about good things that ought to get a boost. I once had a long argument with my deputy minister about these things. He and the minister thought that if you wanted to [get] something done, you had to create the conditions to get it done. They had the responsibility and the experience. I was just a Presbyterian who was appalled by these things."

Although the Liberals scattered tax breaks and exemptions far and wide, in a seemingly haphazard fashion, they were, in fact, practising a form of Keynesian economics. John Maynard Keynes was a Cambridge University professor and adviser to several British governments who, in the mid-1930s, developed one of the most original and powerful economic theories of the twentieth century. Keynes held that governments should use their size and strength to offset the impact of economic cycles. When a country's economy was booming, the national government should cut or restrain spending to build up its financial reserves and avoid setting off an inflationary cycle of rising prices and incomes. The government would then be in a position to increase spending during an economic downturn to create employment and promote growth.

According to Turner, some senior Liberals, including Trudeau, were also being influenced by John Kenneth Galbraith, the Canadian-born author, adviser to Democratic presidents, and Harvard University economics professor. Galbraith was, and remains, a staunch advocate of government borrowing to finance infrastructure and create jobs. "We had John Kenneth Galbraith waltzing up to Ottawa advising the prime minister," says Turner. "Galbraith took things well beyond Keynes, who believed in spending on a cyclical basis, not a constant basis. Keynes recognized that you couldn't get into this kind of situation. I told Trudeau one time, 'I don't want you seeing that guy [Galbraith] without my being there.'"

For most of the 1970s, the Canadian economy seemed to be suffering from precisely the type of ailments that called for a dose of Keynesian stimulation. The economy was not growing as fast as it had during the 1950s and 1960s, and unemployment was consistently higher than it had been in those two decades. But rather than spend directly on public works and capital projects, the Liberals instead tried to use the tax system as a tool to promote growth and employment. In theory, personal tax cuts would put more money into the hands of individual Canadians, who would spend it on consumer goods. Tax breaks and exemptions for business were supposed to stimulate investment in new plant and equipment. This would lead to higher output, more jobs, improved sales, and, finally, increased tax revenues for the federal government.

In reality, nothing of the sort happened. Most economists now agree that the low growth and high unemployment of the 1970s were not caused by a normal slump in the business cycle. These problems were part of a profound structural change in the economy and, therefore, were immune to Keynesian-style fiscal stimulation. "There was a sharp drop in the growth of productivity in 1973–74," says Judith Maxwell, a former chairman of the Economic Council of Canada. "No economist has really been able to pin down the cause of it, although there is a general sense that it was associated with the oil price shock of 1973." Output per worker, which had grown at an average annual rate of 4 to 5 percent from the end of World War Two until 1972, plummeted abruptly and began growing at only 1 to 2 percent annually. Furthermore, the productivity collapse, as some economists call it, has persisted right through to the mid-1990s.

"The source of government revenue is the amount of activity in the economy and, if the economy cannot generate the rates of growth in income, and transactions like retail sales, then you just don't collect as much in taxes," says Maxwell. "That was something that appears to have been completely outside the control of government. People were slow to recognize that this was going to be a permanent, or at least a very long-term shift. People kept thinking, it's just for this year and we'll get back to normal soon. And we're still not back to normal, if you define normal as the rates of growth we experienced in the 1950s and 1960s."

The Liberal tax cuts failed to have much impact on unemployment, nor did they offset the impact of the drop in productivity. They did seriously weaken the federal tax system, however. It became much less effective at collecting revenues to pay for government programs, the very purpose for which it was designed. As Mimoto and Cross noted in their study, federal revenues rose steadily in the early years of the Trudeau era and hit a peak of almost 20 percent of gross domestic product in the 1974–75 fiscal year. Within four years, they had fallen to 16.1 percent of GDP. Revenues did rise in relation to GDP in the early 1980s, but that was largely due to massive new taxes on oil and gas production that were introduced as part of the National Energy Program of October 1980.

—◄o►—

While revenues were declining drastically as a proportion of GDP, the Liberals failed to take any meaningful action to control expenditures. Spending kept on growing, in both nominal and real terms, and the federal government became a larger and larger presence within the national economy. At the same time, Liberal finance ministers stood in the House of Commons year after year and declared in their budget speeches that the government was doing its utmost to control expenditures.

Turner initiated this annual ritual in November 1974 when he presented the first budget of the freshly elected Liberal majority. He announced a 15 percent increase in spending, which was, admittedly, an improvement over the previous year, when a minority Liberal government allowed spending to soar by 25 percent. But as the prominent economist and York University lecturer Fred Lazar noted at the time, "If this was restraint one shuddered to think what an expansionary policy would have been." And in a year when the Liberals were supposed to be controlling expenditures, the deficit nearly quadrupled to hit $5.1 billion.

On March 31, 1977, Turner's successor, Donald Macdonald, a Bay Street lawyer, was humming a variation on the same tune in a budget speech. "We are now seeing the solid results of our commitment two years ago to get government expenditure growth below the growth rate of GDP," he told the House. "Our expenditures for the fiscal year just concluding are estimated at some $750 million less than the forecast contained in the budget of last May." Savings of that magnitude — three-quarters of a billion dollars —

may have sounded impressive. But the Liberals had just racked up a deficit of $6.5 billion. Macdonald added that he hoped to trim another $650 million from the spending projections for the 1977–78 fiscal year. That, too, might have been a worthy objective had the Liberals been even close to a balanced budget. Instead, that year the deficit broke the $10-billion threshold for the first time.

Shortly after bringing in his second budget, Macdonald announced his retirement from federal politics, and Jean Chrétien became Canada's first francophone finance minister. Chrétien made his Commons debut as minister with his budget of October 20, 1977, and it was a noteworthy document for several reasons. Having run eight straight deficits, and allowed the shortfall to sky-rocket from $1.3 billion to over $10 billion in just four years, the Liberals were finally prepared to admit that they had a problem on their hands. But they were not ready to do very much about it, as Chrétien revealed in his budget speech. "The revenues of the federal government are growing more slowly than expected," he said. "As a result, our cash deficits are now so large that our room for manoeuvring is very limited. While my room for manoeuvring is very limited, because of the large deficits in our accounts, I believe we can do more to stimulate the economy."

When it came to making political choices, dealing with the deficit didn't make Chrétien's agenda. He announced tax cuts that would benefit 7.5 million low- and middle-income Canadians and cost the treasury $700 million in forgone revenue. He also revealed that indexation would boost personal tax exemptions by 7.2 percent. "I only regret that the importance of indexation is so often forgotten or ignored in public discussion," Chrétien told the Commons. "That is why I am pleased to repeat it this evening. Taxpayers will benefit from an additional $850-million tax exemption."

Chrétien brought in budgets in April and November 1978, and in both he stuck to the script that he and his fellow finance ministers had been following throughout the 1970s: fight inflation; stimulate the economy; control government spending; and ignore the deficit.

He was, even then, a stay-put politician, always content with the status quo. Trudeau was just the opposite, and demonstrated his penchant for the unpredictable by announcing major spending cuts, later pegged at $2.5 billion, in a nationally televised speech on August 1, 1978. The prime minister's initiative represented a sharp change in direction, since only two years earlier he had advocated a larger role for government, and it was a major embarrassment for his finance minister, who was only informed at the last minute of Trudeau's intentions.

The generally accepted version of this incident is that Trudeau resolved to cut spending after being chastised about Canada's fiscal profligacy by German Chancellor Helmut Schmidt during a Western economic summit. In his *Memoirs*, Trudeau says he acted unilaterally, without any prodding from Schmidt, because Trudeau's ministers had failed to deliver voluntarily the spending cuts he had requested months earlier as part of an effort to control inflation rather than the deficit.

But regardless of motives, the whole episode was a fiasco which had little or no lasting impact on the country's finances. That is clear from the account provided by *Toronto Star* columnist Richard Gwyn in *The Northern Magus*, his 1980 biography of the former prime minister. "Trudeau ordered his ministers to forward him suggestions for spending cuts totalling $500 million," Gwyn wrote. "At the deadline, in June, half the departments sent in no suggestions at all, and the value of the nicks proposed by the remainder added up to just $18 million. At long last, Trudeau realized what everyone had been saying for years: the bureaucracy, his bureaucracy, was out of control."

When Trudeau finally decided to bypass his cabinet, and the bureaucracy, and announce the cuts himself, the results bordered on being farcical. "Seldom in Canadian politics have such important economic decisions been taken by so few amid such confusion," Gwyn wrote. "The public was totally mystified by Trudeau's sudden conversion to such neo-conservative goals as spending cuts and cutbacks in the civil service. Trudeau's own cabinet was equally mystified. The only minister in the know was [Treasury Board President Robert] Andras. Chrétien, holidaying in Shawinigan, heard the news from an aide who himself learned what was going on the way everyone else in the country did, via his television set. He nearly resigned, and would have but for the harm his going would have done to the federalist cause in Quebec."

Trudeau's spending cuts jolted everyone in Ottawa, since cutbacks were basically unheard of in the post-war era. But the shock quickly wore off and life went on as usual. In his final budget before the Trudeau government was defeated at the polls in May 1979, Chrétien drove the deficit and the national debt higher through tax cuts worth an estimated $3 billion.

The deficit finally became an issue of some importance to the Liberals when they were returned to office with a majority government in early 1980, after nine months of Conservative rule. In his budget of October 28, 1980, Trudeau's new finance minister, Allan MacEachen, told the Commons, "I am convinced we must slow down the growth of public debt charges and this is one of the reasons I am determined to reduce the deficit."

MacEachen may have had the best of intentions. But he had the misfortune of being finance minister at the start of the era of astronomical deficits. The problem was that the Liberals had waited far too long before getting serious about the growing chasm between revenues and expenditures. And when they did, the world was in the midst of an economic convulsion. The Islamic revolution in Iran had led to another oil-price shock. Inflation was soaring to double-digit levels. Interest rates were on their way to a catastrophic 20 percent. Businesses were going broke. Unemployment was rising and a deep recession was just beginning. These forces hit the federal treasury with hurricane force. In a three-year period beginning in fiscal 1981–82, government revenues were practically flat, growing from $60 billion to only $64 billion.

Meanwhile, Liberal policies of the 1970s, particularly full

indexation of most social programs, drove federal expenses through the roof. Program spending took off like a sprinter exploding out of the starting blocks. During the three-year period commencing in fiscal 1981–82, expenditures surged from $61 billion to $79 billion. When interest payments on the national debt were factored in, the deficits more than doubled to reach $33 billion. The minister of finance was as helpless as a beetle flipped on its back. MacEachen writhed and flailed, adding to the public sound and fury with his highly contentious tax policies, but he achieved next to nothing.

In his October 1980 budget, he introduced the National Energy Program, under which Ottawa planned to plunder the oil and gas industry of Western Canada and grab almost $17 billion in taxes over a four-year period. A year later, MacEachen announced 150 proposed changes to the tax system that were designed to increase federal revenues by $3.4 billion over a two-year period. The NEP enraged Western Canadians, particularly Albertans. The revisions in the 1981 budget pleased no one and infuriated everyone from farmers and small businesspeople to real-estate developers, stockbrokers, and life insurance executives. Their wrath quickly coalesced into several intense lobbying campaigns and the government was soon retreating.

MacEachen's budgets were the product of a government that had completely lost control of the country's finances and was utterly incapable of exerting any meaningful influence over economic events. "I believe we must reduce our deficit and our borrowing requirements substantially," the minister of finance declared in his November 1981 budget. "I have set myself the task of cutting back the deficit in the next two years." Seven months later, in June 1982, he read another budget speech in the House. Revenues were down sharply from the forecast in the November budget. Debt charges were up. So was spending. As for the deficit, it would be twice as high as expected.

Marc Lalonde, Trudeau's last minister of finance, brought in two budgets — and two deficits exceeding $30 billion. Like many Liberal politicians of the Trudeau era, he made no apologies for his or the government's performance. These unprecedented deficits had been both necessary and good for the country, according to Lalonde. "The deficit has provided considerable support to the welfare of individual Canadians and to the promotion of economic activity through the difficult period of the recession and the first year of recovery," he said in the House of Commons on February 14, 1984. "But government deficits must be reduced as investment recovers and the economy expands."

While the country slipped into a fiscal quagmire, Trudeau was busy elsewhere, first with the constitution and then his peace mission. In his final months in office, he traipsed through the world's most important capitals like some latter-day Don Quixote, preaching disarmament to the likes of Margaret Thatcher, who had recently made war in the South Atlantic, and Ronald Reagan, who had visions of making war in space. The Soviets were between leaders, but in Beijing he met Deng Xiao Ping, the diminutive and Machiavellian master of the People's Republic, who cavalierly told Trudeau that a nuclear war might kill a billion Chinese, but China would survive.

The peace mission was a case of misplaced priorities and misspent energy. Trudeau chose a grandiose international initiative, one that had little or no chance of succeeding, rather than concentrating on the fiscal mess at home, where he may have been effective. But that was typical of Trudeau's approach to economic and financial issues. He added $180 billion to the national debt and made one attempt, in the summer of 1978, to cut federal spending by $2.5 billion. "He was not interested in economics, really," says Maxwell. And Pickersgill, the old Liberal from the St. Laurent-Pearson era, has another explanation: "Trudeau was an economic illiterate."

During his sixteen years in office, Trudeau squandered a century of sound financial management by previous prime ministers and their administrations. His reliance on deficit financing was economically misguided and politically irresponsible. Trudeau presided over a huge expansion of the federal government but asked the public to pay only a portion of the cost. The rest he borrowed. The effect of the deficits was to misrepresent the cost of government programs. People received their benefits, but they did not receive an accurate bill. Had they been taxed in full, they might well have rebelled and said that the price was too high. Borrowing allowed Trudeau and his ministers to spend freely, and often frivolously, without risking their political hides.

Other, equally serious repercussions only became evident after he had retired. He believed in a strong central government, and thrashed everyone from separatists to terrorists to provincial premiers who challenged Ottawa's power. Yet he weakened the federal government by leaving it so burdened with debt and annual budget deficits that it no longer had the capacity to launch new social programs and retained only limited scope for responding to emergencies. He asserted our independence from the United States and its roving multinationals through such initiatives as the Foreign Investment Review Agency and the National Energy Program. Yet he undermined our sovereignty by leaving us dependent upon our lenders, domestic and foreign, to finance the operations of our national government.

Throughout his years as prime minister, Trudeau believed that the state could effectively manage the business cycle, which alternates between growth and recession, but he demonstrated just the opposite. Governments could spend billions, directly or through tax expenditures, and nevertheless do little to create employment or stimulate growth. He and many of his Liberal colleagues believed in Keynesian economics but they demonstrated that it is unworkable in practice, because once they started spending they found it impossible to stop. They set out to create jobs and prosperity and wound up creating massive deficits and a mountain of debt.

3

THE TROUBLE
WITH BRIAN

During their nine years in office, the Mulroney Tories periodically found themselves engulfed in a political tempest that unfolded like this. The prime minister or his minister of finance or another member of his cabinet would announce that spending would be cut, or civil service wages frozen, or social benefits clawed back through the tax system, or a crown corporation privatized. At that point, all hell would break loose.

Opposition MPs would be the first on their feet, thumping on their desks in the Commons, seething with apparent rage, hurling accusations at the government during Question Period and generally behaving with all the decorum of a pack of pit bulls. The scene would then shift to the Commons lobby where the same honourable members would regurgitate their well-rehearsed outrage for a scrum of jostling cameramen and microphone-toting reporters all desperate for their daily dollop of controversy.

Then the special interests would pounce and denounce with the tenacity of angry rottweilers, their rhetoric inflamed, their positions rigid, their commitment unwavering. Within a few days, the combined power of the opposition, the special interests, and the media would turn a local disturbance into a nationwide storm and the Tories would be running for shelter. Rational arguments would be swept aside by a deluge of rhetoric, and passion would rule the battlefield.

This scenario occurred over and over during the Tory years. It happened when the Conservatives tried to tamper with indexing of old age pensions, when they began to claw back the baby bonuses, when they started to trim transfer payments to the provinces, and when they snipped away at the spending plans of the CBC. It occurred when the Tories closed rural post offices, cancelled a few Via Rail passenger trains, and sold off crown corporations like Air Canada and Petro-Canada. To hear the howls of outrage that greeted all these initiatives, an innocent bystander might have concluded that the Mulroney government had dismantled our most beloved institutions, stripped us of our most vital public services, and systematically destroyed the nation.

Moreover, the images and emotions of the moment, coloured by partisan politics and manipulated by special interests, have survived. Academics, social policy analysts, and other commentators have perpetuated the notion that the Mulroney Tories were little more than a party of bomb throwers. These observers have practically created a new literary genre called Mulroney horror stories. In many cases, their rhetoric, criticisms, and conclusions have been nearly as intemperate as those of the politicians, pundits, and special interests who had front-row seats during the Tory years.

Here, for example, are James Rice, a professor at McMaster University's School of Social Work, and Michael Prince, who holds a similar position at the University of Victoria, writing in the 1993–94 edition of *How Ottawa Spends,* an annual review of federal social and economic policy published by the Carleton University School of Public Administration: "The cost to Canadians [of

Conservative social and economic policy] has been a lowering of the social safety net and a weakening of the bonds of nationhood. Families are under greater economic pressure, more children are living in poverty, the unemployment rate is up, more young people have lost the will to look for work, there are fewer new, full-time jobs and housing is harder to find. More people are falling into and through the social safety net."

Knowlton Nash, the former CBC correspondent and anchorman for *The National*, made a fine contribution to the genre in his 1994 book, *The Microphone Wars: A History of Triumph and Betrayal at the CBC*: "Within a few months of coming into office, Mulroney made massive budget cuts in government spending, with a particularly savage chop to the CBC, proportionately far heavier than to other areas of government spending. That, in turn, meant hundreds of jobs would be cut and scores of dramas, documentaries and arts programs would be killed. 'A catastrophe,' was [CBC president Pierre] Juneau's characterization of the cuts. Little did he realize that it was only the beginning of the Mulroney government's slash and burn budget attack on the CBC."

One of the most strident — and wide-of-the-mark — attacks on the Tories was written by former civil servant and Liberal caucus research director Brooke Jeffrey. In her 1992 book, entitled *Breaking Faith: The Mulroney Legacy of Deceit, Destruction and Disunity*, Jeffrey wrote, "The Mulroney Conservatives have no understanding of the importance of such concepts as fairness, equity and equality of opportunity, no recognition of the importance of national symbols. They are determined to eliminate government intervention in the marketplace, reduce social justice and abandon regional equity, all because they see such policies as costly and inefficient. Almost all their initiatives have involved tearing down rather than building. The Mulroney government has created a series of crises where none needed to exist. Through ruthless determination and deliberate policy decisions, they have brought the country to the brink of economic and political chaos."

In fact, nothing of the sort happened under the Tories. Brian Mulroney may have come to office promising pink slips and running shoes for thousands of civil servants, but when he retired in 1993, the status quo had survived unscathed, with a few notable exceptions. The Child Tax Credit, an income-based program aimed at low- to medium-income families, replaced the universally available Family Allowance. The Old Age Security program was no longer universal because Ottawa clawed back most of the money when high-income earners filed their tax returns. Via Rail had absorbed some real cuts at the hands of the Tories. In 1984, the rail passenger service received a $474-million subsidy from the federal government. Nine years later, the subsidy had been slashed to $348 million annually. The Conservatives also imposed some discipline and restraint in many other areas of government spending, particularly through their two-year expenditure control program, introduced in the February 1990 budget.

Yet by any important yardstick, it had been business as usual in Ottawa. Total federal spending went up every year the Tories were in office, rising from $110 billion in 1984–85 to almost $160 billion by the time they were defeated in October 1993. Transfers to other governments, including equalization payments to the provinces, the Canada Assistance Plan, and established program financing, stood at $21.7 billion when the Tories arrived in office and had climbed to $29.4 billion nine years later. In fact, tables produced by Rice and Prince show that total social spending grew at an average annual rate of 5.5 percent throughout the Tory years, whereas the average rate of inflation was 4.6 percent. Benefits paid to the elderly and the unemployed outpaced inflation by an even more comfortable margin, according to Rice and Prince.

Throughout their time in power, the Tories rarely cut spending in the sense that expenditures dropped year over year. Indeed, most average Canadians would probably define a spending cut this way: one dollar in a budget in year one is reduced to, say, 95 cents in year two and 90 cents in year three. But like most Canadian governments, the Conservatives only cut spending projections. In other words, government managers and planners always anticipated that one dollar this year would become $1.05 or $1.10 next year. Instead, the Conservatives would merely trim the increases back to $1.03 or $1.04. Invariably, the opposition parties and the organizations affected by these modest reductions would howl in anguish. This is like a group of unionized workers demanding a 10 percent pay hike, settling for 3 percent, and telling the public that they had taken a 7 percent pay cut. In most places, such an assertion would correctly be dismissed as sheer nonsense. But in Ottawa, it passed for the truth.

The CBC is a prime example of an organization in which these types of cuts were made. The corporation, repeatedly knifed by the Tories, according to its own newscasts and its many boosters, actually saw its annual parliamentary appropriation for operating expenses rise to $1.1 billion in 1993–94 from $808.5 million in 1984–85, an increase of almost $300 million or 36 percent in nine years. Those figures come straight from the corporation's annual reports. The same Conservatives also built the massive, ten-storey CBC Broadcast Centre in downtown Toronto, which was supposed to cost the taxpayers of Canada $381 million but, according to an article in the September 1994 issue of *Saturday Night* magazine, may wind up consuming $1.7 billion. Had the vocal proponents of the organization levelled with the public, they would have said, "The CBC is getting more tax dollars from you each year, but more isn't good enough for us. We need a whole lot more."

Public-sector union leaders also continually bewailed the treatment they received at the hands of the Tories. But their membership figures would lead an average taxpayer to wonder what the fuss was all about. The Public Service Alliance of Canada, the largest union of federal civil servants, lost several hundred members through layoffs and buyouts but maintained its membership at 170,000 throughout the Mulroney years because some government departments were growing. Overall, public-sector employment stood at 401,000 in 1984 and had risen to 406,000 by the time the Tories were defeated, according to figures compiled by Statistics Canada.

—◄o►—

But the deficit and the national debt remain the most telling evidence of Mulroney's failure to reduce the size and cost of government. The Tories inherited a deficit of $38.5 billion from Trudeau. They never managed to get the shortfall below $28 billion. And they left Chrétien's Liberals with a record deficit exceeding $40 billion. The debt was approaching $210 billion when Mulroney became prime minister. It was surging toward $500 billion when he resigned in June 1993. All of this raises a larger question: how could the Tories have failed so completely at managing and reducing the federal deficit?

After all, dozens of Tory MPs arrived in Ottawa in September 1984 fundamentally committed to slashing the shortfall. Some may even have imagined that they could balance the budget. "The issue was front and centre for us," recalls former Ontario Conservative and finance committee chairman Don Blenkarn. Furthermore, Tory caucus members had every reason to believe that their leader, Brian Mulroney, shared their aspirations. His tough talk about government waste, inefficiency, and overspending before and during the 1983 leadership campaign convinced many party members to support his candidacy. And in the election campaign that followed, his well-known opposition to the deficit brought thousands of voters into the Tory tent.

Here is Mulroney delivering one of his standard speeches prior to his second run at the Tory leadership. It was a spring day in 1982. He was president of the Iron Ore Co. of Canada, and he was addressing the Chamber of Commerce in Fredericton, New Brunswick. This was the Mulroney who captivated party members, as well as ordinary voters, who were concerned, even frightened, by the sorry state of the nation's finances. He spoke about "the deepening crisis in Canada's economy," and lamented the legacy of

Pierre Trudeau. "When Mr. Trudeau took office, we had a government in Ottawa that spent $12 billion a year," he said. "Today, we have a government that overspends by almost $18 billion a year. We have a government whose annual interest charges on its debt now exceed $13 billion.

"What would I do?" a brash and frisky Mulroney asked the Fredericton chamber. "I'd cut everywhere and under every circumstance. I'd cut consultants, outside lawyers and accountants, advertising, public service compensation, waste, unproductive subsidies, travel, indexed pensions and fringes, capital construction, capital overruns, and just plain bureaucratic excess, to name but a few examples. I'd cut public expenditures until such time as spending was brought under control and taxpayers began to sense that their dollars were being handled judiciously."

Mulroney reaffirmed his commitment to fiscal prudence in *Where I Stand*, a slender volume published by McClelland & Stewart in the spring of 1983 during the Conservative leadership race. It was little more than a rehash of the speeches he had been making on various national issues as a private citizen. On the first page of the opening chapter, Mulroney scornfully described Trudeau as "our national economic wizard who has managed the remarkable feat of transforming a $500-million deficit in 1968 into about a $26-billion overrun this year." A few pages later, a less partisan Mulroney observed, "When government allows its spending to get out of control, it wastes not only our money but its credibility. It forfeits its leadership role in terms of being able to mobilize public opinion and action in the name of Canada's national interest. How can a government call on a nation to restrain itself and to be more realistic in its collective demands upon our economy when its own record is an unbroken string of fiscal excess? The second problem the Trudeau government has created by its excessive spending is to diminish gravely Ottawa's capacity to act as a stabilizing force within our national economy."

Unfortunately, the closer Mulroney got to the prime minister's office, the more cautious he became. Fifteen months later, in late August, 1983, a ginger and judicious Mulroney sat for a one-on-one interview with the *Toronto Star*'s Richard Gwyn. Mulroney had just won a federal by-election in the riding of Central Nova. He was about to enter the House of Commons for the first time. He was leader of the Opposition and 24 Sussex Drive was just over the horizon. Mulroney and Gwyn met at the spartan and unheated log cabin in Pictou, Nova Scotia, where the Tory leader had lived for the summer with his wife and children while he campaigned.

Mulroney sipped a strong Turkish coffee, smoked cigarette after cigarette, and spoke more candidly than he ever had about how he planned to cut the deficit. "New revenues will come from new economic growth," he told Gwyn. "Certainly there will be restraints. But spending cuts will be fairly modest, a reduction in the rate of increase of spending. The fact is, we've devised in Canada a structure of social programs that in many ways serves us very well. Some people might like to chop it. But this isn't going to happen. We are not Britain. We are not the United States. Those social programs do honor to the character of the country."

During the 1984 election campaign, Mulroney virtually played hide-and-seek with his opponents, the special interests, and the media. They were all anxious to flush him out on the deficit, given his belligerent pre-leadership talk of "cutting everywhere and under every circumstance." But the Tory leader dodged most of their queries. Instead, the central theme of the Tory campaign was newness. Mulroney's speeches were sprinkled with references to new prosperity, new initiatives, new understanding, new promise, and, of course, new spending. By mid-campaign, the *Globe and Mail* had compiled a list of twenty-six Mulroney promises that would require new federal financing. And in a campaign appearance in Vancouver, Liberal leader John Turner accused Mulroney of making 338 such promises.

Under a Conservative government, there were to be 8,000 new jobs in the Canadian military within three years. Via Rail services cut by the Liberals would be restored. There would be more money for arts groups. Offshore search and rescue operations in Atlantic Canada would be upgraded. Agricultural colleges could count on more money, and farmers could expect lower operating costs. In his last major speech of the campaign, delivered August 28 to the Empire and Canadian clubs of Toronto, Mulroney attempted to answer his opponents and his critics in the media by estimating that all his promises would cost $4 billion over two years. As for the deficit, it would be reduced "through a balanced program of strategic investment, economic growth, tax reform and prudent fiscal management."

Despite this last-minute attempt to address the fiscal issue, the Conservative campaign planners did their best to ensure that deficit reduction did not disrupt their crowded and upbeat agenda. For one thing, they were reading the public opinion polls and they knew that spending cuts were likely to flop with the public. Most voters were only vaguely familiar with the country's financial mess and had only recently begun to pay attention to the arguments pro and con that were being batted about in public debate. Most were just beginning to understand the implications of huge annual spending overruns and were not prepared for the radical surgery needed to correct the imbalance. One public opinion poll conducted at the time by Decima Research, the Conservatives' polling firm, revealed that only 2 percent of Canadians cited deficits and the debts as the country's most pressing economic problem. Another firm, Thompson Lightstone and Co., found that 6 percent of the public saw overspending as a top economic issue.

The Conservatives also demonstrated that they were astute students of recent Canadian electoral politics. They knew that asking the voters to make sacrifices and accept some suffering was no way to win at the polls. "If you look at the history of Canadian elections since the middle 1970s, the voters have chosen the easy option almost every time," says Toronto actuary and former Tory MP Paul McCrossan. "In 1974, Bob Stanfield proposed wage and price controls. He said, 'We've got to bite the bullet now to stop inflation.' You had Trudeau saying, 'No, we don't need that. We can work our way out of it.' In 1979, it was [Joe] Clark's turn. Clark was saying, 'We can have mortgage interest deductibility,' and Trudeau was saying, 'We can't afford it.' In 1980, Clark said, 'We have to bring the price of energy to world levels,' and Trudeau was saying, 'No, we don't. We can have a made-in-Canada policy.' We chose the easy option. In 1984, Turner was arguing that we have to get control of the deficit but Mulroney said, 'No. We can do it through better management,' which was the easy way."

Once in power, Mulroney's ambivalence disappeared. He moved deficit reduction and cost cutting from back stage to centre stage. The Tory leader announced his government's first major initiative, the ministerial task force on program review under the leadership of then Deputy Prime Minister Erik Nielsen, on September 17, 1984, a day after being sworn in. The objective was to examine over 1,000 government programs in order to provide better service and improved management and eliminate waste and duplication.

Less than two months later, on November 8, Finance Minister Michael Wilson delivered his fiscal and economic statement in the House of Commons, which was meant to be a sort of official ribbon-cutting ceremony to signal the start of a new era of sound management and fiscal prudence. Wilson provided the philosophical blueprint while Treasury Board president Robert de Cotret provided the bricks and mortar — spending cuts and tax increases that would cost Canadians a projected $4.5 billion over the next sixteen months.

Finally, the May 1985 budget, with its mix of expenditure reductions, tax increases, and partial deindexation of Old Age Security, seemed to confirm that the Tories meant business when they talked about cleaning up the financial mess left behind by the Trudeau government. The budget called for spending cuts of $1.9 billion over two years and tax increases that would bring in an additional $2 billion over the same period.

The Conservatives also announced plans to trim the civil service by 15,000 positions over six years. And they made restraint a long-term priority by committing themselves to a net reduction in federal expenditures of $15 billion by 1990–91. This meant that any new spending would have to be offset by matching cuts and, in addition, the government would find another $15 billion to chop.

For the opposition Liberals and New Democrats, as well as special interests ranging from organized labour to women's groups to arts organizations and beyond, all of whom had grown accustomed to perennial increases in spending, this was radical stuff. They unanimously denounced the Tory initiatives and portrayed them as the start of a neoconservative restructuring of Canadian society. In reality, the changes introduced in the November 1984 economic statement and the May 1985 budget reflected the triumph of moderates over hardliners within the cabinet and Prime Minister's Office (PMO). According to several observers who attended meetings and participated in the deliberations, a vigorous debate occurred during the first few weeks of the Conservatives' mandate over how far and how deeply the government should cut.

Charles McMillan, senior policy adviser to Mulroney between 1984 and 1988, said that the hardliners, led by Wilson, argued that the November economic statement and the government's first budget should contain cuts of at least $7 billion. The moderates argued for cuts of $4 billion, and the prime minister sided with them. The views of the moderates were shaped by senior officials in the finance department and the Privy Council Office, the same Ottawa bureaucracy that many Tories, led by Mulroney, had frequently criticized and ridiculed while in opposition.

"Some of us wanted to go higher," recalls McMillan. "I can recall Wilson standing up at a priorities and planning committee meeting in mid-October and reading from Milton Friedman's *The Tyranny of the Status Quo*, which argues that a government should make the big cuts in the first six months of its mandate. Just before the November statement, Wilson and I and [Deputy Finance Minister] Mickey Cohen flew down to Florida to meet Mulroney, who needed a rest after the campaign and meeting the Queen and the Pope. We presented the options and went through the material. That's when Mickey gave Mulroney the soft option, $4 billion versus $7 billion, and he took it."

By accepting the so-called soft option, the Tories had set the hurdle too low to make any real progress against the deficit, according to some participants in the debate. "I think it was an error and I think history will show quite clearly that it was," recalls William Mackness, dean of the University of Manitoba business school. Mackness, who was a senior vice-president and chief economist with the Bank of Nova Scotia at the time, served as a special adviser to Wilson from September 1984 to September 1985.

"The Conservatives implicitly accepted a gradualist policy that was really handed to them by the public service. The statement that Wilson released in November 1984 was written by the civil service. The government didn't roar up to Ottawa and craft that. However, the government endorsed it. They passed up an opportunity to deal upfront and decisively with the problem. Although there was all kinds of catchy, pro-market rhetoric in the document, the fact was that it was prepared to see deficits run at immense levels for years so that you could have a gentle adjustment.

"There was the option of taking sharp draconian measures or not taking those steps, and there was no shortage of advice that the gradualist option would work. The Ottawa bureaucracy didn't think up that approach for the Tories. They'd been marketing it to the Liberals for the previous ten to fifteen years. It has a wonderful appeal in that you don't have any upfront inconvenience because the planners will figure out how to get the revenue and spending lines to cross over at some convenient period in the future. It's a question of analysis being done by people who have literally no concept of a balance sheet, or the consequences of ruining one."

◄O►

In retrospect, some former Tory MPs and ministerial advisers have concluded that Mulroney's commitment to deficit reduction was lukewarm, at best, and they note that he almost always put political expedience ahead of principle. According to McMillan, one of the key incidents which signalled the prime minister's lack of resolve occurred in April 1985. In the face of intense political pressure from Quebec, Mulroney caved in and approved Ottawa's share of a federal-provincial $150-million interest-free loan for Domtar Inc., a Montreal-based pulp and paper company. "With the Domtar grant, the floodgates opened," says McMillan. "It became an auction. If you gave to one region, you had to balance it off with spending in other regions. Pretty soon, everyone was at the trough."

The most clear-cut example of Mulroney's willingness to bend was the capitulation on deindexing the Old Age Security following a month of mounting protests after the introduction of the May 1985 budget. "That was a key surrender," says Blenkarn. "If we had been able to stare down the seniors we could have stared down the farmers. But by surrendering on pensions we encouraged massive amounts of pressure from all sorts of groups. I don't believe that Mulroney, at any point, was really prepared to bite the bullet on the deficit. I think he was prepared to pretend to play tough but when push came to shove he usually found the money. When it was politically important, he did it. He didn't let philosophy get in the way of making an advance politically."

To make matters worse, the Tories were unable to avoid the pitfalls that face any new government. Ministers quickly became enamoured with their departments. Problems arose that seemed to demand new spending. And then there was the erosion of will that occurs as a government approaches another election. "My argument in November 1984 was that the reason for going early with big cuts was that the ministers are positioned within their empires to make arguments against cutting," says McMillan. "You've got to get them before they've fallen in love with their assets and bought into the spending agenda."

In fact, many Tory cabinet ministers caught the spending bug during their first year in office. University of Moncton professor of public administration Donald Savoie argued in his 1990 book, *The Politics of Public Spending in Canada,* that by the time Wilson presented his first budget, some of his cabinet colleagues were already resisting spending cuts, and their opposition grew from there. Even Wilson's determination seemed to be slipping when he unveiled his second budget on February 26, 1986. The finance minister announced cuts totalling $500 million but gave his cabinet colleagues the discretion to decide where to trim expenditures. He exempted programs touching on "health, safety, security and service to the public."

By this time, the Tories were really resigned to nibbling at the edges of the problem. The cuts were spread across twenty-six departments, and in an era of multi-billion-dollar departmental budgets, employment and immigration took the biggest hit — $76 million — while regional industrial expansion was next in line at $50 million. "Spending cuts were now out of favour," Savoie writes. "Wilson and Treasury Board president Robert de Cotret could hardly work up any interest outside their own departments to launch another round. In fact, it became increasingly clear after Wilson's 1986 budget that spenders were beginning to turn the tide and win some major battles against the guardians."

During the final two years of their first term, the Conservatives completely lost sight of their original budgetary objective — a net expenditure reduction of $15 billion by 1990–91 — and were actually borrowing billions of dollars to fund new programs. In the 1986–87 fiscal year, the Tories provided $1 billion in assistance to Western grain growers who were being hurt by falling world wheat prices. A year later, they provided another $1.1 billion. In both cases, the government borrowed rather than trimming back other programs. "The grain subsidies were horrific," recalls Blenkarn. "The farmers screamed and screamed and screamed, 'You're giving Quebec everything and you're not giving anything to Western Canada.' We had all these members from the West saying, 'What the hell are you doing, Mulroney? We're in terrible shape!' All the premiers were after him. So he gave."

Similarly, the Mulroney administration launched the Atlantic Canada Opportunities Agency in June 1987 with $1.05 billion in borrowed money to be spent over five years. Later that year, they set up the Western Diversification Fund with $1.2 billion in new money. In 1988, an election year, the Tories and the Quebec Liberal government agreed to a jointly funded $1-billion regional development program. As a result of these and other initiatives, federal spending jumped 6 percent in fiscal 1988–89. By comparison, it grew only 1.8 percent in 1985–86, the first full year of Tory rule.

Although they wound up spending rather than cutting, Mulroney, Wilson, and other senior members of the government frequently boasted about the progress they had made against the deficit. "Our challenge in 1984 was to restore fiscal stability and rebuild credibility in the management of government finances," Wilson said in the House of Commons on February 10, 1988, as he presented his final budget of the Conservatives' first term. "That is exactly what we did. We are reducing the growth rate of the national debt to no more than that of the economy by 1990–91. We are achieving steady year-to-year declines in the deficit. The reduction projected for 1988–89 will be the first time in the post-war period that the deficit has declined four years in a row. We are ensuring substantial reductions in the government's financial requirements."

The Tory pitch may have made sense to economists and bank chairmen, but average voters, at least those who were concerned about federal spending and overspending, could not help but wonder how the government was doing better when expenditures went up every year, the national debt kept growing, and the annual deficit remained stuck at close to $30 billion. And once the 1988 election was behind them, the Tories themselves seemed to realize that they had to attack the problem with renewed resolve. "The feeling was that the deficit had not been tamed, and that the whole compounding interest problem was worse than ever," recalls David McLaughlin, who served as a senior aide to several Tory cabinet ministers and as a policy adviser in the Prime Minister's Office. "We were back. We had a mandate. We said, 'Let's get at these things.'"

One of the government's first initiatives was to form a cabinet-level expenditure review committee, which was widely discussed in Ottawa and the national media as a serious attempt to bring spending under control. "It was an internal mechanism to focus the government politically on dealing with the deficit and debt," says McLaughlin. "It was a big committee, major stuff at the time. You would have the minister of finance on it, the president of the Treasury Board, your other senior ministers like Don Mazankowski and John Crosbie, as well as the regional ministers like Bill McKnight from Saskatchewan. It was going to drive the government."

But ERC, as it was known, did not last long, nor did the Conservatives' determination to cut spending. "I remember the committee's first meeting because I ran into a deputy minister who was just coming out of the room," says Savoie. "I asked him if they were biting the bullet, and he said, 'Biting it? They're biting it, chewing it and spitting it out. Boy, they're going to make some tough decisions.' Well, it never came to pass. The prime minister attended the first meeting and never showed up again. That sent a message to a lot of the spending ministers that this is not serious. If the prime minister is not in the chair, no tough decisions are really made. The personality of the prime minister, and the role of the prime minister in this thing is absolutely crucial. No question about it."

The expenditure review committee gradually ceased to function and was supplanted by the operations committee. Known around the capital as OPS, it became the central decision-making body of the government on a day-to-day basis, according to McLaughlin, although Mulroney was not a member. Mazankowski chaired the committee while he was deputy prime minister but turned over the chairmanship to Harvie André after becoming finance minister. McLaughlin, who sat in on many operations committee meetings as a policy adviser to the prime minister, recalls that cabinet ministers were constantly pitching projects that needed funding. They were expected to find some or all of the money themselves, usually by shifting it from other parts of their departmental budgets. But this didn't always happen. More often than not, the finance minister and fellow ministers would strike deals to accommodate political priorities or deal with economic emergencies.

"The economic and fiscal situations were always top of mind," says McLaughlin. "The sources of money and the problem of money were always present. But it's very difficult to tell cabinet colleagues, 'No, you can't have the funding.' Strong ministers make strong cases. Sometimes, they don't take no for an answer. They keep coming back. At the end of the day, you'd have the finance minister saying, 'We'll accommodate it within the fiscal framework. We'll find the money somewhere. We'll take it out of a policy reserve or something. If it takes us off the fiscal framework then when we do the budget a few months from now, something else will have to go.'"

Theoretically, all of the day-to-day wheeling and dealing was supposed to take place within the fiscal framework set out in the annual budget. And in their first two budgets after the 1988 election, the Tories attempted to crack down on spending. In the weeks leading up to the budget of April 27, 1989, the Conservatives took every opportunity to warn Canadians to expect the worst. Then they failed to deliver. They announced expenditure reductions of $3.4 billion over two years, which sounds steep until it is set against total spending of $292 billion during the same period. For all their tough talk, the freshly elected Tories set out to trim federal outlays by a grand total of 1.17 percent. In effect, they repeated the mistake they made in year one of their first mandate: they set the hurdle too low.

The centrepiece of the Conservatives' next budget, unveiled February 20, 1990, was the two-year expenditure control plan. It was projected to cut $2.8 billion from previously planned spending for the 1990–91 fiscal year and $3.3 billion in 1991–92. Under this scheme, a number of programs, including science and technology, the Canada Assistance Plan, and defence, would be limited to 5 percent increases in spending per year. Funding for others, such as the CBC, Telefilm Canada, and the Export Development Corporation, were to be frozen. The Tories cut spending in several other areas for total savings of $51 million, and cancelled three programs, including the Coast Guard's Polar-8 icebreaker. Most of the savings, however, were to be realized through better internal management of the government. Overall, the expenditure control plan was to result in huge savings of almost $20 billion over a five-year period, and a stunning drop in the deficit — from $30.5 billion at the outset to $10 billion in 1994–95.

But two developments, the 1990–91 recession and the government's preoccupation with constitutional issues, demolished those rosy projections and left the Tory deficit-reduction plan in shreds. The recession led to every finance minister's nightmare. Revenue growth stalled as businesses failed and corporate profits dwindled. At the same time, spending soared as unemployment rose and the welfare rolls got longer. While the recession wreaked its havoc, Mulroney and his senior ministers were absorbed in trying to save the Meech Lake Accord, and later became immersed in the lengthy public consultations and negotiations that led to the Charlottetown Accord. They simply failed to devote adequate time and energy to managing the country's finances. By late summer, 1992, as the government prepared to put its latest constitutional package to the people in a national referendum, the results of that neglect became apparent. Mazankowski was the finance minister at the time, having taken over from Wilson, and the revenue, spending, and deficit projections contained in his February 1992 budget were off by several billion dollars.

"The Privy Council Office advised the prime minister in late August to meet privately with Mazankowski before he briefed senior ministers on the fiscal and economic problem," says McLaughlin. "The finance department's tracking was starting to show that we were going to be significantly off-track and it would require decisions about cuts and other things. The dimensions were such that we had to get the two senior people in the government to focus on it. That advice was coming from PCO. But we were dealing with the referendum. In those circumstances, although you may monitor the fiscal situation, you're not going to get the kind of political focus required to make significant decisions related to it."

According to McLaughlin, the cabinet finally got the grim news about the government's deteriorating finances on October 28, two days after the defeat of the Charlottetown Accord. In a bid to steer the government back on course, Mazankowski delivered an economic statement, which amounted to a mini-budget, in the House of Commons on December 2, 1992. By then, revenues for the 1992–93 fiscal year were estimated at $124 billion, down $8 billion from the projection in the February 1992 budget. The deficit was expected to come in at $34.4 billion, up from the $27.5-billion estimate contained in the budget. Two months later, as the 1992–93 fiscal year drew to a close, Mazankowski released new estimates showing that revenue would be $1 billion lower than his December forecast, and the deficit would be $1.1 billion higher at $35.5 billion. In effect, the Tories had lost control of the country's finances, just as the Liberals had in the early 1980s when Allan MacEachen was finance minister and the country went through another debilitating recession.

Although they came to power talking tough about taming the deficit and reducing federal spending, the Conservatives achieved neither. They managed to slow down the growth of government, which was an accomplishment, but a small one given the expectations they created with their November 1984 economic statement and subsequent declarations. As for the deficit, they backed the beast into a corner temporarily, driving it down to $28 billion, but they never wrestled it to the floor. In the absence of real progress, they relied on promises of future progress.

An analysis of the nine Tory budgets, prepared by the Dominion Bond Rating Service in Toronto after the Conservatives were ousted from office, revealed thirty-five different estimates of what the deficit would be in future years. And the estimates were almost invariably wrong. For example, the May 1985 budget called for a deficit of $35.8 billion for the fiscal year, whereas the actual deficit was $38.6 billion, a difference of $2.8 billion. The April 1993 budget predicted a shortfall of $32.6 billion, but the Tories produced a deficit of $42 billion, a $9.4-billion miscue. "The forecasts of the PC governments became progressively worse as their term matured," the credit rating agency concluded. "Accordingly, they addressed the problem through ever rosier forecasts of revenue and economic growth, with a result that Canadians became increasingly skeptical of the government.

"The PCs were aware of their forecasting gaffes and tried to deflect criticism. One of the more inventive commentaries was provided in the 1991–92 budget papers. The government said that 'If revenues and program spending as a percent of GDP had been allowed to remain at their levels in 1984–85, the 1990–91 deficit would have risen from $30.5 billion to $82.7 billion.' Using this analogy, the deficit had been cut $52.2 billion, even though the 1990–91 deficit was actually just $2.4 billion lower than anticipated in the 1984–85 economic statement."

What little progress the Tories made was largely due to higher revenues rather than lower expenditures. In fact, early in their first term they learned a crucial lesson, which they never forgot: raising taxes is a lot easier than cutting expenses. The Conservatives were blessed with an economic boom that lasted seven consecutive years, the second-longest period of sustained growth in the post-war period. While the robust economy of the 1980s in itself would have generated billions of dollars in new revenues for Ottawa, the Tories conducted a major overhaul of the tax system, which dramatically increased the government's take. In their nine budgets and two economic statements, the Conservatives introduced approximately forty-three tax increases. Besides the despised Goods and Services Tax, which sparked the equivalent of a national temper tantrum, they eliminated a number of exemptions and deductions, broadened some taxes, and introduced brand new levies, such as surtaxes for high-income earners. Consequently, government revenues from personal income taxes more than doubled under the Tories. In 1984–85, Ottawa took in $29 billion through income tax. By 1991–92, the yearly toll had soared to more than $61 billion.

This reliance on the revenue side of the balance sheet to address the country's fiscal problems was completely contrary to the stated intentions of the Tories. In his budget of February 26, 1986, Wilson said that as a matter of long-term policy, 70 percent of any reductions in the deficit would be achieved through cuts to government spending. The balance would come through increases in taxes and other sources of revenue. But almost every time the Conservatives attacked the deficit, the tax grabs were heftier than the spending cuts.

The May 1985 budget slashed expenditures by about $1.9 billion over two years and called for tax hikes totalling $2 billion. In that budget, the Conservatives brought in eleven tax measures, which included the elimination of the Registered Home Ownership Savings Plan, the deindexation of the personal tax system, a jump in the Manufacturers Sales Tax, and the first surtax on high-income earners. The next time out, in February 1986, Wilson brought in another ten tax hikes. The Manufacturers Sales Tax went up again. Liquor and tobacco taxes went up. The surtax on personal income was raised. And the list went on. Even as he told the Commons and the Canadian public that the Tories would rely on a 70/30 split between spending cuts and tax hikes, Wilson announced expenditure reductions of $500 million and tax measures worth $1.5 billion for the coming fiscal year. In the subsequent two years, those same tax changes would cost the public an estimated $5.5 billion.

In the two budgets prior to the 1988 election, the Conservatives were simply trying to avoid provoking voters with either controversial spending cuts or painful tax hikes. But once the election was over, they hammered the public again. Wilson's April 1989 budget contained thirteen tax hikes, including the announcement that the GST would be introduced on January 1, 1991. Those tax measures were expected to boost government revenues by almost $11 billion over two years. By comparison, the finance minister proposed to cut spending by only $3.4 billion during the same period. The finance minister also announced changes to the financing for unemployment insurance, clawbacks that ended the universality of Old Age Security and the Family Allowance, and steps to slow down the rate of growth of the Canada Assistance Plan as well as general-purpose transfers to the provinces.

This tidal wave of tax increases unleashed by the Mulroney governments had far-reaching and fundamental repercussions that were both financial and cultural. From a financial perspective, the Mulroney Tories left individual Canadians poorer by taking a big bite out of their take-home pay. The impact is evident in a Statistics Canada report entitled *Where Does the Money Go: Spending Patterns of Canadian Households, 1969–1992*, published in late 1994. Statistics Canada notes that in the period covered by the report, household incomes remained relatively stable once inflation is taken into consideration; but taxes went way up in real terms.

"Personal income taxes rose steadily to 20 percent of total household expenditures from under 13 percent in 1969. This resulted in a smaller proportion being left over for other household expenses," Cynthia Silver, the author of the report, notes. "Taxes are graduated such that those with lower incomes pay proportionately less tax than those in middle or high-income brackets. In 1992, personal income taxes accounted for only 4 percent of total expenditures for the one-fifth of households with the lowest incomes. The proportion rose to 17 percent among the three-fifths of households in the middle-income groups and 29 percent among the one-fifth of households with high incomes."

Another revealing look at the tax burden borne by Canadians appears in the December 1994 issue of *Tax Policy Bulletin*, published by the Toronto-based accounting firm Ernst & Young. In 1992, personal income taxes in Canada stood at 14.5 percent of the country's gross domestic product, versus 10.1 percent in the United States. Total taxes paid in Canada represented 36.5 percent of GDP, compared with only 29.4 percent in the United States. According to Ernst & Young, that seven-point spread means that Canadians are paying the equivalent of $50 billion per year more in taxes than Americans. By comparing taxes in the two countries between 1970 and 1992, the company showed quite clearly that the gap widened significantly during the Mulroney years.

From a cultural point of view, Mulroney and his finance ministers tested and discovered the public's tolerance for tax increases. This had an immediate impact on the mood of the electorate. Canadians may have been deferential and acquiescent toward their government and their leaders at the beginning of the Mulroney years but they were surly and cynical at the end. The uproar that greeted the GST, the revolt against excessive tobacco taxes, and the growth of the underground economy, with its cash transactions and tax avoidance, all attested to the new mood among Canadians. Mulroney's mania for tax increases also changed the public's underlying attitudes toward government. The surliness and cynicism turned into permanent resentment of tax increases of any kind. In the post-Mulroney era, politicians at every level have had to talk tough and strive mightily to bring in budgets that do not impose new financial burdens on their constituents. Similarly, candidates for public office at the federal, provincial, and municipal level now chant the line "No new taxes" with mantra-like predictability.

Long before the Conservatives' defeat in October 1993, it had become evident to most observers, even those on the left, that the Tories had failed to make any meaningful improvement in the country's finances and frequently failed to meet their own deficit projections. Furthermore, their deficit-reduction strategy was ultimately a political disaster because it alienated voters on the right, on the left, and in the centre of the political spectrum. Those on the right, who wanted real reductions in dollars spent and a balanced budget, were left jaded and disillusioned, and fled in droves to the Reform Party. Those on the left, who remained wedded to perpetual and unlimited spending increases, viewed Mulroney's tepid cuts as radical and dangerous. And those in the centre, who had to bear the brunt of the Tory tax increases, were simply infuriated.

While Mulroney ran the country, his political opponents on the opposite side of the house, and his adversaries on the left, consistently portrayed him as an ideologue and a deconstructionist who was bent on dismantling Canada's social safety net. That is essentially a false portrait. Mulroney was a tinkerer, and a timid one at that. His lack of resolve and his failure to bring about fundamental change in our social programs and in the size of the federal government left us with a sky-high national debt and increasingly precarious finances and ultimately contributed to his party's electoral disaster in October 1993.

But in Mulroney's failure there is a more enduring lesson for Canadians, and it is this: we cannot grow our way out of our deficit-debt crisis. There will be no easy solutions. Mulroney inherited a dreadful financial mess from Trudeau but was blessed with the second-longest uninterrupted economic boom of the post-war era. Even the smoking economy in the 1980s, however, did not generate the windfall revenues required to balance the federal budget. In the uncertain 1990s, it is becoming increasingly clear that there is only one way out of our dilemma: spending must be cut. Everywhere and under every circumstance.

4

CHRÉTIEN'S
CRAFTY LIBERALS

So there was Jean Chrétien, on the first anniversary of his 1993 election victory, seated on a small stage at the centre of a large, high-ceilinged meeting hall at the University of Ottawa. The CBC's Pamela Wallin was at his side and several dozen ordinary Canadians sat around them. Wallin was the host and Chrétien the guest at an electronic town hall, one of those carefully orchestrated encounters with a group of average voters, who had been selected to represent a cross-section of Canadians. There were Maritimers and Quebeckers, Ontarians and Westerners, men and women, Caucasians and people of colour, businesspeople, civil servants, and blue-collar workers.

The questions spanned the spectrum of issues: crime, health care, education, unemployment insurance, Quebec, social policy reform, and the country's debt crisis. An auto worker from Scarborough, Ontario, asked Chrétien whether he had a mandate to push a Progressive Conservative agenda of deficit reduction and cuts to social programs. A small businessman from Edmonton exhorted the prime minister to balance the budget as quickly as possible. A woman from Prince Edward Island expressed her fear that the government would cut seasonal UI benefits that pump millions of dollars a year into her province's economy. A woman from Edmonton accused the prime minister of behaving like Reform's first cousin.

Throughout this grilling, there were two Jean Chrétiens on stage — the one we heard and the one we saw. This was a televised event, and TV is an audiovisual medium. It consists of images, words, and sounds. We watch and we listen, in that order, because pictures are more arresting than words. Given this hierarchy of the senses, the visual elements of Chrétien's presentation, his delivery and style, did more to shape our perceptions than did the content and substance of his answers. And from a visual perspective, our incongruous prime minister performed flawlessly. He was sincere, down-to-earth, and earnest. He was never prickly or combative like Trudeau or stuffy and overbearing like Mulroney. He was polite when his questioners were aggressive. He was patient when they were tedious and windy. He vigorously defended his government but never seemed to be lecturing the audience. In short, Chrétien displayed all the qualities that sent his popularity soaring to record levels during his first year in office and kept it aloft in year two.

But when we listened, a different Chrétien emerged, one who was aurally jarring and intellectually dissonant. Chrétien speaks the way most people think: in a stream of consciousness that consists of disjointed, incomplete sentences or rambling strings of clauses posing as complete thoughts. Yet his decades of political experience were abundantly evident from his performance. He never tripped or faltered or boxed himself in. He could be evasive and equivocal. He rarely made a firm commitment and rarely ruled anything out. He was there but he wasn't there. Nobody could touch him.

He answered all the questions, yet his answers did not add up to a compelling or coherent statement about where he was going or why the public should follow. Instead, the substance and content of his responses exposed the inherent contradictions of some of his government's policies. He talked about growth when he knew he must cut spending. He preached optimism when he knew that his government would inflict pain. But, Chrétien has never been bothered by such contradictions. It is not his style. Contradictions are only troublesome for those preoccupied with detail. Chrétien has always let others read the fine print. He concentrates on the big picture. Bureaucrats produce fat briefing books. He prefers the one-page memo. Others fret over policy. He worries about positioning. And at his anniversary town hall, the prime minister cleverly used the voices of the ordinary Canadians seated around him to illustrate where he stands. "I've been in politics a long time," he said. "Being a Liberal is you're always trapped in the middle. I'm too far to the right for the left winger and too much of a left winger for the right winger."

Chrétien led the Liberals into office with a detailed program, contained in their famous Red Book of campaign promises, but no firm ideas about where he wanted to take the country. His biggest ambition was simply to win the 1993 election, and to restore the Liberal Party to its accustomed place at the helm of the government of Canada. By fulfilling that ambition, he ensured that the twentieth century will be remembered as a Liberal century, with Laurier at one end, Jean Chrétien at the other, and King, St. Laurent, Pearson, Trudeau, and Turner in the middle.

The Liberal victory was a testament to his extraordinary skill as a politician. His abiding popularity during the first half of his mandate was a reflection of his personal charm and his ability to read the public mood. What Chrétien sensed upon taking office was that after Trudeau and Mulroney, the public was tired of political and economic adventurism. Between 1980 and 1993, Canadians witnessed, experienced, or endured two devastating recessions, the first Quebec referendum, the patriation of the Constitution, the fight over the National Energy Program, the debate over free trade, the introduction of the GST, the Meech Lake crisis, the referendum on the Charlottetown Accord, and numerous petty scandals. Chrétien's primary objective, once he was ensconced in the prime minister's office, was simply to deliver good, honest government.

One problem awaited him, however, that would demand more than competence and integrity, and that was the country's debt crisis, which was growing at a rate of $85,000 a minute, according to the government's own figures. It can only be solved by a leader who is prepared to make fundamental changes, one who is capable of redesigning the federal government and reshaping public expectations of government. Chrétien's response to this crisis, combined with his handling of the Quebec problem, will determine whether he is viewed as an average prime minister, a good one, or a great one. But Chrétien's temperament and aspirations may prevent him from being anything more than average. He is by nature calculating rather than daring, clever rather than brilliant, more a manager than a visionary, and he has only reluctantly accepted the job of cleaning up Canada's fiscal mess.

This was apparent during his anniversary town hall. Members of the audience kept asking variations of the same question: they wanted to know how Lloyd Axworthy's social policy review could lead to a stronger social safety net while Paul Martin talked about lopping billions from the federal deficit. But Chrétien danced around the question, as he did whenever it was put to him in the fall of 1994. "To be a Liberal, you care about people," he said. "You are preoccupied with the problems of the unemployed; how can we use money to train them. That's the Liberal way. For us, we would like to have a budget with no deficit. The reality is I had, when I came here, a huge debt, $500 billion. I did not create it but I have to pay the interest on it. I have no choice. It's a very complex situation."

-◦-

For Chrétien, fiscal conservatism is necessary rather than desirable. He has adopted a fiscally prudent approach to governing more out of expedience than conviction. He and his cabinet colleagues came to understand the enormity of the problem and the potentially disastrous consequences — a plummeting dollar, skyrocketing interest rates, and perhaps even an international lenders' strike — that awaited the country if they failed to act. They also realized that they could take drastic, un-Liberal actions and still remain popular, because the Canadian public had finally accepted the need for reform.

In effect, the arithmetic of debt, our impatient international lenders, and an awakened electorate pushed the country's fiscal crisis to the top of the political agenda, and have pushed the Chrétien government down the path of fiscal conservatism. This was an unexpected turn of events for the Liberals, who campaigned on a platform of creating jobs and stimulating economic growth. They convinced themselves, as well as the electorate, that they had their own comprehensive and carefully crafted game plan, and were prepared to implement it. The Red Book, they said, was full of ideas and initiatives merely awaiting the approval of the voters to become policy.

But their plan to reduce the deficit to 3 percent of GDP from 5.2 percent within three years of being elected was designed more to help win the election than to solve a fiscal crisis that had been two decades in the making. The Liberals promised to lower spending by "cancelling unnecessary programs, streamlining processes and eliminating duplication." For good measure, they even threw in a few specific cuts. They would cancel the purchase of new military helicopters, slash defence spending, chop the $4.1 billion Ottawa spent annually on consultants by 15 percent, cut grants to business, and trim the budgets for cabinet ministers' offices, as well as the PMO. Despite those details, this was an essentially vague plan that avoided mentioning anything painful.

The Liberals' long-term fiscal objectives were even fuzzier. "Any responsible government must have as a goal the elimination of the deficit," the Liberals concluded in their campaign booklet. But when that would occur, or how they would get there, was anybody's guess. They were not saying during the 1993 campaign, and after two years in office, they still had not set a date. For an opposition party, the ambiguities were an asset rather than a liability, because they allowed the Chrétien Liberals to stickhandle the dicey issue of deficits and debt through an election campaign far more skillfully than any other party or political leader.

During the 1984 election, John Turner promised to cut the deficit in half within seven years. The unfortunate Turner came across as a desperate politician with a dangerous idea. He managed to spook an electorate that was already deeply skeptical about him. In 1993, Preston Manning promised to balance the budget within three years by adopting a slash-and-pray approach. He proposed to slash federal spending by $19 billion and pray that an economic recovery would generate sufficient tax dollars to close the remaining gap between revenues and spending. Like a consultant who has spent too many years at workshops and seminars, Manning used charts and graphs to show voters precisely which programs would be gored and which would be gouged to reach his targets. He no doubt managed to frighten some voters — and terrorize others. Then there was Kim Campbell, who could keep a straight face while promising to balance the budget in five years without raising taxes or cutting social programs. Campbell, however, did not scare anyone. Most voters correctly saw that her plan had no substance and no credibility.

Chrétien and his team were clever enough to realize that a deficit-reduction plan that talked about enormous spending cuts would inevitably frighten voters. They knew that seniors would fear for their pensions and the jobless would worry about the security of their unemployment cheques. Businesspeople would see their subsidies evaporating. Artists, athletes, feminists, ethnic groups, and dozens of others would see their grants disappearing. Civil servants would have nightmares about layoffs or pay freezes. Any talk of big budget cuts during an election campaign would automatically unleash vigorous and vociferous opposition. The special interests, the social activists, the arts groups, the public-sector unions, sometimes even business organizations, would begin banging their drums, preaching doom, and ensuring that a rational discussion was impossible.

By the very simple expedient of talking percentages rather than dollars, the Liberals managed to avoid all the abuse normally hurled at deficit cutters. Their promise, put in plain English, meant that they planned to cut the deficit from about $40 billion to $25 billion in three years. But cast as a percentage of GDP, the Liberal plan sounded positively harmless, and it generated none of the usual overheated rhetoric that we have come to associate with the deficit debate. There was no talk of scorched-earth policies, slash-and-burn tactics, vicious cuts to social programs, or frontal assaults on equality.

With their deficit plan, the Liberals deftly claimed the cherished middle of the political spectrum. They sounded concerned and competent without posing a threat to the status quo. They were not as reckless or naive as the New Democrats, who were prepared to ignore the deficit or even allow it to grow. Nor were they harsh and draconian like the Reformers. Perhaps equally as important, the Liberal policy wonks had come up with a compromise that would unite the left and right wings of their own party. The fiscal conservatives, who wanted tough action, and the free spenders, who had railed and wailed from the opposition benches every time the Tories tried to cut a nickel or a dime, could both embrace the plan outlined in the Red Book.

The deficit-reduction plan created the illusion that the Liberals were prepared to take decisive action. But their first budget, delivered on February 22, 1994, by Finance Minister Paul Martin, revealed a serious lack of resolve. Having won the election by promising to create jobs and opportunity, the budget made "economic renewal and revitalization" the government's top priority. However, Martin and his minions offered, at best, Chamber of Commerce–style solutions to the country's economic problems. The budget spoke of relief from taxes, better access to capital, fewer regulations, and "a true strategy for research and development, one with real priorities, real direction, and a real review of results."

Martin's first budget was laden with such bulging rhetoric. He told the Commons that "we need a new architecture — for government, for the economy," and declared that "this budget sets in motion the most comprehensive reform of government policy in decades." Amid this barrage of standard political bravado, some clear thinking occasionally surfaced. "For years," he said, "governments have been promising more than they can deliver, and delivering more than they can afford. That has to end. We are ending it."

But while the finance minister diagnosed the problem correctly, he failed to prescribe the proper medicine. He promised "fundamental reform," yet left the status quo intact. Program spending was slated to rise by $800 million in 1994–95 and by $100 million the following year, which were minuscule increases by Ottawa's standards but increases nonetheless. Martin anticipated that public debt charges would jump by $3.5 billion over the same two-year period. But even as program spending and interest payments continued to grow, he predicted that the budget would bring down the deficit by $13 billion to $32.7 billion within twenty-four months. In essence, Martin was playing the same game as the dreadful and duplicitous Tories even as he steadfastly claimed to be different. He was betting on the miraculous power of economic growth to generate billions of dollars in new tax revenues and he was hoping to avoid the trauma of real cuts. His cuts, like those in the Conservative budgets, were largely cancellations of previously announced spending increases. And just as Wilson and Mazankowski had done, Martin opted for the budgetary equivalent of Rolaids when major surgery was required.

Eight months later the results were evident. On October 18, 1994, one day after releasing major discussion papers aimed at charting new economic and fiscal policies for the country, Martin told the Commons finance committee that rising interest rates had made a shambles of the plan, contained in his budget, to reduce the deficit to 3 percent of GDP within three years. The government's debt-servicing costs for the year would likely hit $44.3 billion, $3 billion more than he had anticipated. To put the problem in context, he pointed out that the additional and unexpected interest costs exceeded federal spending in each of the following areas: research and development, agriculture, and cash transfers for post-secondary education. In the absence of new and meaningful cutbacks, he would miss his 1995–96 deficit target by at least $2.3 billion and his 1996–97 goal by as much as $5 billion.

These were large and difficult admissions for a finance minister to make, but absolutely necessary after the Trudeau and Mulroney years, when each new pronouncement about spending cuts was greeted with increasing skepticism and, finally, scorn. Those were the years when our ministers of finance routinely overestimated revenues and underestimated spending, and almost always racked up a bigger deficit than promised. Spending cuts were rarely reductions in the actual dollars spent but mostly reductions in previously planned increases. By the end of the Mulroney era, the financial markets of the world, which were financing our governments to the tune of $160 million a day, had come to expect that federal budgets would contain fiscal tricks and sleights of hand, conjured up for political advantage.

As he attempted to set the country on a new fiscal path, one of Martin's biggest challenges was to convince our lenders, upon whom we had become utterly dependent, that he had rejected the practices of his predecessors and was prepared to make fundamental changes. "For ten years, governments have talked about cuts, but in reality did not live up to the billing," Martin told the finance committee. "As is clear, program spending still went up, not down. All that government did was slow the rate of growth in spending. In fact, between 1984 and 1994, program spending increased by an average of 4.2 percent every year. That game is over. Any talk of a freeze is simply outdated. It is clear that for the future, total program spending will have to be much lower than it is today. In the past, government would chip away at its operating costs without looking at the programs themselves. We will not make that mistake. We can't afford big government. We need smaller government. But what we also need — now more than ever — is smarter government."

Fundamental change was needed, he argued, because the problem was simply too big to outrun or outgrow, and recent history proved that point. In fact, without decisive government action, the country was destined to continue sliding further into the red because the national debt would keep growing faster than the economy. "Now, there are those who think we can just grow our way out of this bind," he said. "We can't. The recovery of the late seventies did not solve our debt problem. The recovery during the 1980s didn't do it either. We simply caught our breath before climbing the next flight on the debt stairs. For those who think the recovery alone will do it today, history is not on their side."

From Martin's comments to the finance committee, it was apparent that his thinking had evolved substantially in the months since his first budget. He now recognized that the country had fallen into a debt trap. "We are borrowing to pay the interest on the debt," he told his fellow MPs. "And what we borrow simply gets added to the principal. Interest payments keep getting larger as the debt keeps getting larger. In effect, our interest payments as a country are going up because the principal of the debt is going up — and the principal is going up because the interest payments on the stock of debt are going up. That's the curse of compound interest."

Martin's message in October was substantially different than the one he delivered in his February 1994 budget. The fuzzy thinking had been replaced by a clear understanding of the frightening dimensions of the problem. According to Peter Nicholson, a vice-president with Bell Canada Enterprises and one of Martin's closest advisers during this period, the ugly arithmetic of compounding interest finally persuaded the minister: "We did some simple calculations, which showed that if we didn't do something dramatic, and simply let the problem continue to compound for another five years, our annual interest payments would go up by $20 billion a year. We were paying about $40 billion in interest a year ago. In five years time, at today's rates, if we have exactly the same spending-revenue relationship, the likelihood is we would be spending $60 billion a year. And, of course, that amount would be compounding, so if you let it go for ten years, it's out of sight.

"Martin said, 'My God, $20 billion a year just in higher interest payments.' He compared that with old age security which was costing about $20 billion a year, defence which was about $10 billion, Indian and northern affairs, plus native health, at $5 billion. I mean, you're talking two to four or five times these other gigantic expenditures; that's the rate at which our interest costs are expanding. I'm sorry, but this will destroy the federal government. All the talk of social conscience and all the other objectives are meaningless in the face of the arithmetic. He really came to believe that profoundly because it wasn't really a debatable issue. It wasn't a question of ideology or opinions. The numbers were there."

Nicholson concedes that the Liberals based their Red Book deficit-reduction plan on what he calls "very imperfect knowledge." He also notes that, while in opposition, they had put more energy into criticizing the Tories than thinking about the feasibility of their own program. And Martin initially questioned the numbers and the scenarios developed by his officials in the finance department. "He's a guy who loves to debate," said Nicholson. "He's instinctively a skeptic. Whatever you say, he'll say the opposite. He'll say, 'I don't believe that. Convince me.' I think it's fair to say that as he had time, which he didn't have before the 1994 budget, to get into the details of the numbers, look at the scenarios and explore the projections about growth and interest rates, then his convictions and his understanding deepened. He came to understand vividly that we were going to be consumed by compound interest. And once he becomes convinced, he's really quite a bulldog."

◄O►

The arithmetic of debt may have been as indisputable as the laws of gravity. And Martin may have turned into an anti-deficit bulldog. Still, there was no guarantee that Chrétien would unleash Martin on the problem. The political mood of the country had to be right. The prime minister is a cautious politician who never allows himself to get too far ahead of, or out of synch with, the voters. He is also leader of a party that for fifty years has subscribed to the notion that the well-being of the nation depends upon the size of the government. But, several things occurred between October 1994 and February 1995 to indicate that the mood was right, and that stiffened the government's resolve to act.

First, the Commons finance committee held pre-budget hearings across the country, and the dozens of private individuals and business groups who appeared were nearly unanimous in demanding an all-out assault on the deficit. Second, Liberal MPs detected a virulent public opposition to any new tax increases, a sentiment that was communicated to them directly by constituents and indirectly through the consumer revolt in January 1995 against arbitrary increases in cable television rates. Next, there was the Mexican peso crisis, a sharp devaluation of the currency that created economic havoc, and which Martin would later describe as "a wake-up call . . . a concrete demonstration of a nation's vulnerability to global financial markets." Finally, New York–based Moody's Investors Service, the world's most influential bond-rating agency, announced that it was putting government of Canada debt under review.

Martin's personal conversion to fiscal conservatism, combined with the external pressures for change, turned his second budget, introduced on February 27, 1995, into a landmark political event. Its significance was evident from the opening lines. "There are times in the progress of a people when fundamental challenges must be faced," the minister told his colleagues in the Commons and his fellow citizens across the country, "when fundamental choices must be made, and a new course charted. For Canada, this is one of those times. Our resolve, our values, our very way of life as Canadians are being tested. The choice is clear. We can take the path, too well trodden, of minimal change, of least resistance, of leadership lost. Or we can set out on a new road of fundamental reform, of renewal, of hope restored. Today we have made our choice. Today we take action."

The budget contained measures aimed at saving the federal government $29 billion, of which $25.3 billion would come from spending cuts, over the following three fiscal years. By 1996–97, program spending is slated to fall to $108 billion from $120 billion in 1993–94, the year in which the Liberals took power. The list of departmental cuts, to be implemented over a three-year period, is long and comprehensive: $1.6 billion from defence; $1.4 billion from transport; $900 million from human resources development; $900 million from industry; $600 million from natural resources; $550 million from regional development agencies; $550 million from international assistance; $450 million from agriculture; and $200 million from fisheries. Subsidies to business were slated to tumble to $1.5 billion from $3.8 billion over the same three years. Grain transportation subsidies for Western farmers, which had emerged out of the Crow rate of 1897, were eliminated. Transfers to the provinces for health care, post-secondary education, and social assistance were set to fall by $4.5 billion by 1997–98.

Undeniably, this was strong medicine. It represented a radical departure from the practices of the past two decades. Every year, just as surely as Canada geese fly south in the fall and return in the spring, the federal minister of finance has started out with spending increases and ended with budget deficits. Martin put a stop to one part of the equation by announcing actual reductions in program spending. But for all its significance, this budget could not solve a crisis that was twenty years in making. It merely represented "a new course charted," to use Martin's words. It put us on "a new road to fundamental reform." What we now face is a long, arduous journey down that road, and Martin has been as candid about that as anyone in the government.

The Chrétien government's goal of reducing the deficit to 3 percent of GDP is nothing more than a first step that is going to take at least three years to achieve and add almost $100 billion to the national debt. It can do no more than stabilize the country's finances by slowing the growth of the debt in relation to the economy. That would be a substantial change from the status quo in which the debt has been growing much faster than the economy because of our huge, and perennial, budget deficits. The second step on the road back to financial health must be the elimination of the deficit altogether, which would stop the growth of the debt. This, too, is merely an interim measure, and could take several years to achieve once the government has met its 3 percent target. The third phase of a meaningful fiscal recovery must involve a commitment to keep the budget balanced permanently so that the size of the debt falls as a percentage of the economy through several complete business cycles of expansion and recession.

In November 1995, during an appearance before the Commons finance committee, Martin finally announced plans to move beyond the 3 percent goal. The government intends to cut the deficit to 2 percent of GDP by the end of fiscal 1997–98. And in a major speech to an international bankers' conference in Jackson Hole, Wyoming, in early September, 1995, the finance minister assured his audience that he is under no illusions about the magnitude of the challenge before us. "Coming into office in the fall of 1993, we expected to find a nasty fiscal situation — the combination of misplaced priorities, which is the stuff of politics, and compound interest, which is the stuff of the inexorable laws of arithmetic," he said. "It became clear that a very long period of restraint would have to be endured to turn the debt momentum around."

Martin concluded his Jackson Hole speech on the crucial point that cleaning up the country's finances means more than merely smaller government, as measured by "head counts and spending volume." The role of government must be redefined, and public expectations of government must also change. In essence, our collective challenge is to rethink our attitudes, values, and beliefs about the place of the state and the responsibilities of the individual. "We do believe that government should only do what it can do best — and leave the rest for those who can do better — whether business, labour, or the voluntary sectors," he said.

"In metaphorical terms, it is to become more like the tiller of a sleek, modern sailboat than the paddle wheel of a nineteenth-century steamer. Yet achieving this transformation still poses a very large challenge. This is because the habits and incentives of bureaucrats and politicians, and the institutions they have created over the past fifty years, have all been adapted to the fiscal growth of government. We have not yet learned how to act creatively as we must in the new environment of static or shrinking financial resources. That constraint is forcing us, as never before, to concentrate on the setting of priorities and on discovering how to do what is genuinely needed without spending a lot of taxpayers' money.

"What is called for here is not only a change in attitude; it is a sea change in the nature of politics as it has been practised in the affluent democracies over the past five decades. The job of getting government right, or reinventing government, or whatever the phrase, is much more than a slogan. Creating a public sector where it can truly be said that 'less is more' is the greatest challenge we face."

It is apparent from his Jackson Hole speech, from the opening lines of the 1995 budget, and from his comments to the finance committee in October 1994 that Martin was motivated by conviction rather than expedience. There was a believer, rather than a mere pragmatist, behind the statements. Martin was speaking with increasing clarity and confidence. He had become the most powerful minister in the cabinet and had emerged as the voice of the government. He was driving the agenda. He was defining the goals and objectives.

Some cabinet colleagues bought into Martin's agenda and successfully embarked on substantial reforms. As the intergovernmental affairs minister, Marcel Massé conducted a year-long program review that will lead to an overall reduction of almost 20 percent in departmental spending by 1997–98. As Treasury Board president, Art Eggleton was responsible for eliminating 45,000 civil service jobs, a 15 percent cut in the federal workforce. And as transport minister, Doug Young quietly but efficiently made wholesale changes to both the size and role of his department.

By the end of fiscal 1996–97, Young's initiatives will have cut the departmental operating budget by 50 percent and the workforce to less than 4,000 from 20,000 when he took over. He turned over federally owned airports to organizations known as local operating authorities. He allowed consortiums comprising airlines, pilots, and other partners to run the country's air traffic control system. He launched a review of Canada's marine transport system with a view to ensuring that the St. Lawrence Seaway and most major ports operate on a subsidy-free, commercially sound basis.

In making these changes, Young was guided by clear ideas about the proper place of government in the country's transportation system. "We're not putting these people on the street," he says of employees removed from the departmental payroll. "We're actually taking people who are working in what should be a business and commercial environment, and putting them in the business community. We are going to remain at Transport Canada with what I think the role of government should be: an oversight role for safety, security and policy, and whatever regulatory role is left, which will probably be fairly limited."

Where Young, Eggleton, and Massé have joined Martin's anti-deficit express, other members of the government, who had the misfortune to pursue contradictory or conflicting objectives, were simply flattened by it. The most prominent victim was Axworthy and his social policy review. The review was launched, with the blessing of the prime minister, in the first days of the mandate. At that point, the

Liberals were still sorting out their priorities. They believed, naively as it turned out, that they could afford to take their time, and perhaps even spend some money on a proper overhaul of the country's social programs. Axworthy laid out his vision of what needed to be done in his discussion paper entitled *Improving Social Security in Canada*, which was released in October 1994 along with Martin's papers on fiscal and economic reform.

Axworthy began with grandiose ambitions. He invited his fellow citizens "to help shape a new vision of social security for the 21st century." His review would encompass almost $39 billion worth of programs, including unemployment insurance, the Canada Assistance Plan, post-secondary education, and child tax benefits, and it would be guided by sound principles. Our social programs should be fair and affordable, Axworthy said. They should create opportunity, enhance mutual responsibility, and prevent future problems. He identified several current social ills, all deserving serious consideration, all worth attempting to solve. Long-term unemployment, defined as a year or more without work, was three times as high in 1994 as it was in 1976. There were too many repeaters on UI: almost 40 percent of those who were collecting in 1994 had filed three claims in the past five years. And a scant 10 percent received any job counselling, meaning most unemployed Canadians were poorly prepared to re-enter the labour force.

The discussion paper was full of ideas, few of which could be transformed quickly or cheaply into programs. Furthermore, Axworthy did not receive the support he anticipated from his constituency — social policy analysts, experts, workers, and advocacy groups. "He expected some sympathy, on the basis that mild reforms by a left-leaning Liberal were better than being cleaned out by Martin, but he just didn't get it," recalls Allan Moscovitch, a professor in the School of Social Work at Carleton University in Ottawa. "At one high-profile public forum in Toronto in early 1994, he was attacked throughout the whole meeting. There was just no real communication."

That rift doomed the entire social policy review. Axworthy and the social policy community failed to realize that the federal government could no longer afford to deliberate, study, or experiment, not when the country was plummeting into the red at a rate of more than $30 billion a year and when heavily indebted nations were increasingly vulnerable to the whims of the world's financial markets. The government had to act, and it did. Martin and the finance department usurped Axworthy's role and dictated the terms, timing, and parameters of social security reform in the 1995 budget.

For many members of the social policy community, the results were startling, if not shocking. The most unexpected development was the creation of the Canada Health and Social Transfer, under which each province will receive an annual lump sum payment to cover Ottawa's share of welfare, health care, and post-secondary education. The CHST eliminates Established Programs Financing (EPF), a block fund scheme for transferring money to the provinces for health care and post-secondary education. It also means the end of the Canada Assistance Plan (CAP), through which the federal government covered up to 50 percent of the cost of provincial welfare programs.

Having unilaterally established the new health and social transfer, the finance department arbitrarily imposed cuts in the amount of money it gives the provinces. Under EPF and CAP, Ottawa was scheduled to transfer $29.6 billion in 1996–97 and the same amount the following year. Martin has slashed those transfers to $26.9 billion in the first year of operation and $25.1 billion in the second, for a two-year cut totalling $7 billion. The role of the minister of human resources development in the creation of the CHST, which comes straight from the 1995 budget, has been limited to developing with the provinces a "set of shared principles and objectives" to control the use of the money.

But many social policy experts contend that in creating the new transfer scheme, and cutting its financial contribution to social programs, Ottawa has forfeited its power to set national standards for health care and social assistance. They predict that this will inevitably lead to fragmentation and growing inequities. "Without question, the Canada Health and Social Transfer will give the provinces greater scope to redesign their health care and human services," according to Ken Battle, director of the Caledon Institute of Social Policy in Ottawa, a private, nonprofit research organization. "The future social policy landscape across Canada is sure to become more uneven and more rocky."

National standards have been sacrificed, Battle and others argue, because the finance department is driving social policy, all in the name of deficit reduction. "The hand of finance is just so obvious," he says. "Cost-sharing is anathema to people who are trying to do financial planning and forecasting. What CAP meant was that the feds had to pay half the shot of whatever the provinces did on welfare and social services. In times of recession, when welfare caseloads increased, Ottawa was faced with increasing expenditures that were not controllable. By shifting to block funding, the federal government is saying, 'Here's the money. It doesn't matter whether you're hurting. This is all you're getting.' That, of course, is going to be a smaller amount each year because it's not indexed to inflation."

But some experts contend that it is wrong to conclude that less federal money means less federal control over program spending. Arthur Kroeger, a former federal deputy minister who now lectures on social policy at Queen's University in Kingston, Ontario, argues that the federal government always had limited control over how the provinces spent their transfer payments. "Health care is the only area where the federal government has played a significant role at all," he says. "The transfers for post-secondary education are so unconditional that they don't even have to be spent on education. Ottawa has no say whatsoever about what the provinces do with that money. As for welfare, there are no national standards, and there are certainly no national rates. The provinces may tell the federal government, 'You reduced your payments so you ought to shut up.' Morally, that argument may have some weight. But the fact is, in 1998, the federal government is still going to be transferring over $20 billion a year to provincial governments. If Ottawa wants to use that as leverage to enforce standards, it can."

While Martin and the finance department presented the CHST as a *fait accompli*, they gave Axworthy slightly more leeway to reform UI and old age pensions. In his budget speech, Martin announced that Axworthy would be releasing a discussion paper on unemployment insurance in late 1995. The budget also stipulated that they would jointly prepare a paper on Old Age Security (OAS) and the Guaranteed Income Supplement (GIS), although the release of this paper was delayed indefinitely due to Chrétien's promise, during the Quebec referendum, to protect pensions. In both cases, Axworthy was responsible for the details, but finance set the basic course that the government would follow. Martin ordered a 10 percent cut in UI spending — for savings estimated at $1.6 billion — through further restrictions on eligibility and the length of claims. He was prepared, however, to allow some of the money to be diverted into a new Human Resources Investment Fund comprising several programs developed by Axworthy and his department and aimed at getting jobless Canadians back into the workforce.

As with UI, Martin went beyond merely announcing that pension reform was imminent: he also laid down the principles that would be followed. An overhaul is necessary because OAS and GIS currently cost over $20 billion annually, one-sixth of the government's program budget. Without major changes, benefits could increase by 60 percent to roughly $32 billion over the next fifteen years due to the aging of the population. In his budget, Martin stipulated that the federal government would continue to protect seniors of modest or less than adequate means. But the OAS, which is currently paid to everyone over the age of sixty-five and is clawed back from high-income seniors at tax time, is destined to go only to those in need. "They have got to address old age pensions if they want to meet their deficit targets," says Kroeger. "One of the problems with seniors, as far as governments are concerned, is that they all vote. That's been a constraint on other governments, and it's probably a daunting prospect for the present government."

The fact that the Chrétien government was reviewing, reforming, and even abolishing some of Canada's most important social programs, all created by previous Liberal administrations, revealed that power had been a sobering experience. A huge change in thinking occurred at the cabinet table during the first half of the mandate. But for all that, the Liberals did not achieve very much. They developed a budgetary plan to reduce the deficit to 3 percent of GDP by the end of their mandate. They had not put anything before the public to indicate how they would balance the budget. They had not begun a public discussion about how they would reduce the debt or how big a debt would be acceptable. Nor had they turned their attention to two crucial questions that must be addressed: how do we avoid this type of financial mess in the future; and how do we ensure that future governments balance fiscal prudence with social compassion? So, there were legitimate reasons for remaining deeply skeptical about where the government was going and how far it was prepared to go. And the questions began with the prime minister.

Chrétien clearly sided with Martin in the cabinet and caucus debates leading up to the 1995 budget. Yet, he has never displayed much enthusiasm for dealing with the deficit or the debt. On the contrary, his approach has been essentially negative. In the early days of his administration, he confided to close associates that one of his principal objectives was to keep the International Monetary Fund out of Canada. In other words, he would not allow the crisis to become so acute that outside intervention was required. But nor would he set out to alleviate the problem. That is the mindset of a minimalist, and Chrétien's pronouncements following Martin's second budget reinforced that image.

One of the prime minister's few extended public discussions of the debt crisis occurred on CBC's *Morningside* a few days after the release of the budget. "We don't do these things out of joy," he told host Peter Gzowski. "We had to do it. The big burden we all carry is this debt, that is, 544 billion dollars. And we had to stop the growing of that." Later in the interview, he returned to this theme: "It's our responsibility to make sure we don't hit the wall. It's why we have done what is needed. It's not out of pleasure, sir, I have to tell you that. I'm not a doctrinaire right winger. I'm a liberal. I feel like a liberal and it's painful. But it is needed."

Circumstances have forced him to take action but Chrétien has proved to be a reluctant reformer. He is a career Liberal who cannot do what Liberals have been doing for half a century: launching programs, hiring civil servants, creating departments, setting up crown corporations, and generally increasing the size of the state and enhancing its role in the affairs of the nation. He has found it difficult "to act creatively . . . in the new era of static or shrinking financial resources," as Martin insisted, in his Jackson Hole speech, that we all must do. Hence, in the first half of his mandate, Chrétien made no attempt to define the type of country he wants to build. Nor has he hinted that a better country can emerge from the restructuring and retrenchment of government.

Instead, he reverted to a mantra: we had no alternative and we take no pleasure in what we have done. Occasionally, he revealed the magnitude of changes he thinks are necessary. "Medicare is something all Canadians will want to maintain," he told Gzowski. "Medicare is costing close to 10 percent of GDP to the Canadian taxpayer. In the U.S., it's 15 percent. In Europe, they manage to have universal medicare for 8.5 percent or less of their GDP. So, in my view it has to be improved. It has to be reduced." And later he told Gzowski, "We have to review what is medicare. In some provinces, for example, they pay for the ambulance, in others they don't. It's not exactly the same program everywhere. So it's why we have to examine what is the essence of medicare."

Once in a while, he mused about the changes that have occurred in our social programs since their inception. Yet, he never went so far as to say that we should return to the original objectives: "In the beginning, medicare was to make sure that the dignity of everybody will be protected, that nobody will lose his home because somebody is sick in the family, or needs major surgery. Eventually from election to election it was expanded. So we have to decide what is absolutely necessary for the Canadian citizens to have a free, universal, public administered health service, portable from province to province."

Chrétien has become a peekaboo prime minister. He says little and does less. He dodges problems, delays decisions, and almost never reveals where he stands. This could be seen as weakness and uncertainty. In fact, it is the work of a clever and crafty politician who knows how to create some space for himself when circumstances have granted him next to none. Chrétien has been dealt a weaker hand than any other post-war prime minister. Ottawa's ability to tax, borrow, or spend has been completely depleted. At the same time, the economy has been weak, unemployment high, and the prospects for growth shaky. The financial markets have become increasingly unpredictable and inhospitable, and the separatist threat in Quebec poses an even more direct and dangerous constraint on the government. So, Chrétien has led from behind. He has allowed others to play their cards first and hoped that their mistakes or the right set of circumstances would produce a solution.

The prime minister relies on ambivalence and procrastination because he recognizes his own limitations. Chrétien had no ambitions to be a reformer on a grand scale when he became prime minister. He is unlikely to persuade a reluctant public or recalcitrant provinces through the force of his personality, the strength of his ideas, or the power of his intellect. Instead, he set out to win the trust and affection of the public and to make Canadians feel good about themselves. In this he has succeeded like no other national leader of the post-war era, as is evident from his ratings in the polls.

But the times demand more than a merely popular prime minister. What we need today is an effective prime minister, one who can use our trust, affection, and good will as the basis for acting decisively. We need leadership that is proactive rather than reactive. Keeping the IMF out is not sufficient. At some point, the prime minister must step out of the shadow of his minister of finance and become the voice of his government. He should lead a parliamentary and public debate aimed at creating a consensus on a sustainable level of debt. And he should begin to play a role in defining the goals of a reformed welfare state, one in which fiscal prudence and social compassion are both core values. Otherwise, he runs the risk of being a hugely popular but quickly forgotten prime minister, whose impact on the country will be as fleeting as footprints in freshly fallen snow.

5

WHO IS RIDING
THE GRAVY TRAIN?

For years and years, the answer to that question was short and simple: almost everyone. In the early 1990s, our governments were borrowing money at a rate of $7 million an hour, and the sad fact was that they were giving it away even faster. And nobody seemed concerned about results, redundancy, or duplication, either within or between governments. Ottawa subsidized business. So did the provinces. Ottawa had all sorts of grants and tax breaks for farmers. So did the provinces. Ottawa provided financial support for the arts. So did the provinces. Ottawa pumped money into multiculturalism. So did the provinces. Thousands of federal and provincial civil servants, employed in dozens of departments and administering hundreds of programs, devoted their careers to reviewing applications, approving grants, writing cheques, and increasing our indebtedness hourly. Everyone was generous to a fault, but nobody outperformed the federal government.

Ottawa's motto might well have been: no group too small, no

cause too zany. And its *modus operandi* could have been: come one, come all; line up, sign up. The government had a grant or a subsidy for anyone who could fill out an application. The parade of petitioners stretched from coast to coast to coast and embraced every segment of society. It included Laotians and Lithuanians, bums and billionaires, farmers, feminists, and fiddlers, poets, painters, and sculptors, bowlers, bocce players, and badminton buffs. If you were planning a workshop or a symposium, holding a rodeo, building a ski resort, or expanding the local zoo, no problem. Ottawa could help.

A tidy summary of this deluge of subsidization and redistribution of national wealth appears annually in an obscure and rarely read set of documents called the Public Accounts of Canada, in which the federal government tallies up how much money it took in during the previous fiscal year and how the money was spent. In the 1992–93 accounts, for example, Section 8, Volume II was devoted entirely to transfer payments, which were defined as "any grant, contribution or other payment made by the government, for which no goods or services are received, and which is made for the purposes of furthering program objectives." In other words, Ottawa handed out the money but did not receive anything tangible in return.

Transfer payments included everything from multi-billion-dollar programs such as old age pensions and funding for post-secondary education, right down to the tiniest grant to an artist or ethnic group. In the fiscal year ended March 31, 1993, these federal transfers totalled $66 billion, with close to $61 billion going out in the form of major social programs and slightly over $5 billion in grants and subsidies. For the sake of brevity, the public accounts mention individually only those grants exceeding $100,000. Yet in fiscal 1992–93, this list ran to 115 pages and contained the names of over 12,000 recipients. Various government departments also keep their own detailed records of grants under $100,000, and these lists fill hundreds more pages and encompass untold thousands of recipients.

Section 8 of the accounts, with its phone book–like columns of names, addresses, and numbers, will never make a bestseller but does provide a fascinating glimpse into the all-encompassing and often bewildering world of Ottawa's grant-giving. A government which by any objective measure was technically bankrupt in 1992–93 nevertheless provided two grants worth a total of $450,000 for improvements to the golf and country club in Baie-Comeau, Quebec, Brian Mulroney's home town. It awarded $150,000 to the 1992 World Motorboat Championships, which were held in Valleyfield, Quebec, and $187,500 for an international marathon swimming race across Lac-St-Jean in the Saguenay region of Quebec. The Hockey Hall of Fame, financed largely by the National Hockey League and some of the largest corporations in Canada, including Ford, Molson, and Imperial Oil, received $1 million from the government of Canada. Curiously, the Hall of Fame, which is located at Yonge and Front streets in downtown Toronto, got its grant under a Department of Communications program aimed at subsidizing cultural infrastructure projects in Quebec and Alberta.

When it comes to free public money, some organizations just cannot get enough of a good thing. The Vancouver-based Asia-Pacific Foundation collected two grants, worth a total of $1.75 million, from External Affairs, then hit the Western Economic Diversification office for another $388,000. The Ducks Unlimited national office, located near Winnipeg, raked in $153,500 from the Environment department and $240,750 from Western Economic Diversification. The Regina Open Door Society and its Saskatoon counterpart each received two Employment and Immigration grants. Their total take: almost $750,000. New Experiences for Refugee Women, a Toronto organization, received $153,500 under one Employment and Immigration program and $161,000 under another program run by the same department. La Société du Théâtre Capitol in Quebec City accepted a $1-million regional development grant and a $150,000 grant from the Department of the Environment. The Commonwealth Games Society of Victoria was the big winner in the duplication derby: it got $10 million from Health and Welfare and $104,000 from the Department of Communications.

Trade associations, many of whom have repeatedly called for spending cuts and deficit reduction, apparently have few qualms about using public funds to further the economic interests of their members, the vast majority of them private companies. One of the chief culprits is the Ottawa-based Canadian Chamber of Commerce. The chamber reeled in a $1.5-million grant from Employment and Immigration as well as $2.3 million from External Affairs to promote trade in the Asia-Pacific region. Similarly, the Toronto-based Canadian Manufacturers Association received $193,000 from the Department of Industry, Science and Technology and $241,000 from Energy, Mines and Resources.

Other associations that were riding the federal gravy train included the following: the Shoe Manufacturers Association of Canada, the National Optics Institute, the National Institute for Magnesium, the Canadian Advertising Foundation, the Pulp and Paper Institute of Canada, which in 1992–93 received three grants, the Canadian Apparel Manufacturers Association, the Canadian Association of Fish Exporters, the Canadian Pulp and Paper Association, the Canadian Wine Institute, the Canadian Wood Council, the Council of Forest Industries of B.C., the Fisheries Council of Canada, the Fur Council of Canada, and the Quebec Association of Furniture Manufacturers.

The federal government was also dead serious about promoting economic development, and did so by showering money on private companies and nonprofit groups from Atlantic to Pacific. In 1992–93 alone, the Atlantic Canada Opportunities Agency distributed $225 million while the Western Economic Diversification agency pumped $166 million into the four Western provinces. Ottawa was, and in all likelihood remains, deeply committed to keeping Montreal afloat economically. Federal initiatives aimed solely at Quebec's largest city in 1992–93 included the Southwest Montreal Housing Program, the Montreal Development Fund, the

Corporation for the Economic and Social Renewal of Southwest Montreal, the Recovery Program for East Montreal, the Assistance Program for Montreal Regional Development, the Centre d'Initiative de la Technologie de Montréal, and the Société du Centre de Conférence Internationale de Montréal. Besides these efforts, the government contributed a total of $4.26 million under two programs toward the city's 350th-anniversary celebrations. Finally, 104 other Montreal companies, associations, and nonprofit organizations received federal money to promote growth and create jobs.

Athletes and academics were big recipients of federal largesse. The Department of Health and Welfare spent almost $45 million in 1992–93 supporting top international competitors such as Kurt Browning and Silken Laumann, as well as pillars of the national sporting scene like the Canadian Five-Pin Bowlers Association, the Canadian Water Polo Association, and the Canadian Team Handball Federation. Moving from the playing fields to the ivory towers, the government provided the Social Sciences and Humanities Research Council with about $40 million for grants. The money was distributed to university professors studying such pressing matters as slavery on the Caribbean island of St. Barthélemy in the eighteenth and nineteenth centuries and the social history of baseball in the Maritimes and New England from 1860 to 1960.

Then there were the volunteer groups, nonprofit societies, and nongovernment organizations that qualified for federal funds under numerous soft and fuzzy programs. Health and Welfare distributed $14 million in 1992–93 under the New Horizons program, which enables senior citizens "to become more actively involved in the life of their communities." The Department of the Environment contributed $600,000 to "networking organizations for community support initiatives." Secretary of State, which was rolled into the new Department of Canadian Heritage when the Tories restructured the government shortly before their October 1993 defeat, handed out $20.4 million under programs aimed at promoting "a better understanding amongst Canadians" and "furthering participation in Canadian society." And in a typical year, the federal government gives away around $25 million to promote what the public accounts call "cultural development," a bland, innocuous phrase for multicultural grants.

Multiculturalism, like many other federal programs, has become a little world unto itself, with its own buzzwords, rhetoric, and swirl of events. Taxpayers' money was used to sponsor and support conferences, forums, symposiums, workshops, roundtables, and dialogues. It was used to subsidize the creation of books, movies, documentaries, and theatre productions, and to educate teachers, police officers, businessmen and women, students, library workers, municipal workers, and health care providers, to name a few. The objective of all this activity, according to multiculturalism's many supporters, is to build a better society by promoting tolerance, diversity, pluralism, full inclusion, cross-cultural awareness, and strategies for change.

The building block for this new and improved Canada is the multicultural grant. Every year, our civil servants approve thousands of these handouts to groups large and small, prominent and obscure. The Mulroney Tories, during their final year in office, funded Chinese, East Indian, Jewish, and Muslim associations in Newfoundland and Labrador, as well as the African Society of Prince Edward Island. They provided Zion United Baptist Church in Truro, Nova Scotia, with $2,890 for a one-day problem-solving dialogue. The objective: "to prove our people are capable of working." Ottawa chipped in $28,000 for a feature film, entitled "Another Planet," about the experiences of a black teenage girl in rural Quebec, $28,000 for a video about expatriate Chilean poets in Montreal, and $5,600 for a documentary about Japanese-Canadian farmers in Alberta. The Boys' and Girls' Clubs of Greater Vancouver received $7,500 for a celebration of diversity project, while the Cranbrook Women's Resource Society got $5,000 for "strategic planning on race relations in the East Kootenay." Police departments in Vancouver, Saanich, Port

Moody, Matsqui, and Delta received money to hire summer students from visible-minority communities.

Various business and professional associations have also displayed a fondness for multiculturalism money. The Ottawa-based Conference Board of Canada picked up almost $300,000 to pay for a two-year research project on "the importance of diversity in Canadian economic prosperity." The Toronto-based Canadian Advertising Foundation collected $116,000 for a study on "how to include and portray visible minorities in advertising." And the ubiquitous Asia-Pacific Foundation got $28,500 for a series of roundtable discussions on the relationship between diversity and international trade.

Handing out grants and subsidies has become such an enormous government enterprise that even our civil servants cannot keep track of all the programs. And that is hardly surprising, according to Gary Taylor, a Toronto businessman who publishes two annual directories to help the uninitiated search for public money. Taylor's 325-page *Guide to Canadian Grants and Assistance Programs* and his 180-page *Guide to Canadian Arts Grants* contain names and descriptions of 1,200 federal and Ontario programs which give away money. The directories, says Taylor, are very popular with civil servants. "They buy them because they have all these programs but they don't seem to communicate very well with each other. If somebody comes in and asks them about one that they're not running, they usually don't know where to send the person. For the most part, though, I get orders from businesses, small, medium and large. It gives them a good overview of all the programs without spending a lot of time looking for them. It can wear you down just trying to find the right one. Many businessmen feel like it's just not worth it, yet they know there's money sitting on the table."

After leafing through Taylor's guides, or scrutinizing Section 8 of the public accounts, the average taxpayer might well conclude that the proliferation of grants and subsidies over the past twenty-five to thirty years has been haphazard and unfettered by any over-arching fundamental principles. We seem to have decided that as a society we will deny ourselves nothing. Our political leaders, regardless of party affiliation, seem to have believed that they had to litter the country with largesse in order to win elections. And once in office, they threw as much money as humanly possible at every perceived problem or noisy special interest. By attempting to appease so many special interests, we have seriously compromised — perhaps ruined — the one thing in which every man, woman, and child has an overriding interest: the solvency of our country.

We are not the only nation to have strayed into such perilous waters. The prominent Swedish economist Assar Lindbeck made a similar observation about his country in an October 1993 lecture sponsored by de Nederlandsche Bank of Amsterdam: "The traditional welfare state, chiefly designed to provide economic security and to wipe out poverty, may after a while turn into a 'transfer state' with free-for-all distributions to various groups of citizens at the expense of the general taxpayer. Politically determined redistribution may, in this context, largely become a complicated system of tax and transfer lotteries, which are often loaded in favour of politically powerful groups. As these redistributions may severely hurt the national economy, the general interest of society simply cannot be regarded as the sum of unco-ordinated special interests."

During their first year in office, Jean Chrétien and his ministers served notice that they intended to change the rules for the businesspeople, cultural groups, multicultural organizations, athletes, academics, and myriad other special interests who have long enjoyed unquestioned access to free public money. Finance Minister Paul Martin initiated the change in his February 1994 budget with the following low-key announcement: "Fiscal reality requires that the government review its policy on funding interest groups. Our goal is to encourage greater reliance on funding from other sources."

The prime minister then asked his cabinet colleague Marcel Massé, the minister for public service renewal and intergovernmental affairs, to supervise a comprehensive review of all federal program spending outside of social programs. Throughout the spring and summer of 1994, senior civil servants in every department evaluated the programs under their control on the basis of six criteria: the public interest test, the role of government test, the federalism test, the partnership test, the efficiency test, and the affordability test. In essence, several questions were asked of each program. Is it serving the public? Is the government fulfilling a legitimate or necessary need? Could it be delivered better by the provinces, the private sector, or voluntary groups? Can it be delivered more efficiently? Is it affordable?

In late September, 1994, Massé released a public statement and met the Ottawa press corps to reveal the broad outlines of the reforms. "The central objective is to identify the federal government's core roles and responsibilities and to re-focus our resources in order to provide modern, affordable government," Massé said. "There is no doubt that, at the end of this process, if we're successful, we're going to have a downsized federal government with a smaller public service."

There was nothing loud, brash, or extravagant about Massé's announcement. He presented the program review to the public in the equivalent of plain brown paper rather than gift wrap, causing barely a stir in places like Kenora or Kamloops but sending ripples of anxiety through Ottawa. Besides being the seat of government, the nation's capital is a head-office town, not for private companies, but for dozens of nonprofit, nongovernment, and volunteer organizations, as well as crown corporations, which rely on the federal government for all or part of their operating budgets. Take a glance at the city's telephone directory, under the letter C, and you will find listings for everything from the Canadian Broadcasting Corporation to the Canadian Hard of Hearing Association. It is a veritable potpourri of special interests and advocacy groups, including, among others, the Canadian Fitness and Lifestyle Research Institute, the Canadian Mediterranean Institute, and the Canadian Mushroom Growers Association.

For these groups and the people who work for them — executive-directors, program managers, publicists, resource persons, and clerical staff — there was nothing modest about Massé's announcement. The objective, he said, was to save billions, not mere millions. Yet, the program review was more than simply an effort to cut spending. It represented a strategic retreat, a 180-degree turn, by the federal government after half a century of uninterrupted growth and expansion. Ottawa would be withdrawing, rather than advancing. In the past, particularly during the debates over deficits and debts in the 1980s, special interests invariably saved their favourite programs by focusing on goals and objectives. If it was designed to reduce regional economic disparities or promote equality or eliminate barriers or strengthen Canadian identity, a program was simply beyond reproach or rational analysis. The Liberals, with their review, attempted to shift the emphasis to outcomes and results. They began asking hard questions: Why are we doing this; what are we achieving? Consequently, for the first time in decades, financial rather than social considerations were driving the national agenda.

The response from some quarters was quick and curt, and signalled the start of an emotional and protracted battle between the government and hundreds of the organizations it funds. Massé announced his plans on a Wednesday. Within twenty-four hours, CBC vice-presidents Alain Pineau and Michael McEwen appeared before the House of Commons heritage committee to launch the corporation's defence of its $1.1-billion annual subsidy. Pineau peppered the parliamentarians with statistics to demonstrate the CBC's contribution to Canadian identity and culture, compared with those of private broadcasters. McEwen cleverly argued that the corporation's five radio and four television services cost each Canadian taxpayer the equivalent of ten cents a day. The next day's

Globe and Mail captured the essence of their presentation with a snappy headline: "CBC worth every dime, its officials say."

These arguments were clearly debatable. But the CBC's position on the program review was not. The corporation, and many groups that depend in whole or in part upon the taxpayers, adamantly opposed the government's plans for a very simple reason: they feared their survival was at stake. And generally speaking, large organizations were far more vulnerable than small ones. In times of profound change and dwindling resources, the small, the quick, and the agile can be expected to fare better than the big, the slow, and the cumbersome. By any measure, the CBC falls into the latter category. It is a sprawling organization, with a huge number of employees, a bureaucratic management, a highly unionized workforce, and little or no inclination to change. It also relies on the government for about 90 percent of its operating budget. As such, Canada's public broadcaster, despite its size and might, had more to fear from Liberal cutbacks than quaint and obscure outfits like the Canadian Luge Association or the Canadian Team Handball Federation.

In fact, some of these organizations were displaying an admirable resourcefulness rather than passively awaiting their day of reckoning. "We're fighting like hell to survive," said Jacques Goulet, executive-director of the handball federation, which relies on the government for 45 percent of its annual budget. "We would like to be self-sufficient, which won't be possible for five to seven years. But if we don't do anything, we're dead."

The handballers cover just over half of their operating budget through membership fees and fundraising activities. In 1994, the federation hired a marketing co-ordinator to replace an outgoing administrator as part of its drive for self-reliance. Dave McDuff, managing director of the luge association, was looking for the type of sponsorship deal that is now common in the sports world. But instead of Molson Hockey Night in Canada or Labatt's Blue Jay Baseball, McDuff was contemplating something like the Petro-Canada National Luge Team. The attraction for a sponsor, he said, would be having its name tied to a team that competes at the winter Olympics and world championships. "If we're going to survive, we're going to have to be self-supporting," he said.

Other organizations, however, were contemplating potential casualties. Jocelyn Beaudoin, executive vice-president of the Montreal-based Council on Canadian Unity, said that the council already raises close to $5 million annually from corporate and individual donors to cover operating costs. It counts on the federal government for an annual grant to pay for its Encounters with Canada program, which brings 2,000 high school students to Ottawa during the academic year for one-week study sessions. They get to observe the operation of various federal institutions, such as the House of Commons and the Supreme Court. Without the federal money, the program would be cancelled and twenty employees laid off, said Beaudoin.

Another prominent organization, the National Action Committee on the Status of Women, was also facing layoffs if its federal funding was cut. Executive-director Beverly Bain said that NAC depends on Ottawa for about one-third of its $940,000 annual budget. NAC also relies on fundraising projects and cash donations from members. But the government has been a source of stable funding, and the federal grant covers salaries as well as administrative expenses. "If we lose even part of our funding from the federal government, we're going to lose staff," said Bain. "We're going to protest as much as possible. There are other places for the government to cut. Slashing social programs and women's programs is not going to fix the deficit."

◄○►

The Chrétien government's efforts to reduce grants, subsidies, and contributions to special interest groups demonstrates the insidious nature of our deficit/debt crisis and the dilemma facing any political leader who attempts to solve it. Our governments have been borrowing huge amounts of money, but they redistribute that money, plus revenues raised through taxation, in the form of transfers to individuals, organizations, and companies, all of whom come to depend on these funds in different ways. Grants and subsidies are used to pay the salaries of people employed at the head offices of volunteer associations, advocacy groups, and nonprofit societies. The same government money keeps hundreds of these organizations afloat and allows them to run their programs or push their causes.

The political leader who attempts to reduce a government deficit by eliminating such subsidies immediately collides head on with a whole host of irreducible human problems. Jobs are jeopardized, incomes threatened, organizations imperilled, programs and services endangered. The leader, along with his ministers and caucus, must inevitably deal with the ferocious lobbying, elaborate arguments, and anguished pleas of aroused and frightened interest groups. At the same time, the government receives a steady flow of advice and analysis from senior bureaucrats, outside economists, and think tanks like the C. D. Howe Institute, all warning of the dangers of chronic deficits and escalating debt.

The battle over deficits, then, becomes a very human drama. It is a struggle to sway the individual politician, with one side appealing to the mind, the other to the heart, one to reason, the other to emotion. For the political decision-makers the choices are clear: the public interest or the special interest. The public interest is often distant and intangible — a balanced budget, a sound treasury — while the special interest is often immediate and concrete — preserving jobs, maintaining programs. This explains why Brian Mulroney and so many other leaders have avoided making painful decisions and, in effect, evaded their responsibilities. It was an understandable but flawed response because whatever they accomplished by appeasing special interests could never outweigh the damage done to the public interest, that is, the financial health of the country. And this demonstrates a simple truth: If we add up all our special interests, the sum will never equal the national interest.

The Chrétien government's program review was an attempt to restore some balance between public interest and special interest. The Liberals acknowledged that the government could no longer afford to fund these groups at current levels. They recognized the need for a complete overhaul of Ottawa's multitude of assistance programs because the federal government, quite simply, had drifted badly off course. Our governments once devoted most of their energy and resources to legislating, regulating, negotiating, and providing basic services. In the post-war era, they have built an elaborate cradle-to-grave social safety net, and taken on a plethora of new and questionable responsibilities. As Section 8 of the public accounts reveals, Ottawa has become deeply immersed in promoting, encouraging, and subsidizing hundreds of unrelated activities. But in attempting to satisfy every conceivable demand, very often for political advantage, we have ended up with what Lindbeck calls the transfer state, a socially driven, unaffordable free-for-all.

"All over the Western world, central governments expanded through the 1950s, 1960s, and 1970s," says Osbaldeson. "I think there was a belief that central governments could bring certain benefits, so people sought the intervention of their governments. I'm now persuaded that the systems which central governments put in place to deliver those benefits have proven to be inefficient and ineffective. I think people would be relieved if the government would stop doing these things because they see this inefficiency and ineffectiveness, they have paid taxes for them, and they are getting things they don't really want.

"And I'm absolutely convinced that governments have taken on too much. I've looked at other countries around the world and asked what's the right number of departments. I found that there are about fourteen that are common to all. They are pretty basic activities, like defence, justice, finance, transport, culture, health, external affairs, and revenue. But they are core activities because every government has found it necessary to perform those functions. What you don't find is things like urban affairs, consumer affairs, forestry and fisheries, tourism, and small business."

Besides shrinking or even eliminating peripheral departments, there is a second, equally important way in which the federal government can return to what Massé called "core roles and responsibilities." Osbaldeston said that, in many cases, Ottawa should stick to passing laws and setting national policy but should forget about running costly programs to support or enforce its laws and policies. It may be perfectly legitimate for the federal government to set national environmental standards, he said. There is no need, however, for Ottawa to conduct its own inspections. That can be left to the provinces, the municipalities, or even the private sector, eliminating duplication and preventing jurisdictional squabbles. This type of division of responsibilities already occurs in the area of law enforcement. The federal government has created the Criminal Code of Canada but has never attempted to enforce it everywhere. This it leaves largely in the hands of local police departments.

Multiculturalism is one of the most startling cases of governments going overboard, of legislating for the common good and then plunging energetically into the whole dubious business of promoting, assisting, and subsidizing. We have created in this country a strong and comprehensive body of laws that prohibit discrimination and promote tolerance. Human rights law, an expression of our shared values and objectives, begins in the constitution, which guarantees that each individual will be treated equally under the law, and without discrimination "based on race, national or ethnic origin, colour, religion, age, sex or physical disability." To reinforce this commitment, Parliament and the provincial legislatures have each passed human rights acts. They have adopted human rights codes that spell out in simple language the principles contained in the laws. They have set up human rights commissions to enforce their laws and have given the commissions the power to launch investigations, hold quasi-judicial hearings, subpoena witnesses, render verdicts, and impose penalties.

Our laws provide every citizen with a means of seeking redress if he or she has been the victim of discrimination. They should be sufficient to ensure that, over the long haul, equality and harmony prevail among the populace at practically no cost to the federal treasury. But more importantly, we should put our faith in the common sense and good nature of ordinary Canadians. Canada is one of the most fluid and open societies in the world, a nation remarkably free of class or caste, ghettoes or slums. We have an economy in which ability and ambition almost always supersede rank and privilege.

It wasn't always so. The history of this country is littered with incidents of hatred and violence, inspired by race, religion, and ethnic background. French have fought English. Catholics have battled Protestants. Europeans have clashed with aboriginals. Newcomers have imported old feuds and animosities from their homelands. But Canadians have never become permanently hung up on their differences. We have never become obsessed with retribution and revenge. We have generally found amicable or civilized ways to resolve our disputes and settle our differences. We may be hyphenated Canadians, but we end up being Canadians first, and Poles or Britons or Jamaicans second.

Our big cities have Chinatowns, Little Italys, Greek districts, Portuguese sections, and East Indian retail strips. But none of these ethnic enclaves could be considered ghettoes, because people live or work there by choice. Over time, these areas tend to shrink or disappear altogether as the inhabitants move to the suburbs to pursue the same dreams as other Canadians: a single-family home, a quiet street, a safe, clean neighbourhood. We have become a multicultural society of our own accord.

Nevertheless, Ottawa and the provinces insist upon spending millions of dollars every year to promote multiculturalism. "One has to ask how much of this is policy and how much is politics or patronage or pork barreling," says Osbaldeston. "If, for example, there is not a vibrant German community in Kitchener-Waterloo,

Ontario, I don't think any amount of money you put into the German cultural clubs is going to create one. I doubt very much that any government grant flowing to the Kitchener-Waterloo Oktoberfest makes or breaks that activity. It does allow some MP to present a cheque to Oktoberfest. A lot of politicians refer to that as 'presence.' In other words, if people don't see the federal government at work, there is no value to the federal government."

Although the usefulness of multiculturalism grants and many similar types of promotional funding is highly suspect, these programs have acquired large and devoted constituencies. Pat Lorje, a Saskatoon psychologist, a member of Roy Romanow's NDP government, and one of the most provocative New Democrats in the country, has become something of an expert in the behaviour of these constituencies, and has coined her own term for them. She calls them the conferencing classes. "We've created an unacknowledged group of people who are constantly on the move in this country, booking tickets with airlines, collecting air miles, and checking into hotels," says Lorje. "They belong to groups that have historically felt disadvantaged and oppressed: women, visible minorities, aboriginals. Business groups are probably doing the same thing. They go to conferences and talk, and wring their hands, and say isn't this awful and isn't that awful.

"They've become a tremendous lobby, and they spend so much money on airlines and hotels that these industries have come to rely on them, and I'm sure they're not even aware of it. I wonder what would happen to this country if we simply called a halt to all these conferences for a year. Would the Canadian way of life disappear, or would it be substantially improved?"

Of course, before they can hold their conferences or workshops or roundtables, these groups must first obtain their grants. And applying for funding has become a cottage industry in Canada. Margaret Wente, editor of the *Globe and Mail*'s *Report on Business*, explained how the process works in a column she wrote in September 1994. Wente noted that the federal Department of

Human Resources Development hands out about 500 grants each year, worth a total of about $10 million, to women's organizations across the country. "In the past decade, women's causes have become a major new customer of the government grant-giving machine," Wente observed. "A vast subculture exists of social workers and other people in the helping professions who spend much of their time having conferences, conducting studies and devising action plans about women's problems.

"I asked the department to send me a list of the grants in Ontario since the whole list was too long. It is a gold mine of information on how to get money from the government. The secret is to squeeze into your project as many of the following hot buttons as possible: mention the word violence; be francophone; be aboriginal; be a visible minority immigrant group; mention abuse; be disabled; be old; mention harassment. And since entrepreneurship is also fashionable these days, you might get somewhere if you include the word networking in your group's name."

The list of grants which Wente received included $9,000 to a group called Women for Change, which was planning a project called Making Changes. It was described as "popular theatre and dialogue presented to service providers/institutions on issues such as family violence and poverty." An organization called the Action Centre for Social Justice received $21,000 for a "low income women's brainstorming conference." Another, called Kitchener-Waterloo Business Women in Networking, got $12,000 for a study that identified "the gaps in entrepreneurial training programs for women."

After coming to the end of the list, Wente arrived at the following conclusion: "We have in this country hundreds of thousands of women and children who live in crushing poverty. We have governments trapped in a debt crisis. And yet they persist in handing out money to programs, not people; to professional students of poverty, not to the poor. A group in my neighbourhood got $12,000 to hold a conference about immigrant women and illiteracy. If you gave that money to actual immigrant women, think how much babysitting and bus fare it would buy so that they could go to English class."

In Saskatoon, the maverick NDPer Pat Lorje has come to precisely the same conclusion. If we are going to spend the money, she says, let's spend it on services rather than conferences. She thinks that governments would be better off hiring anti-racism officers to talk to business executives about the advantages of hiring visible minorities, or to talk to students about the origins and consequences of racism. Rather than sending people to conferences about violence against women, governments would do better by diverting the money to service agencies that deal directly with domestic abuse. But Lorje is not optimistic that such reforms are imminent. "There is a tyranny that has grown up," she concludes, "and it says we can't look at the problems some of these so-called solutions have created."

In the context of a federal budget that exceeds $160 billion a year, the money spent on individual programs to promote multiculturalism, amateur athletes, or environmental groups, to cite a few examples, looks positively puny. Collectively, however, Ottawa allocates several billion annually to these programs. This in itself is probably enough to make them an inviting target for a deficit-ridden government that is desperate to save money. They are even more vulnerable because they fall into the category of discretionary spending. The federal government can cancel the programs under which interest groups are funded without amending laws or consulting the provinces.

Business subsidies and regional development grants were vulnerable for similar reasons, and Martin took an axe to them in his 1995 budget, promising to reduce total handouts to $1.5 billion a year by 1997–98 from $3.8 billion in 1994–95. Based on recommendations coming out of Massé's program review, he cut or eliminated rail transportation subsidies for Western grain growers and businesses in Atlantic Canada, production subsidies for dairy farmers, and various subsidies for cultural industries such as magazine and book publishing. The minister of finance also promised to scale back Industry Canada's freebies for business and announced that the regional development agencies would be providing loans and repayable contributions rather than handing out grants.

Subsidies to private companies were cut for a couple of other reasons, as well. First, their effectiveness is highly questionable. And second, for years business executives and the organizations which speak for them have noisily implored our politicians to cut spending, eliminate the deficit, and balance the budget. Indignant bank presidents and irate chief executives have routinely delivered anti-deficit speeches at service club luncheons, annual meetings, and similar events. Every year, in the weeks leading up to the federal budget, groups like the Business Council on National Issues, the Canadian Chamber of Commerce, and the Canadian Manufacturers Association have met the minister of finance and urged him to rein in social programs, lower taxes, and tackle the debt problem.

Yet some of these organizations, and undoubtedly many of their members, have eagerly accepted government largesse. In other words, they were part of the problem, and occasionally a leader of the business community acknowledges as much. One such executive is NOVA chairman Newell. "Money has been squandered on almost totally unsuccessful regional diversification grants and agencies, on public sector investment in business, and on rescue packages for terminally ill businesses, all at a huge cost to the taxpayer," he told a group of investment dealers in Toronto in September 1994. "And all too often, members of the business community were either there at the trough or, at best, were silent spectators."

But the most basic knock against grants and subsidies to business is that they rarely create lasting jobs or real economic opportunity. Instead, they are mainly political playthings set up by cabinet ministers who are trolling for votes. The Western Economic Diversification Fund and the Atlantic Canada Opportunities Agency are two classic examples of highly politicized decision-making. Through the Speech from the Throne in the fall of 1986, the Mulroney government announced that it intended to dismantle the Department of Regional Industrial Expansion and would create new agencies to stimulate economic development in the Atlantic and Western provinces. Mulroney then asked the University of Moncton's Savoie to prepare a report on the requirements of the Atlantic region and the type of organization it needed.

By Christmas of 1986, Savoie had submitted his report. He recommended that the government make $250 million available to the new agency over a five-year period. He also suggested that the money come from existing programs that would be scaled back. But that is not what happened. "The Atlantic Opportunities Agency was launched June 5, 1987, and the Tories allocated $1.05 billion in funding, most of it new funding and all of it borrowed," Savoie recalls. "The Western fund was established one month later and got $1.2 billion, an extra $150 million. If you want to know why it was created, don't look any further than Don Mazan-kowski. It was Maz's baby. He oversaw its development from day one, pure and simple. There was an election coming in 1988. All of that was no coincidence."

The Tories established a third such agency, the Federal Office of Regional Development – Quebec, which handed out money under a number of programs. The results were often appalling. Thomas Courchene, a Queen's University economist and author of several penetrating studies on social spending in Canada, remembers touring Quebec's Gaspé Peninsula and being shocked at the brazenly politicized nature of some of the subsidies: "You'd have a federal fish plant and a provincial plant in the same community, a federal facility that made ice for its plant and a provincial facility that made its own ice. Both plants were working at 17 percent of capacity because

119

there were no fish left. But Ottawa was involved so Quebec said, 'This is our bailiwick and we're going to outspend them.'"

Over the years, various economic studies and analyses have reinforced the anecdotal evidence about the ineffectiveness of regional development grants. The Ottawa-based Canadian Labour Market and Productivity Centre, a think tank jointly funded by business and labour, published an article about regional economic disparities in the spring 1990 issue of its quarterly journal. The centre estimated that in 1961, per capita personal income in Ontario was two-thirds higher than in Atlantic Canada. By 1988, the gap had fallen to one-third, a drop of 50 percent in less than three decades. Yet in 1989, Atlantic Canada's unemployment rate was two and a half times as high as Ontario's. By comparison, it was less than twice as high in the late 1960s.

These numbers raised the obvious but intriguing question: why would the employment situation in Atlantic Canada deteriorate even as personal income was rising in relation to the most prosperous province in the country? The centre concluded that the federal government had made a significant impact on incomes through unemployment insurance, equalization payments, and other transfers. But Ottawa had failed to have any real impact on the economy even though it spent billions of dollars to lure business to the region. "Subsidies to businesses to establish new industry may often be ineffective while direct government job creation in many cases offers limited possibilities for long-term employment. This suggests that the government has had much less control over job creation than income generation." In short, Ottawa could transfer money; it could not create opportunity.

Courchene maintains that regional development policies have failed because the federal government attempted to impose the wrong model on Atlantic Canada. "Ottawa was trying to duplicate Ontario's manufacturing economy," he says. "One reason you couldn't do it was that their wage rates were too high relative to their productivity so they were uncompetitive. I think we have to put an end to regional economic development and have one equalization program that is up-front and visible and makes payments to the provinces. We also have to focus on people rather than places. I think that the wealthy provinces will still give money to their fellow Canadians if it's to enhance human capital and education. But if it's some hare-brained scheme to attract resources from other parts of the country, that game is over."

Regardless of the strength of such arguments, there is no guarantee that they will carry the day should the battle over the Liberal program cuts begin in earnest. The 1995 budget merely flagged the government's intent to begin trimming back. That was the painless part of the exercise. As Osbaldeston observes, "The easiest part of reorganizing the government is deciding what should happen. The most difficult part is making it happen. Too many reformers believe their task is accomplished when the announcement is made. In fact, it has only begun."

The Liberals managed to blunt the potential opposition by ensuring that some of the victims of their cuts received big financial cushions to protect them temporarily. For example, Western grain growers quietly accepted the termination of their transportation subsidies, effective August 1, 1995. But the Liberals offered them transition packages worth almost $2 billion over several years. A much more typical response was the outcry that greeted the announcement that Ottawa intended to cut off funding for Toronto's Harbourfront Centre, a multi-purpose arts and cultural facility that attracts an estimated three million visitors per year. When the protest over the cutbacks threatened to become a public relations fiasco for the government, the Liberals meekly retreated and restored Harbourfront's money.

That is exactly what too many governments have done in the past because fiscal reforms inevitably cause anguish, anger, and protests of one sort or another. Everyone has a doomsday scenario. But these laments should arouse our skepticism since they are usually part fact, part fiction. Unquestionably, some publicly-funded organizations will fold when they lose their grants or subsidies. Some people will lose their jobs, and some programs will disappear. In most cases, they will expire because there is little or no public demand for them and never was.

We should also remember that previous battles over spending cuts have been remarkable for their lack of balance. The advocates of government spending have always relied on a simple tactic: paint it black. They use strong language to defend their positions. They talk of slash-and-burn techniques or scorched-earth policies to create in the public mind images of degradation and destruction, waste and want. We are supposed to conclude that nothing will be left standing and nothing will grow here afterward. In these battles, truth is usually the first casualty. The advocates' imagery and the conclusions they draw are frequently exaggerated because both neglect human nature.

The Liberal program review, and other attempts to cut spending, would be more accurately likened to a carefully planned, timed, and controlled forest fire. There will be damage. But there will also be regeneration, because human beings, like other living things, are inherently dynamic. In the context of the program review, many small, obscure organizations will defy the odds and surprise the skeptics by surviving and flourishing, because those organizations have found alternate sources of financing or they are filling a legitimate public need or they have reinvented themselves. Large organizations will also endure, provided they are capable of reforming themselves and adapting to the country's new fiscal realities. The big mistake that our governments made in the past was to assume that they had to fund hundreds of diverse and unrelated activities or nothing would get done. In doing so, they seriously underestimated the initiative and enterprise of ordinary Canadians.

6

WHO IS PULLING
THE STRINGS?

For most Canadians, the world's financial markets are as remote and mysterious as the gods they worship. Evidence for this, ironically, can be found in the incredible boom in mutual fund sales that has occurred in this country in the past decade or so. In 1984, Canadians had just under $7 billion invested in dozens of funds. By 1994, the figure had skyrocketed to $127 billion and the number of funds available had soared to over 800. But most people put their money into mutual funds largely to minimize their risks and because they do not consider themselves knowledgeable enough to invest directly in the smorgasbord of products — from common and preferred shares to warrants and options — that are available in the markets.

Then there are the twenty-four-hour-a-day global currency and bond markets that are so far removed from the daily life of the average citizen that they might as well be operating on another planet. These are the markets where the big institutional investors play — the pension funds, life insurance companies, and mutual funds, which may buy and sell hundreds of millions of dollars worth of bonds and currencies every day. Yet, as Canada has slid further and further into debt over the past two decades, the financial markets have become increasingly important to our collective well-being. They deliver the billions of dollars in borrowed money, both domestic and foreign, that we require to keep our government operating.

Most of the time, the markets operate smoothly, quietly, and efficiently. But occasionally, the money managers, speculators, and traders who handle these huge flows of currency and government paper react or overreact to political events, economic trends, natural disasters, or other newsworthy developments. The result is usually a brief but unnerving tempest that catches people's attention and increases the cost of mortgages, business loans, and consumer credit. The most obvious signs of turmoil are a falling currency and rising interest rates. Depending on the duration and severity of the turbulence, national governments can sit back and hope the storm passes, they can wade into the market to restore calm, or, in the most dire cases, they can issue a plea for help from international financial agencies or the U.S. government.

Over the past fifteen years, Canada has been buffeted, on average, once a year by a blast from the markets. In the spring of 1980, international investors temporarily turned sour on Canada over the impending Quebec referendum. Four years later, it was the news that the federal deficit had hit a record $38.5 billion. In early 1986, investor anxiety over what would be contained in the second Tory budget sent the Canadian dollar to its all-time low of 69.3 cents against the American dollar. The collapse of the Meech Lake Accord, the rejection of the Charlottetown Accord, and the election of the Liberals in October 1993 all triggered turmoil in the markets.

In each case, jittery traders in New York, Tokyo, and other financial centres began dumping their Canadian dollars, which caused the currency to drop in value against the world's benchmark currencies, such as the U.S. dollar, the Japanese yen, and the German mark. Most of the time, the Bank of Canada attempted to act as a stabilizing force and break the fall of the dollar by spending some of its foreign currency holdings to buy up surplus Canadian dollars. The country's central bank was usually forced to bump up interest rates to ensure that domestic and foreign lenders kept buying government bonds. Fortunately, the upheavals since 1980 were short-lived and had little lasting impact.

For veteran market watchers, those financial squalls have become almost routine. "We have had extensive experience with currency crises in this country," economist Sherry Cooper concluded in a February 1995 issue of a weekly newsletter published by Toronto-based investment dealer Nesbitt Burns. "With so much experience we can make several observations. The downdraft typically precedes a critical political or economic event and the average time from peak to trough is only one to 1 1/2 months, with a cumulative decline in the currency of 2 to 6 percent. The blow off triggers a significant and rapid widening of short-term interest rate spreads vis-a-vis the U.S. In virtually all cases, at least 70 percent of the currency's loss is recouped within two months of the trough. Roughly 90 percent of the widening in interest spreads caused by the currency turbulence was retraced over the subsequent nine to ten weeks."

Cooper wrote her commentary in the wake of the currency crisis of January 1995, which was triggered by the collapse of the Mexican peso and growing international concerns over Canada's mammoth debt. This spasm in the markets was, in many respects, similar to all the others of the past decade and a half. It ied to a huge selloff of the Canadian dollar that pushed the currency to a low of 70.27 cents and forced the Bank of Canada to boost its rates by more than a full percentage point in the space of a month. But there were a couple of crucial differences. This crisis convinced many ordinary Canadians, in a way that endless political speeches and economic studies never have, that the nation's finances had sunk to a deplorable and dangerous state. And it aroused visceral fears that the remote and mysterious forces of the market now controlled our destiny.

Over a two- to three-week period, newspaper headlines and newscasts carried daily reports of the carnage inflicted by these impersonal, unseen powers. "Bank rate climbs, dollar sinks," read one headline. "Canada hit by foreign sell wave," said another. And so it went. "Dollar's battering continues." "Panic situation points to further rate increases." "Bank rates soar to defend dollar." "Interest rates rewriting budget."

Then, amid all this alarming news, the *Wall Street Journal* published an editorial on January 12 entitled "Bankrupt Canada?" "Mexico isn't the only U.S. neighbor flirting with the financial abyss," the *Journal*, one of the most widely read and influential business newspapers in the world, said in the opening paragraph of its editorial. "Turn around and check out Canada, which has now become an honorary member of the Third World in the unmanageability of its debt problem. If dramatic action isn't taken in next month's federal budget, it's not inconceivable that Canada could hit the debt wall and, like Britain in the 1970s or New Zealand in the 1980s, have to call in the International Monetary Fund to stabilize its falling currency." The editorial concluded with this warning: "What is clear is that Canada can no longer dawdle over its tax and debt burdens. It has lost its triple-A credit rating and can't assume that lenders will be willing to refinance its growing debt forever. Before Canada hits the wall it must put on the brakes and take its government in a new direction."

Pundits, politicians, economists, and various other experts immediately attacked the editorial, or dismissed it. Prime Minister Chrétien, on his way into a cabinet meeting the day after the editorial appeared, trivialized the author of the piece by telling a group of journalists, "The Monday morning quarterbacks, you know, they write articles, they don't run a government." Ontario's NDP premier at the time, Bob Rae, responded with disparaging comments about the U.S. "If you want to talk about Third World," he said, "compare health care in an inner city in this country to health care in Washington, D.C., or New York City."

Toronto Star columnist Dalton Camp, normally one of the country's more astute and articulate political commentators, led the most sustained attack in the media. In three different pieces, Camp bashed and belittled both the paper and the editorial writer. "The portrait of Canada as a country of high-livers awash in debt is being sedulously cultivated by right-wing organs in the United States and by minor league organ-grinders in the Great White North," Camp wrote in the January 29 edition of the *Star*. "As a generality it is partly true Canadians live longer and healthier lives than do Americans. It is an American opinion, shared by the *Wall Street Journal,* the insurance industry, and the private health care business, that we can't afford to do so much longer."

After the paper ran a second editorial about public finances in Canada, Camp dismissed what he called its "hysteria and hyperbole." He added that "My own opinion is that the *Journal* has a Canada fetish, and its senior editors soon will be going to lunch dressed as Mounties." His final word was that the editorials, and the fuss they created, were utterly inconsequential.

In reality, the newspaper's assessment of our finances, and particularly the assertion that Canada had become an honorary member of the Third World in terms of its unmanageable debt, had a jolting effect on public opinion. And there was a good reason for that. The appearance of the first editorial was as though a voyeur had stepped out of the bushes and startled a group of skinnydippers. Ordinary Canadians felt exposed and vulnerable. They realized that outsiders with clout were scrutinizing our affairs, and that those outsiders did not like what they were seeing. On a normal business day, fewer than 25,000 Canadians read the *Wall Street Journal.* But the January 12 editorial led to anxious discussions in living rooms and coffee shops across the country about "hitting the wall" and the imminent arrival of the IMF.

More than anything, it demonstrated that the country's fiscal crisis was real rather than hypothetical. This was not just an arcane academic debate between left-wing and right-wing economists but a problem with potentially devastating consequences for the average taxpayer. Over the past twenty years, the government of Canada, as well as the provincial governments, has issued enough bonds and treasury bills to paper a mountain. Investors have bought these securities and expect to be repaid in full with interest. The currency crisis of January 1995 was one of those moments when the doubts of individual lenders coalesced and ordinary Canadians nationwide felt the reverberations.

The turmoil also taught Canadians a harsh lesson: the calamitous growth of the national debt and the excessive reliance on foreign lenders has eroded our independence to a degree unmatched even by free trade and globalization. As a *Toronto Star* editorial writer put it, "By dumping Canadian dollars on foreign exchange markets, the unequivocal message to Ottawa was that foreign capitalists could take their money out of Canada at any time — unless the government sees things their way. The purpose of these warnings is to demonstrate to Ottawa that it has relinquished its economic sovereignty to those who hold its massive $550-billion debt."

The Dalton Camps of the world may have been able to dismiss the market turmoil as inconsequential, but others recognized the gravity of the situation and the necessity of assuaging our nervous creditors. On January 18, 1995, six days after the *Journal* editorial appeared, New York–based Salomon Brothers Inc., one of the world's largest investment dealers and a major marketer of Canadian government bonds, held a "global conference call on Canada and the provinces" for its institutional clients. The call attracted about 150 money managers, most of them from U.S. pension funds and insurance companies with hundreds of millions of dollars invested in Government of Canada bonds.

In his opening remarks to the money managers, Peter Plaut, the Salomon vice-president who hosted the call, went to great lengths to explain what he saw as the substantial differences between the Mexican and Canadian economies. He said that Canada remains a sophisticated developed country, as opposed to an emerging market like Mexico. Plaut also told his listeners that this nation has a diverse, resource-rich economy, a broad tax base, a record of political stability, and a long record of meeting its debt-repayment obligations.

Despite these strengths, international investors have become much more cautious about Canada than they once were, because of the size of our debt and our inability to get it under control. "Over the last couple of years, attitudes toward Canada have changed," Plaut said. "People used to be willing to take a chance that things would get better magically. Now they are taking a wait and see attitude before they significantly increase their exposure to Canada. They're not jumping in without doing their credit homework. Clearly, what will maintain confidence in Canada is fiscal austerity."

Given our precarious public finances, the federal and provincial governments have been working diligently behind the scenes in recent years to prevent a sudden loss of confidence among both the investment dealers who market their bonds and the rating agencies like Moody's Investors Service in New York and the Dominion Bond Rating Service in Toronto, which assess their creditworthiness. "There isn't a government in this country that doesn't speak often and very confidentially to the credit rating agencies," said Edward Neufeld, a former chief economist with the Royal Bank. "Many of them, the provinces, private corporations, and even the federal government, take trips to New York to meet with them. We're skating on thin ice. When you're as close to trouble as this country is, in terms of its debt burden, you don't want to make any mistakes. You don't want to give people any nasty surprises, which cause sharp reactions the morning after a budget. So while you can't show them what's in the budget, you can sit down with them and talk through the issues and speak generally about it. You make sure they don't have an enormous negative reaction."

According to several sources, the traffic between Ottawa and New York became unusually heavy in the weeks leading up to Martin's second budget as officials from the federal government attempted to prevent any adverse reactions among investors. On one such excursion, a finance department delegation comprising Suzanne McKellips, Rob Henry, and Rick Egelton, who has since left the civil service, visited about a dozen New York investment dealers in mid-February, 1995, and put out the message that the budget would contain cuts in the range of $12 billion to $16.5 billion over two years. "It was an off-the-record session," said an economist with a Wall Street investment house who participated in the meetings and agreed to be interviewed provided there was no attribution. "I wasn't able to tell anyone that they had been here. They were attempting to manage expectations, and trying to signal what they were planning to do in the budget. That way, people wouldn't be surprised when it came out.

"I said I thought spending could be cut by as much as $16.5 billion under certain circumstances," the economist said, "and I was pretty much told that that figure was too high. So I said, 'Okay, let me go back to my worksheets.' I revised it down because I knew other people were looking for cuts of $12 billion and I found out that that was too low, according to them. So we knew the cuts were going to be somewhere between $12 billion and $16.5 billion."

The fact that the finance department dispatched a delegation of senior officials to sound out Wall Street before the 1995 budget was presented to Parliament reflects our growing dependence on foreign lenders. Traditionally, Canada's minister of finance has had to worry about how his budget would be received by the Canadian public, the opposition parties, regional interests, and special interests such as business and labour. Today, the country's finance ministers must address a powerful new constituency — our creditors. And the further we plummet into debt, the more important their judgement becomes. In fact, they are now arguably the single most crucial audience for a federal budget. After all, the voters can bring down a government only once every four or five years when they go to the polls. Our lenders could disrupt the economy and destroy a government at any time, simply by dumping their Canadian dollars and bonds or by refusing to buy up an issue of treasury bills or bonds.

As Martin prepared his second budget, the country's foreign lenders cast long, deep shadows over all his deliberations. On February 16, 1995, Moody's, the world's largest credit rating agency, stunned the government and increased the pressure on the finance minister by announcing that it was putting Canada's ratings under review. That decision immediately knocked half a cent off the Canadian dollar and forced the Bank of Canada to increase interest rates. The Moody's announcement was one of those dry, bloodless institutional responses to a crisis. But financial analysts and money managers, who were quoted at the time in the business press, revealed the real mood of the markets. It was, in a word, nasty. "They better come across this time," snapped Patrick Paradiso, a vice-president at Deutsche Bank Capital Corp. in New York. Jerry Ficchi, a market analyst with Technical Data of Boston, added this dire warning: "If Martin doesn't produce it could get extremely ugly. There will be a new low for the Canadian dollar within five minutes."

At the same time, the government faced a major test of the market's appetite for Canadian debt in the weeks following the budget. Several old bond issues worth a total of $3.725 billion, originally sold to investors between 1984 and 1990, matured on March 1. Another issue worth $3.8 billion was due March 15. And $1.35 billion came due April 1. Since the government does not have the financial resources to pay off its old debts as they mature, it has no choice but to borrow more money by selling new bonds. The proceeds from the new bond issues, in this case $8.675 billion, were used to pay off holders of the old bonds. On top of that, the government had to borrow about $2 billion in new money during that same period to finance its 1995–96 operations. Faced with borrowing needs of that magnitude, almost $11 billion in the space of a month, Martin simply could not afford any budgetary miscues that might irritate or upset the lenders.

The finance minister also had to deliver a budget that would stand up over time because, according to some observers, the federal government's credibility in international markets has slipped badly due to the Mulroney government's track record of repeatedly missing its deficit-reduction targets. Investors now want realistic objectives, and they want them met. "The department of finance people have acknowledged that, at the end of the Mulroney years, they knew their deficits were going to come in over the budget projections but they didn't want to mess up going into an election," said the same Wall Street economist. "You'll never get anybody to tell you to what extent they were overestimating revenue and growth, but the finance people will acknowledge that there was an element of that in the budgets. The Tories did not do what they could have done at the end, and that's really when the biggest deterioration in the deficit occurred.

"We went to Germany in 1994, and the response I got from some of the clients was, 'We're just so tired of hearing the department of finance or the government of Ontario saying they're going to hit this target or that target every year, and then they miss it.' These are investors, typically mutual funds, who have significant holdings of Canadian bonds. We're not talking $500 million here. We're talking billions of dollars. The Mulroney government's deficit-reduction targets were just moving targets. The Tories didn't look at them as being serious so we learned not to look at them as being very serious. That's why Martin has gone in the opposite direction of setting targets that are fairly easy to meet. But rebuilding confidence in the government's projections is going to take years. This problem is not going to go away overnight."

As the country's fiscal position has crumbled, lenders have begun to scrutinize our affairs much more closely than they once did. Many are demanding detailed financial statistics from brokerage firms and are doing some of their own analysis rather than relying entirely on the rating agencies. "Every time somebody from the government comes down here, I tell them they need better stats," the New York–based economist said. "I'm getting a lot of requests from the investors for information on Canada. They want to look at the debt ratios, the current account deficit, the budget deficit, interest payments as a percentage of expenditures, all the things you look at for highly indebted countries. They want to understand what they're getting into and what the risks are."

Despite the signals that our creditors were growing impatient, there remained in this country a large and diverse constituency comprising commentators like Camp, left-leaning Liberal MPs like Warren Allmand, activists like Maude Barlow, and labour leaders like White, who insisted that we should disregard all these rumblings from abroad. The threat to our well-being, they assured us, had been greatly exaggerated. From their perspective, the volatility in the markets in early 1995 was no more significant than a few days of bad weather.

Indeed, while the financial markets threatened to hammer our currency and drive up our interest rates, some members of this camp were engaged in a specious debate about how we got into this mess in the first place. Barlow and her Council of Canadians, an Ottawa-based public advocacy group, were the principal proponents of this position. They attempted to divert attention from the implications of the problem to the origins of the problem. This was like looking through a telescope from the wrong end. Inevitably, their perceptions were distorted, their assumptions shaky, and their conclusions faulty.

Their main line of argument was based on a highly contentious 1991 Statistics Canada study by analysts Mimoto and Cross allegedly showing that social programs accounted for only 2 percent of

Canada's debt. The real causes of the country's fiscal problems, Barlow and her supporters maintained, were high interest rates and tax breaks for corporations and the wealthy. Since social programs were not the cause of the problem, they reasoned, there was no justification for cutting them. "There are alternatives," the council said in an open letter to Martin, which was signed and sponsored by about 750 individuals and several dozen labour, social justice, and religious organizations. "You can reduce the deficit and improve social programs by creating jobs, controlling interest rates and ensuring that corporations and the very wealthy pay their fair share. It's a question of choices, Mr. Martin. What kind of society do you want to live in? One that protects its most vulnerable citizens, or one that casts them aside?"

Barlow and her followers created a stir and made some noise. But there was a Lilliputian quality to their efforts. In the end, even if they were right about the origins of the problem, they were wrong about the solutions. And to argue that we still have a choice between taxing and cutting represented a monumental misjudgement. We are a small country with a small population that has borrowed billions of dollars a year from foreigners over a period of several years, all to support a level of consumption and a standard of living that we cannot afford. We are long past the point at which we can even contemplate a made-in-Canada solution to our fiscal problem that does not take into account the wishes of our creditors. In fact, they do not have the slightest interest in the scope or state of our social safety net. Thus, to expend enormous time and energy proving that interest rates and tax breaks, as opposed to social spending, caused our debt is like going to war to resolve a dispute over which end of the egg we ought to crack.

Barlow and Camp and all the others who raged against the markets simply misunderstood what the country was up against. They may as well have been arguing with an Arctic cold front. *New York Times* foreign affairs columnist Thomas L. Friedman captured the character and power of the markets in a column he wrote about

Canada shortly after Moody's had zapped the Chrétien government by putting the country's debt on a credit watch. Quoting a senior finance official in the Clinton administration, Friedman wrote, "It is almost spooky dealing with market powers. At least with the Russians there was a hotline with someone's voice at the other end. But with the bond market, you can't argue with it, you can't bargain with it, sometimes you can't even find it. It is an impersonal arbiter, and governments just have to get used to it." Friedman concluded with this observation: "Moody's and the bond market are now imposing on democracies economic and political decisions that the democracies, left to their own devices, simply cannot take."

What we witnessed in early 1995, then, was much more profound and fundamental than mere bad weather. It was closer to climactic change. After twenty years of budget deficits caused by too much spending, too many tax giveaways, and lacklustre productivity growth, we were experiencing a calamitous slide into bankruptcy, a disastrous descent from financial strength and self-sufficiency into dependency and vulnerability. We have left ourselves exposed to the whims of nameless, faceless traders and investors around the world. They are demanding a stiff interest rate premium to keep buying our bonds. And they could, without warning, put the federal government into default simply by refusing to take up a new issue of bonds or to roll over a maturing issue. Furthermore, we are the first generation of Canadians to have put ourselves in such a position.

"Ever since Confederation, Canada has never once defaulted on its debt," says Neufeld. "Even in the Great Depression of the 1930s, when things were really dreadful for all kinds of reasons, the soundness of the nation's finances was never questioned. One or two provinces had problems, but not the government of Canada. That soundness carried over to our financial system, as well. In the U.S., they had a collapse of their financial system in the 1930s, but we never did. To get into a situation where we could not meet our obligations would be, without question, the worst financial crisis in our history. It would leave a blemish on our record. I think the people in power and authority have begun to get a glimmer of the magnitude of the issues. We have made an historic mistake by undermining our national finances."

He is correct about the historic implications for two reasons. Our conduct will reduce the level and quality of public services available to the next generation of Canadians, and will likely lead to a drop in their standard of living. In other words, the demolition of the country's finances will have a major impact on the future, and the impact will almost certainly be negative. Our conduct also represents a sharp departure from the past, and a rejection of the values and practices that served Canadians well for generations. There was a time when Canadian politicians and businessmen borrowed sensibly and spent or invested wisely. Businessmen aimed to make a profit. Politicians aimed to balance their budgets. They did so because fiscal prudence was part of the genetic code of the country.

Canadian governments, companies, and crown corporations have always had to borrow money from foreign lenders because, for most of our history, Canada has been asset rich and cash poor. Explorers, fur traders, pioneers, and everyone else who landed here discovered that this country was a warehouse full of natural resources. They found fish, fur, lumber, and fertile land, raging rivers that could be harnessed to produce electricity, minerals ranging from gold and silver to nickel and copper, and eventually they discovered petroleum. However, we lacked the population base and the private savings required to finance the development and exploitation of our resources. We had to import capital in order to turn a northern wilderness into a thriving free-enterprise economy.

Occasionally, Canadian businessmen and promoters borrowed far too heavily, and their carelessness or miscalculations threatened the stability of the governments that backed their schemes and guaranteed their debts. This occurred during the railway and canal building booms of the 1850s, during the turn-of-the-century railway building bonanza, and arguably toward the end of the Alberta energy binge of the 1970s. But those excesses and brushes with disaster were the exception. Most of the time, foreign capital was successfully employed to finance the construction of productive assets such as mills, mines, factories, electrical generating stations, and a transcontinental railway. Raw resources were converted into marketable goods that generated revenues and incomes, profits and taxes. Workers, capitalists, investors, and governments reaped the benefits.

Canadian governments have periodically borrowed heavily as well. But they managed, until now, to avoid leading the country to the brink of financial disaster. And they achieved this without the sophisticated economic and statistical tools available to the contemporary politician or civil servant. Prior to World War Two, for example, the Dominion Bureau of Statistics was capable of producing only rudimentary estimates of the rates of unemployment and inflation. In the years between the wars, federal statisticians periodically attempted to measure the overall size of the economy, what we now call gross domestic product, but they did not succeed in developing a comprehensive measure until the end of World War Two. And they certainly had no way of forecasting economic growth. But what our former leaders lacked in technical tools and specialized knowledge, they undoubtedly made up for in common sense. Even a cursory glance at the record suggests that our predecessors never lost sight of the simple fact that too much debt could be ruinous.

At Confederation, Canada's national debt stood at $94 million. By the turn of the century, it had risen to $292 million. Despite that growth, interest payments were consuming only 20 percent of the federal budget in 1900, down from 29 percent in 1867, meaning that economic growth had outstripped the rise in the debt. To put those numbers in perspective, the debt tripled in thirty-three years under Sir John A. Macdonald and Sir Wilfrid Laurier. It increased twentyfold in twenty-five years under Trudeau and Mulroney. Similarly, interest payments absorbed 12 percent of federal revenues at the start of the Trudeau years, and about one-third at the end of the Mulroney era.

One of the key measures of our current difficulties is the debt-to-GDP ratio, which tells us how big our debt is in relation to the entire economy. In the mid-1990s, that ratio was rapidly approaching 80 percent. It has reached such levels before, but only in the most trying times, namely the Great Depression and World War Two. Although Dominion statisticians only developed their measure of GDP toward the end of the war, they used it to estimate the size of the economy on an annual basis back to 1926. In that year, our debt-to-GDP ratio stood at 62 percent. By 1933, in the darkest days of the Depression, it had reached 117 percent, due to the utter collapse of the economy. (Between 1929 and 1933, our GDP shrank from $6.1 billion to $3.5 billion, a drop of 42 percent.) At the start of the war, the country's debt was down to 91 percent of the economy, but by the end of the conflict, it had reached 108 percent.

For a little over two decades after World War Two, we played by the old rules. Fiscal prudence and common sense guided our actions. It is worth noting that during this period, specifically from the late 1940s until the late 1960s, we laid the foundation of our welfare state. We maintained our belief in balanced budgets and the dangers of carrying too much debt. At the same time, we built a caring and equitable society. In effect, prudence and compassion, or efficiency and equity, as the U of T's Simeon put it, were deemed to be perfectly compatible.

In the twenty-three years between 1947 and 1970, the federal government recorded roughly an equal number of surpluses and deficits. The shortfalls were small by current standards and kept the growth of the debt in check. At the end of the war, Canada's net public debt, the amount we owed our lenders minus recorded assets, was $12.7 billion. By the mid-1970s, the debt had grown to $25.6 billion. But the economy had grown much faster. As a result, the debt had fallen dramatically to 17 percent of the value of the economy, probably the debt's lowest level this century. The provinces, for the most part, kept their fiscal houses in very good shape as well. Quebec and Nova Scotia both introduced fourteen consecutive balanced budgets between 1948 and 1968. New Brunswick had fifteen balanced budgets and Manitoba twenty in those two decades. Saskatchewan, the birthplace of social democracy in Canada, recorded six deficits in the thirty-five years between 1947 and 1982, while B.C. had a mere five.

Federal finances began to come unglued during the early to mid-1970s, and fell apart completely in the 1981–82 recession. Coming out of that recession, provincial finances also went into a tailspin. Surpluses were transformed into deficits, and provinces that had been running small deficits wound up with shortfalls of hundreds of millions or even billions of dollars. Patti Croft, senior economist and a vice-president of Toronto-based Wood Gundy Inc., points out that in 1979–80, the combined deficits of the provinces totalled about $3 billion. By 1982–83, they had surged to $10 billion, and they remained at roughly that level until the recession of the early 1990s. Then they hit an astronomical $20 billion per year.

Most economists argue that our governments turned to foreign lenders in the early 1980s partly in search of cheaper interest rates but also because our domestic capital markets could no longer meet their demand. But Ottawa and the provinces made no efforts to co-ordinate their borrowing or to set ceilings on how much they should rely on foreign lenders. By contrast, former federal finance minister John Turner and some of his provincial counterparts set up some informal arrangements in the 1970s to ensure that they didn't go overboard. "When I was minister of finance," recalls Turner, "I had a deal with Charles McNaughton, who was treasurer of Ontario, and later Darcy McKeough, Raymond Garneau, who was Robert Bourassa's minister of finance, John Crosbie in Newfoundland, and the late W. A. C. Bennett, who was premier and treasurer in B.C. We had an agreement not to borrow more than 5 percent of our total requirements in foreign currency. It fell by the wayside after I left in September 1975."

In the 1980s and early 1990s, Ottawa and the provinces borrowed whatever they needed from anyone who was prepared to lend. And with combined federal-provincial deficits that eventually hit the $60-billion range, our governments were seized with a dizzying demand for money that foreigners were eager to fill. The age of the mega-deficits coincided with two significant changes in the way financial markets worked, and these also triggered an unprecedented flow of foreign money into federal and provincial coffers.

First, in the mid-1980s, the national governments of most Western industrialized nations deregulated their domestic financial services industries. They lifted or relaxed a number of long-established rules governing their life insurance companies, pension funds, mutual fund companies, banks, and brokerage firms. One of the major changes was to give these institutions greater latitude to buy foreign securities. This led to huge flows of capital from one country to another. The movement of Japanese money into Canadian government bonds is illustrative. In 1978, Japanese investors held 32 percent of the Canadian bonds owned by foreigners. By 1990, they had increased their holdings to 45 percent and had overtaken the U.S. to become the largest foreign investor in Canadian bonds.

The second major change was the introduction of computerized trading, which led to vast increases in the speed and volume of transactions and, more importantly, the integration of financial markets around the world. Brokerage firms and banks located in the world's financial centres — Toronto, New York, London, Tokyo, and elsewhere — set up their own trading floors and linked them to each other electronically. A large trading floor in this country might be the size of an NHL ice surface. A big one in New York or Tokyo might be two to three times as large.

To the uninitiated, trading floors are cluttered chaotic places. Hundreds of traders sit at tidily arranged work stations, intensely scrutinizing small computer screens that provide a steady flow of information about that day's prices and interest rates. They also keep an eye on headline news or all-business television stations to stay abreast of political or economic developments anywhere on the globe that might affect the markets. The traders are generally grouped according to what products they handle. Some trade stocks. Some buy and sell government bonds. Some deal in currencies. Others specialize in bullion, still others in arcane products such as futures, options, and derivatives. There is always a buzz in a trading room, created by so many people conducting business simultaneously with their counterparts who may work for a company down the street or a continent away. It is a frantic environment in which trillions of dollars worth of paper changes hands worldwide every day.

"There are lots of people out there who can sell $300 million in Canadian bonds at the snap of their fingers, in less than a second," observes Satish Rai, a thirty-one-year-old vice-president of the Toronto-Dominion Bank who manages eleven mutual funds worth over $5 billion. "I sometimes trade $50 million or $100 million or $300 million in a day. If I want $50 million in Canadian bonds, I call my broker and tell him what I want and he says, 'You've got it.' The broker tells the salespeople on his desk and each of them might have ten clients. They get on the phone and try to find the bonds. Within seconds they get them. It happens at the speed of light."

For all their mesmerizing speed, and the loathing which they arouse among critics, the traders are really only a small part of a bigger picture. That is because the financial markets ultimately consist of hundreds of millions of ordinary citizens around the world who put their savings into mutual funds, contribute to pension plans, or purchase life insurance policies. Their savings or contributions or premiums are pooled and become multi-billion-dollar funds. The companies entrusted with the management of these funds have but one obligation: to preserve their value over time. That means investing the money prudently to ensure that it grows by at least the domestic rate of inflation, so that the ordinary Canadian, American, or Japanese has a mutual fund, pension fund, or life insurance policy that is worth something ten or twenty years down the road.

Over the past decade, fund managers have pumped billions of dollars into the financial markets. They have done this directly by turning over their assets to brokerage houses or banks and giving these institutions the authority to invest on their behalf. The fund managers designate what proportion of their portfolios will be dedicated to currencies or bonds or other products. Ultimately, it is the traders who put the money into various financial products and handle day-to-day transactions. They typically represent one fund and buy from or sell to another. So, they are essentially middlemen, and whether they are speculating in currencies or trading Canadian government bonds, they are almost always handling huge sums of money that belong to other people. Hence, they have a moral and legal obligation to protect the value of that money.

This explains why Canada eventually began to give the markets a bad case of indigestion, and why the markets reacted adversely. Those Japanese pension funds or British life insurance companies or American mutual funds, which have been entrusted with money of their fellow citizens, must have the confidence that our governments can pay the interest on the bonds they issue and, eventually, can repay the principal. But as our appetite for foreign money grew over the past decade and a half, we tested the patience of our lenders, we began to lose their confidence, and we paid a high price. "We are more addicted to capital inflows than any [other] developed country in the world," says Croft. "Our interest rates contain a pretty fixed premium for fiscal risk, which reflects that dependence, and it's not going to go away unless we turn things around dramatically."

In 1980, nonresidents held $55 billion in Canadian government and corporate bonds. By the end of 1993, their holdings had more than quadrupled to hit $266 billion. In the process, a historic change occurred in our borrowing patterns. Up until 1990, nonresidents always had larger sums of money invested in Canadian companies and stocks than they did in government bonds. And left-leaning, nationalistic Canadians had warned the public from the

1960s onward that too much foreign investment in the economy was dangerous because we risked surrendering control of our economic affairs to outsiders. They argued hard for controls, and they got them in the Foreign Investment Review Agency as well as in the foreign ownership provisions of the National Energy Program. They also waged fierce campaigns against the Canada-U.S. Free Trade Agreement and the North American Free Trade Agreement on the same grounds.

Yet these same nationalists either ignored or underestimated the threat posed by rising foreign ownership of Canadian government debt. In fact, they remained silent even as the balance between non-resident investment in the Canadian public and private sectors finally shifted in 1991. By the end of that year, foreigners held $158 billion worth of government bonds, compared with the $153 billion they had invested in Canadian companies and stocks. And that gap widened in each of the next two years. As this was occurring, the attitudes of our creditors were changing. To some observers, the dangers were obvious long before the appearance of the *Wall Street Journal*'s famous "Bankrupt Canada?" editorial. "Basically, the problem is that we've been pumping out bonds at such a terrific rate in the world credit markets that we've become very unwelcome," says Leo deBever, a vice-president of the Ontario Teachers' Pension Plan Board. "Canada is a minor part of the world's economy. We account for about 2 percent of world output, but we probably represent 7 to 8 percent of the demand for credit."

From 1991 to 1994, deBever was a Toronto-based senior economist with the Canadian branch of Nomura Securities, a Japanese company that is one of the world's largest investment dealers. His job was to provide about 200 of Nomura's big institutional clients, many of whom held Canadian bonds in their portfolios, with information about this country's economic and political affairs. During his stint with Nomura, deBever made four to five trips to Japan, as well as several to Europe and the Middle East to meet with clients. He spent weeks on the road and days in meetings. If one thing became clear to him, it was this: we need their money a lot more than they need our bonds.

"We think about these financial issues in all kinds of emotional and philosophical terms. But to a foreign lender, we're just a commodity. His only objective is to maximize the return for his clients. I remember once very distinctly walking into a meeting in Japan and the guy said, 'I really don't have a lot of time to spend on this because Canada is not very important to us. It's not a very large part of our portfolio.' So I asked him what proportion it was, and he said around 2 or 3 percent. I said, 'How big is your portfolio?' And he says, 'A hundred billion.' He holds $2 billion to $3 billion of our debt. I figured out during my first year with Nomura that you could have ten or twelve guys in a room and they would hold $45 billion out of the $50 billion in Canadian bonds held by the Japanese. But the people who directly managed the Canadian holdings were often very junior, very inexperienced, and they had only the vaguest notion of what we're all about. They would react on impulse to news stories coming over the wire that had very little content in them. They were headline investors, and that made me very uncomfortable.

"You have certain left-wing politicians and commentators who like to think of traders and money managers as evil speculators. But these guys are salt of the earth. Their job is simply to take the money of their clients and make it grow as much as possible. If your country happens to be a convenient vehicle in that process, fine. The problem from a Canadian point of view is that, because we haven't managed our finances very well, that external exposure has become more and more volatile. Essentially, our governments have become glorified debt managers. No matter what they do, they always have to look over their shoulders to make sure that the people holding our debt are not going to be displeased and start dumping it."

DeBever left Nomura toward the end of 1994 because he became morally queasy about what he was doing. In theory, he was providing Nomura clients with objective information they needed to make sound decisions about investing in Canada. But there was always an underlying sales pitch aimed at keeping the money flowing into Canadian government bonds and T-bills. He was facilitating the flow of savings from one country to another, which was putting Canada further and further into debt and, on occasion, doing nothing for the lender. This became clear to him one day during a business trip in Manila. "I was in a taxi and we got stuck in a traffic jam. The taxi driver shuts off the engine, takes out a book, and starts reading. For the next half hour we're stuck there. I look out the windows and here are these people living in total, abject poverty. Their houses are no bigger than a shed, they're cooking their dinner on the sidewalk, and I'm on my way to the Asian Development Bank to convince them to buy Government of Canada bonds. Something just didn't add up."

7

SQUIRMING ON THE LEFT

"Claims that Canada has hit a spending wall, a tax wall, a debt wall, convey the impression that we have been living beyond our means, that we can no longer afford our social programs, that there is no alternative but to decide which programs should be cut and by how much. These claims are completely false."
— *From The Alternative Federal Budget, 1995. Prepared by the Canadian Centre for Policy Alternatives and CHO!CES: A Coalition for Social Justice.*

And so it goes in the social justice, the labour, and the women's movements. So it goes with arts organizations, environmentalists, and the federal New Democratic Party, all of those whom we loosely call the left in Canadian politics. Read any issue of *The Canadian Forum*. Take a glance at the policy statements of the Canadian Labour Congress or the National Action Committee on the Status of Women. Listen to Bob White or Linda McQuaig or Maude Barlow or any number of less prominent but equally articulate voices from the Canadian left.

They keep telling Canadians that the deficit-debt crisis is nothing more than a ruse erected by rich and powerful businessmen with visions of a lean, mean, dog-eat-dog society. It is part of a right-wing, corporate conspiracy to dismantle social programs, reduce the cost of government, and lower taxes for the wealthy. They like to lay the blame for Canada's national debt, which is now approaching $600 billion, at the feet of one man, former Bank of Canada governor John Crow, who drove up Ottawa's debt-servicing charges with his high-interest, zero-inflation crusade in the late 1980s. They keep telling us that what we need is more government intervention in the economy, more generous social programs, greater redistribution of wealth, increased public ownership, and heavy doses of regulation. Tune in long enough and it is like being caught in an echo chamber.

Here is Paul Browne, a research fellow at the Ottawa-based Canadian Centre for Policy Alternatives, writing in the *Globe and Mail* in April 1994: "Canada's social security system has only come under attack because rising unemployment has pushed up social spending at a time when hysteria is being whipped up about the national debt. Only job creation can reduce the deficit, by lessening the need for social spending while enlarging the tax base."

Now cut to CLC president White, writing in the *Globe* in October 1994: "Can Canada move ahead to create a stronger system [of social security]? Perhaps. But not if we are blinded by myths that prevent our exploring all options. It will be a fruitless debate if we accept that our system is generous and wasteful. Or that we cannot spend any more on social programs without destroying our public finances. Or that social programs are 'bad' for the economy. Social spending is not money down the drain. It's money that stays in the economy and keeps activity going. Unlike the economic high flyers who want to dismantle the system, the recipients of social security benefits don't put their money in Caribbean tax-shelters or hide it in Swiss bank accounts."

Or put the tape on fast forward, and hear what *Canadian Forum* editor Duncan Cameron had to say about Paul Martin's February 1995 budget. In an editorial entitled "A Budget to Hate," Cameron wrote, "Martin looks a lot like a Third World finance minister. His budget was crafted first and foremost for the New York money market. The strategy is to cut government spending in the hopes of attracting more foreign buyers for Canadian securities. Inflows of foreign currency would push up the value of the Canadian dollar and, so the hope goes, allow the Bank of Canada to lower interest rates. The 1995 budget makes about as much sense as the free trade deal. In fact, it goes a considerable distance in completing the Americanization of Canada."

In the Canada of the 1990s, the left is on the defensive. The fire-brands sound angry, frustrated, defiant. The moderates, with their penchant for reasoned and moderate argument, cling precariously to their composure. But who's listening? "In the last federal elec-tion, we got 7 percent [of the vote], and we're going down," White told delegates to the CLC annual convention in May 1994. "I have watched other social democratic movements come apart and I don't want to see it happen here." Union leaders attending the gathering were bewildered to learn that many of their members had voted Reform, the party that, in their view, epitomizes neoconserv-ative extremism. The magnitude of the NDP electoral disaster is evident from the following observation by former New Democrat MP Steven Langdon. Writing in the *Toronto Star,* Langdon noted that in October 1993 the party had attracted less popular support than its predecessor, the Co-operative Commonwealth Federation, earned in the 1935 election, the CCF's first campaign.

These are tempestuous times. Old truths are crumbling. Traditional alliances are fracturing. Political labels can be mislead-ing. Many of the old players have new roles. The right now attacks the status quo and demands change. The left, for decades the agent of change and the source of progressive ideas, has become the voice of reaction. Members of the left feel betrayed by their own kind, the provincial NDP governments they helped elect.

Here's how the world looked to former *Globe* columnist and disenchanted leftist Ann Rauhala in the spring of 1994. "It's my party, sort of, and I'll cry if I want to," Rauhala wrote. "You don't have to scratch very deep beneath the surface of any gathering of self-described progressive types to unearth a cold, clay-like lump of disappointment and fatigue with the New Democratic Party. Ask an environmentalist about B.C. Premier Mike Harcourt. Ask an anti-poverty activist about Ontario Premier Bob Rae. You get the same sad shake of the head. The same regretful recounting of a feeling of betrayal and disillusionment. The same resignation about the lack of serious alternatives. Among unionists, feminists, anti-racism activists, environmentalists, gay-rights supporters — everywhere among those we stereotype as the left in Canada — the subject of the NDP and its failures, like a rancorous family scandal, casts a pall over conversations."

Leftists of every stripe are still reading from the same playbook. They quote their dogma chapter and verse. But their cohesion has become the source of their disarray. They cling to their ideas like lobsters with lockjaw, to borrow a phrase from Arthur Meighen. They have become the Orangemen of Canadian politics. The lifeblood of their movement has always been government intervention, public ownership, subsidization, regulation, and protectionism. They believe in these ideas as deeply as the Orange Order believed in the monarchy and Protestantism. As Canada became increasingly urban, multicultural, and secular in the second half of the twentieth century, Orangemen could not or would not adapt and their order is now nearly extinct.

The left in Canada is now facing equally fundamental changes. During the 1980s, government downsizing, deregulation, privatization, and open markets became public policy in most Western industrialized nations, including Canada. Our deepening financial crisis has ensured that those policies did not disappear with the demise of the Mulroney Tories, who had borrowed them from their original sponsors, conservative ideologues such as Margaret Thatcher and Ronald Reagan. Instead, the historically moderate, centrist, and opportunistic federal Liberals, who have pilfered ideas from the left throughout this century, have had to embrace the same conservative agenda that they denounced with vigour and passion while in opposition.

If the left wing hopes to remain a relevant and effective force in Canadian public affairs, then it has no choice but to make some accommodation with the market economy and develop a new set of policies recognizing the primacy of the market in the creation and allocation of wealth. In this, the New Democrats, along with their allies among organized labour, the women's movement, and other left-leaning groups, are facing the same challenge that has bedevilled social democrats throughout the Western world. But the Canadian left is several years behind its European brethren, many of whom learned, after a decade in the political wilderness, to accept some central conservative ideas.

In a June 1994 cover story headlined "A future for socialism," Britain's highly respected weekly newsmagazine *The Economist* observed that social democratic parties were experiencing a resurgence across northern Europe, in part because they had abandoned what it called traditional ideas and old policies. "By the end of the 1980s, most of Europe's left-of-centre parties already advocated (albeit begrudgingly) slimmer government, lower taxes and privatization — measures to which they were once bitterly opposed," the magazine noted in a lead editorial. "Where parties called 'socialist' are doing better, it is partly because they no longer espouse socialism."

At the same time, most of these parties have experienced great difficulty shaking their old hostility toward market economics and their belief in state intervention to regulate and control the market. "Such thinking is profoundly misguided," the magazine declared.

"In a sense, market failure is pervasive. Competition is imperfect, and markets fail to allocate resources precisely, as they would in the textbook world of basic economics. But this century's most important economic lesson is that, except in textbooks, government failure is broader, more damaging in economic terms and much more threatening to individual liberty than market failure.

"If leftist parties could bring themselves to believe that the market is wonderful (not merely useful if kept in place), that it has delivered the vast majority (not a privileged minority) of people in the West to material well-being which they would never have attained otherwise, that it must be trusted to co-ordinate the great bulk of society's activities, then they could be far more effective in pursuing their aims as social reformers."

Can Canadian social democrats make such a leap in their thinking? That is, could they ever concede that the market should "co-ordinate the great bulk of society's activities," while they concentrate on attempting to reduce poverty, eliminate inequality, and provide good public services? The answer to those questions, based on the responses of left-leaning groups to many major government initiatives of the past decade, is a resounding and unequivocal no.

What we get most often from the left these days are incessant demands for more taxes and higher spending, combined with abrasive rhetoric about big business and all the misery it would like to inflict on a vulnerable public. A fine example of this approach can be found in a document entitled "The *Other* Red Book," published in late 1994 by the Canadian Auto Workers in response to Axworthy's social policy review. The deficit, according to the authors of this punchy little polemic, is "the ultimate weapon for those who want to weaken Canada's social programs.

"The real purpose of the social security review is to set the political stage for a weak, U.S.-style social security system, one which undermines workers' bargaining power, cuts wages and makes us even more dependent on employers for economic security," the authors contend. And they foresee a grim future of increased output and pay cuts if the government and the business community succeed in imposing their agenda. "The results will be falling wages, widespread poverty (even among employed people) growing inequality, violence and despair."

The Alternative Federal Budget for 1995 reiterated and expanded on these ideas. It was prepared by the leaders of twenty-five organizations, including women's groups, peace activists, child care advocates, and unions representing auto workers, teachers, postal employees, nurses, and civil servants. Their top priorities are job creation and "the restoration and improvement of our social security system." They ostensibly support the federal government's objective of reducing the deficit to 3 percent of GDP by the end of fiscal 1996–97. But they believe this can be achieved by ministerial fiat rather than hard work, sacrifice, and perseverance. The prime minister and his minister of finance need only order the Bank of Canada to lower interest rates, thereby cutting the government's debt-servicing charges, and they could increase revenues by imposing higher levels of taxation on wealthy Canadians and profitable companies.

The authors of this document would reduce our reliance on foreign lenders by having the Bank of Canada buy more government debt, presumably through the simple expedient of printing money. They would also consider regulations forcing individuals to invest a set portion of their registered retirement savings plans in government bonds, and similar restrictions would apply to company pension plans.

At a time when public-sector budgets of every description are shrinking, and the public has lost confidence in the ability of governments to solve problems, the Canadian left retains an unshakeable and childlike faith in state actions and initiatives. These social democrats advocate "an additional $3 billion a year in new program spending." There would be more money for health care, education, and the elderly. Social assistance rates would be raised, 1 1/2 million new nonprofit day care spaces would be created by the year 2005, and the unemployment insurance program would be made more generous in several ways. "Given our income and wealth, our social programs are not only affordable, they can and must be strengthened," the authors declare. "Furthermore, we believe that our governments have an obligation to make up for the constant failure of the market economy to generate sufficient jobs."

It would be easy to dismiss such musings as irrelevant since the public largely ignored them when they were published. However, these documents help explain why the NDP's renewal process, an attempt to resurrect the party after the electoral disaster of October 1993, has been stalled from the start. The Alternative Budget and "The *Other* Red Book" represent the thinking of some of the largest labour and social policy advocacy groups in the country, including the Canadian Labour Congress, the National Action Committee on the Status of Women, and the National Anti-Poverty Organization. The leaders of most of these organizations are active in the federal NDP and some, like the CLC's White, are political heavyweights who wield considerable influence over party policy. What they brought to the renewal effort was outright hostility to free markets and a rigid opposition to any changes in the scope of our social programs. In short, intellectual sclerosis.

The most visible part of the NDP renewal process, and the most obvious sign of its inability to adopt meaningful reforms, was the selection of Alexa McDonough as party leader to replace the outgoing Audrey McLaughlin. A former social worker, and for fifteen years the head of the Nova Scotia provincial New Democrats, McDonough captured the leadership in what was surely one of the strangest first-ballot victories in the history of Canadian political conventions. She finished second behind B.C. MP Svend Robinson and ahead of former Saskatchewan MP Lorne Nystrom in the first round of voting at the party's national convention in Ottawa in October 1995. After dropping out of the race, Nystrom threw his support behind McDonough, which probably would have pushed her to victory on the second ballot. The extra round proved unnecessary, however. Robinson stunned everyone, particularly many of his youthful supporters, by conceding defeat and endorsing McDonough as the new leader.

The machinations on the convention floor reflected the personal, political, and ideological baggage each candidate brought to the leadership race. Robinson offered the party a brand of radicalism that attracts plenty of media attention, arouses the animosity of caucus colleagues and, in all likelihood, would have totally alienated the bulk of mainstream, middle-class voters. Nystrom represented a pragmatic social democracy that has kept the New Democrats in power in Saskatchewan for most of the post-war era. But with its current emphasis on deficit reduction and fiscal prudence, the Prairie party's approach was seen as an unacceptable tilt to the right by most convention delegates. So McDonough was a compromise between Robinson's abrasive individualism and Nystrom's cautious socialism.

She was the least likely of the three to take the party in a new direction. "She is widely perceived as old guard, by which I mean the [Ed] Broadbent era, and she is," says Rick Williams, a fisheries consultant in Halifax and a close observer of the Nova Scotia New Democrats. "The issue is: can she reinvent herself as the source of a new approach, a new idea, a new paradigm within the party?" Based on her leadership convention speech, and her campaign literature, McDonough has no inclination to transform herself or the party. "Under my leadership, there will be no retreat from the bedrock values on which this party was built. Not now, not ever," she declared.

Along with a rigid adherence to party doctrine, the new leader displayed a remarkable lack of fresh or compelling ideas in her pitch to the delegates. There was nothing provocative or inspiring or original in what she said, only a promise that, somehow, the New Democrats would offer a real political alternative. Platitudes took precedence over substance, and her rhetoric had a hollow ring to it, as in: "The debt and the deficit must be dealt with but it can be done our way, with innovation and fresh ideas, with compassion and respect for the needs of people."

Besides selecting a new leader, New Democrats have also been attempting to develop a relevant and winning set of policies for the next federal election, which will likely be held in 1997. That effort was built around five large regional conferences held in Ottawa, Toronto, Vancouver, Halifax, and Winnipeg between August 1994 and June 1995. Smaller conferences were held in about a dozen other cities, usually in conjunction with events such as meetings of provincial councils or councils of federal ridings. NDP members participated in panel discussions, listened to debates, and submitted dozens of papers dealing with party principals, mission, relations with labour and advocacy groups, party structure, as well as economic policy, social policy, and globalization.

A twenty-four-member renewal committee, chaired by former MP Dawn Black and former Quebec NDP candidate François Côté, then drafted a discussion paper that attempted to draw a consensus out of the views of the members. That paper served as the basis of the policy debates at the leadership convention. The party also planned to hold two large policy conferences in 1996, to hammer out a detailed platform for the next election. But the general shape and content of party policy were evident from the discussion paper that emerged from the regional and provincial conferences.

Most of the ideas developed through the renewal events were in fact old ideas that were dusted off, rewrapped, and recycled. For example, party members declared their commitment to sustainable full employment, which "is economically sustainable, [and] built on the basis of a strong, innovative, high-skill, high-wage, high value-added economy." Almost everyone would agree that full employment is desirable. But those who believe that governments possess the wisdom or resources to fulfill such objectives are few and far between. And most of the NDP proposals for reaching full employment have been proposed or tried many times before. The party would rely on reinvigorated crown corporations, new rules to encourage pension funds to invest in job-creating ventures, and federal action to increase access to venture capital.

Despite the selection of a new leader, and the long policy debate that began in August 1994, the federal NDP remains a party in which conventional wisdom and political orthodoxy are deeply entrenched. A few mavericks challenged the membership to change direction, with little success. For example, John Richards, a professor of business administration at Simon Fraser University in Vancouver and an NDP member of the Saskatchewan legislature in the early 1970s, presented a paper at one of the renewal conferences urging party members to adopt the philosophical position of the Romanow government. "The Saskatchewan experience illustrates what I take to be the key intellectual change that party leaders must make if the NDP is to survive as a meaningful political party," he said. "They must accept the validity of limits to government intervention."

Having uttered what many NDPers regard as a heresy, Richards then committed several others. He made the case that we have too much government in Canada. Experience throughout the Western industrialized countries has shown that middle and upper income earners are reluctant to accept levels of taxation required to support governments that exceed 45 percent of a national economy, the result being perennial deficits. And they refuse to pay when government exceeds 50 percent of gross domestic product. In Canada, the three levels of government — federal, provincial, and municipal — now account for about 51 percent of the economy.

"Middle and upper income Canadians will never voluntarily agree to pay the taxes required to balance the budget at present expenditure levels," Richards argues. "We should admit that there is much dubious spending to cut — from megaproject subsidies such as Hibernia, to an inefficient UI system to an excessively generous public sector payroll. The NDP should advocate energetic federal expenditure reductions over the next two years. We should make a social democratic case for a balanced budget by the end of this parliament in 1998–99."

Richards continues his attack on the universal truths of social democracy in Canada by arguing that governments should recognize the value of the market economy and avoid meddling with it, except when absolutely necessary. "Unless there are well identified market failures that justify it, government intervention cannot generally improve economic efficiency," he argues. "Why? Government inevitably creates its own set of failures, the worst of which is probably the universal tendency of people to divide into narrow interest groups seeking benefits for members at the expense of non-members. Interest groups — including groups such as unions which we like to consider as progressive — constantly promote inefficient and inegalitarian public policies."

That leads to his most radical proposal: the NDP should sever its ties with organized labour, which Richards regards as a privileged and distinct society within the party. "Over the last generation, public sector unions have grown in relative importance; they now dominate the councils of organized labour," he writes. "It is simply not credible that a social democratic party present itself as efficient managers of a generous welfare state, and as the political agent of public sector unions. A divorce between organized labour and the NDP should be friendly but final."

Richards sees the Saskatchewan NDP as an effective social democratic movement, one worthy of emulation by the federal New Democrats. The Saskatchewan party, from the days when it was led by Tommy Douglas and known as the CCF, created a generous welfare state and balanced the books. Allan Blakeney maintained this mix of compassion and prudence in the 1970s, and Roy Romanow has relied on the same approach in the 1990s after inheriting a provincial treasury that Grant Devine and his Progressive Conservatives had depleted and nearly ruined. "The NDP in Saskatchewan has understood the public demand for fiscal restraint and, during its first term in office, proved able simultaneously to eliminate the provincial deficit and preserve the core of social programs," Richards contends.

In fact, some members of Romanow's caucus attempted, with the same lack of success as Richards, to sell this moderate and pragmatic style of social democracy to their fellow New Democrats at the national level. "Clearly, in Saskatchewan, we've managed to demonstrate that austerity is not a bad thing," says Lorje, the NDP member for the provincial constituency of Saskatoon-Wildwood and one of the speakers at the national party's Ottawa renewal conference in August 1994. "We've shown that you can cut in a reasonable and balanced way and still maintain social programs."

Lorje told party members that creative renewal could occur only if they were willing to question some of their most sacrosanct positions. "We have to trot out our orthodoxies and look long and hard at them," she said. "If you're on the left, you have to oppose free trade. You believe social programs like unemployment insurance must be universal. You never ever question multiculturalism or immigration. You totally endorse expanding the social safety net and, most important, you must not talk about it as a cage. Let's think the unthinkable, talk the untalkable, correct the uncorrectable."

Social programs, she said, have not eliminated poverty or solved many of the problems they were designed to solve. At the same time, they have created new problems, like welfare dependency, and attracted huge constituencies. Lorje argued that six million people, about one-quarter of the population, rely on a government cheque to support themselves, and in 1993 families with above-average income received benefits totalling $22 billion. An estimated 85,000 government employees manage and administer transfer programs, a workforce larger than the army, navy, and air force which defend our borders. "No wonder we haven't been able to clean up the system; 85,000 people want to keep their jobs," she said. "That's the dark side of universality. That's what needs to be changed."

Lorje is undoubtedly correct. But the federal NDP won't be putting forward any ideas to deal with the "dark side of universality" because the party is stuck on the notion that social programs must be available to all, without regard to need or cost. The party has chosen a new leader and begun to develop new policies but failed to renew itself, because hardliners have triumphed over moderates, and ideologues over pragmatists. The renewal process has been a victory for those with little or no experience in government, namely the Ontario-centred labour organizations, women's groups, and other special interests who dominate the national party and who swept aside the ideas of those most skilled and experienced in governing, the Saskatchewan New Democrats.

This should come as no surprise. The party and its supporters on the left have failed to come to terms with one of the fundamental political realities of our day. Our ability to raise taxes or borrow more money has been completely depleted by a generation of politicians who came into office with grandiose and expensive plans and then allowed themselves to be pushed even further by opposition members who often behaved like arsonists at a bonfire by constantly demanding more spending. Our leaders were cowed by the ferocious demands of special interest groups and flayed by a press so dazzled by special interests that it lost sight of the public interest. Consequently, public money, the fuel that would fire the furnaces of any left-wing, labour-driven program, is gone. It was burned by Pierre Trudeau and Brian Mulroney, David Peterson and Bob Rae, Don Getty and Grant Devine, prime ministers and premiers, Liberals, Conservatives, and New Democrats, Easterners and Westerners.

Our current politicians, from the prime minister to the premiers, have no stomach for further borrowing. And the public has no tolerance for further tax increases. The middle class in Canada is already footing the bill for two massive transfers of wealth. There is the money we shell out to the less fortunate in our society in the form of welfare, UI, old age security, and transfer payments to the have-not provinces. And there is the $40 billion a year in interest charges on the national debt. It goes to the wealthy individuals and huge institutions that buy our Government of Canada bonds. We cannot tax, spend, or borrow any more because, contrary to the assertions from the left, we have hit the wall in all three areas, the wall being a psychological barrier rather than an objective, measurable obstacle.

Faced with this unprecedented situation, our social democrats are confused and resentful. They resemble the Plains Indians in the late 1800s when the buffalo were wiped out. Their fundamental resource — public money — has disappeared, and their ability to function has gone with it. Bereft of workable or affordable ideas, Canada's battered armies of the left have sought refuge in a moral position. They would have us believe that they are concerned, caring, and compassionate, while their opponents are greedy, narrow-minded, and indifferent to the plight of others. They have cloaked themselves in righteousness and sanctimony.

They see Canada as a country of two classes, rich and poor, and base most of their positions on this essentially flawed perception. This has proved to be a fatal error because it ignores the 85 to 90 percent of Canadians who are neither rich nor poor but middle class. This country's social democrats have not anticipated the anxieties, understood the concerns, or addressed the interests of that group. And the results are evident: the New Democrats plummeted to 7 percent of the vote in October 1993, without having formed a government, and they're stuck there. Middle-class Canadians have deemed the left irrelevant and deserted it.

This is evident, not only at the polls, but in most of the crucial public policy debates of our day. Left wingers lost the free trade debate during the 1988 federal election because they assumed that they had a monopoly on patriotism. In their view, they believed in

Canada. The free traders believed in profits. They assumed that they could carry the day simply by proclaiming their love of country and by denouncing the greed of their opponents. And some of the most passionate and articulate voices of the left continued to see the debate in those terms long after it ended. In her 1990 book, *Parcel of Rogues*, Maude Barlow describes free trade as a story of "greed, ambition and betrayal . . . how Canada's most powerful political and business leaders delivered this country to a foreign power at the cost of our history, traditions and culture."

From such rhetoric it is clear that the left misunderstood the dynamics of the debate and the motives of their opponents. The free trade debate was not just another battle between elites, in this case the corporate right and a coalition of left-wing special interests. It was participatory democracy at its best, a gut-level, shop-floor issue that was argued at dinner tables, coffee breaks, and social gatherings. It divided families, friends, and colleagues. Those who supported free trade believed in their country just as passionately as those who were opposed.

Free trade, for its supporters, was the only way to secure the prosperity of the country, maintain our standard of living, and preserve our social programs. Many of the advocates of free trade were ordinary Canadians with aging parents who need their pensions and kids who need a good education. They believed in Canada's medical system, and our safe and civil society, and had no desire to see it transformed into a mini-America rife with guns, ghettoes, and homelessness. To suggest that the proponents of free trade were prepared to trade away Canada's public pension plans and universal health care simply to enrich themselves was insulting and absurd, and ultimately bombed with the electorate.

The left is now making the same fundamental mistake in the deficit debate. They see no need to argue their position on merit because they believe that they alone occupy the moral high ground. From their point of view, they are defending equality, generosity, and compassion, all the values that distinguish us from our neighbours to the south, while their opponents in the corporate world are motivated by greed and self-interest.

One of the most forceful and articulate presentations of the left-wing position is found in Linda McQuaig's 1995 book, *Shooting the Hippo: Death by Deficit and other Canadian Myths*. McQuaig, a Toronto journalist with a reputation for being incisive and iconoclastic, has written an extended argument in favour of the status quo. She contends that public perceptions about our fiscal situation have been shaped by an elite comprising Bay Street moguls, compliant governments, and an unquestioning media. And she is prepared to ignore the most obvious evidence to the contrary, namely, election results. Since 1991, voters in Alberta, Saskatchewan, Manitoba, Ontario, and New Brunswick have all elected or re-elected governments committed to fiscal prudence. Somehow, it is difficult to imagine the public or the politicians in any of these provinces, except perhaps Ontario, being manipulated by Toronto-based financiers and media outlets.

Nevertheless, McQuaig pursues her thesis with vigour. This elite, naturally, is largely made up of wealthy and powerful individuals who care not one whit for the well-being of their fellow citizens or the country. "Perhaps ordinary people want the government to focus on jobs while the elite wants it to focus on deficit reduction because the two groups have somewhat different interests," McQuaig writes. "Jobs are the highest priority of ordinary people, who rely on a buoyant labour market to give them job security and prevent downward pressure on wages. Members of the elite, however, generally have jobs or ample means of support. The solutions proposed for deficit reduction — cutting back government spending — are exactly what the elite wants. It is quite willing to pay for its own services privately — from medical insurance to private schools — if it can be spared having to contribute to the cost of providing these services for everyone else."

McQuaig would have us believe that Bay Street financiers, who are the real drivers behind this unholy triumvirate, have virtually manufactured a deficit crisis to achieve their own nasty ends: low wages and low taxes. They have misrepresented the nature of the country's financial problems, blaming them entirely on overspending, to justify an attack on social programs. The astonishing truth, she says, is that governments have not overspent during the past twenty years, even while piling up debts of $600 billion: "Contrary to media images of overindulgent Canadians living beyond their means, we have been a frugal, thrifty bunch, paying rising taxes and enjoying diminishing services."

The author reaches this conclusion through an elaborate statistical analysis that can charitably be described as massaging numbers and ignoring reality. She argues, without presenting any figures to support her position, that "the Mulroney government cut federal spending substantially." On the contrary, spending rose to $160 billion from $110 billion under the Conservatives. She contends, on the basis of unpublished research by StatsCan analyst Hideo Mimoto, that spending on social programs has not risen in relation to the economy over the past twenty years. This may be true, but it is a small truth. Compare government spending today with government spending early in the post-war period, when the welfare state was still being erected and expanded, and a far more accurate picture emerges.

Economic and fiscal reference tables produced by the Department of Finance reveal that total spending at the federal, provincial, and municipal levels rose from 30.5 percent of the economy in the early 1960s, during the Diefenbaker years, to 51.4 percent in late 1992, toward the end of the Mulroney era. During those same three decades, federal expenditures, including debt charges, jumped to 23.9 percent of GDP from 16.8 percent, an increase of 42 percent, while total provincial expenditures almost doubled. By the early 1990s, the provinces accounted for 32 percent of the economy, up from 16.2 percent. Spending increases of that magnitude are hardly consistent with thrift and frugality.

The heart of McQuaig's thesis is that high interest rates, rather than excessive spending, are the real cause of our financial crisis. Furthermore, she attributes most of our interest rate problems to former Bank of Canada governor Crow. She portrays him as an inflation-obsessed zealot who coldheartedly cranked up rates between 1988 and 1992 to achieve price stability. His crusade caused a recession, threw thousands of people out of work, and drove our deficits and debt into the stratosphere.

McQuaig's analysis, however, does not support her rhetoric. She cites several economic studies of the impact of Crow's monetary policy and concludes that high rates unnecessarily added $50 billion to the national debt. This is undoubtedly an enormous sum of money. But it is still less than 10 percent of the country's debt. The question that remains is this: What about the other $550 billion in debt accumulated under Trudeau, Mulroney, and Chrétien? How did we get stuck with that? She offers no explanation.

McQuaig differs from most left-wing commentators in that she says we have an interest rate problem whereas the others generally argue that our deficits have been caused by inadequate revenue growth and collection. The common denominator in both approaches is a refusal to recognize spending as a problem. And both lines of argument are dead ends. McQuaig's high-interest thesis explains, at best, 10 percent of our enormous debt. And those who suggest that we can find a solution on the revenue side of the balance sheet never actually make their numbers add up.

York University political scientist James Laxer made a typically futile effort in a *Toronto Star* column that appeared in the spring of 1995 under the headline, "Liberals should slash tax breaks, not social programs." Laxer argued that, if lower interest rates created 250,000 jobs over a two-year period, all three levels of government would reap a revenue windfall totalling $15 billion. If we assumed, for argument's sake, that the money was shared equally, then

Ottawa, the provinces, and the municipalities would each reap about $2.5 billion annually.

Laxer then goes on to propose several changes to the federal tax system, and he examines the financial implications for Ottawa. Eliminating tax exemptions, such as the 50 percent deduction for business meals and entertainment, could yield $3 billion annually. An inheritance tax could produce about $2 billion per year. Getting rid of several corporate tax breaks would add up to $2 billion. Lower contributions ceilings on RRSPs would contribute $3 billion. Laxer, like McQuaig, comes up with a big number — $12.5 billion in additional revenues — but no real solution. At the time he was writing, the federal government was headed for a deficit of almost $36 billion.

The question that this argument raises, and inevitably fails to answer, is this: Where would we get the remaining $24 billion in new revenues required to balance the budget? Laxer and others of his ilk never address that issue because their entire position rests upon a faulty premise. No matter how many tax loopholes and expenditures it closes or eliminates, the federal government cannot come up with the more than $30 billion per year required to balance its budget without spending cuts.

That, at any rate, is the position of many informed and objective people. Here, for example, is David Perry, senior research associate with the Canadian Tax Foundation, addressing the Commons finance committee prior to the 1995 budget: "The public perception of tax expenditures may be a little out of date. No longer do we have a system ridden with loopholes, where those with means can, with impunity, eliminate their responsibility to support public services. Tax shelters have been attacked on a consistent basis since 1982, the first round of tax reform in Canada. Subsequent reforms . . . have drastically reduced tax expenditures. There is not the fat in the tax system that the public seems to think."

But in debates about our national finances, left-wing commentators are rarely restrained by the facts. They rail, as if by rote, against spending cuts and, even more frequently, wealthy individuals and large corporations, who apparently never pay their fair share. They love to leave the impression that there are untold billions of dollars lying in private bank accounts and corporate treasuries that rightfully belong in government coffers. But here again, rhetoric and reality are miles apart.

In the 1994 edition of *Taxation Statistics*, Revenue Canada reported that in 1992 only 253,380 individuals, or 1.9 percent of those who filed tax returns, had incomes exceeding $100,000. They earned 10.8 percent of the total income reported by Canadians yet they paid almost 18 percent of all income taxes. The number of high income earners who did not pay federal tax totalled 2,270 and they earned about $473 million. It is without question scandalous and obscene to think that someone earning over $100,000 a year is not paying any federal tax. But it is also obvious that fewer than 2,300 people earning less than half a billion dollars a year cannot possibly solve the country's deficit problem.

There is additional, equally convincing evidence that we cannot tax our way out of our current financial bind whether we target high, middle, or low income earners. Canadians are suffering from tax fatigue after a decade and a half in which taxes rose more quickly in this country than anywhere else in the twenty-four-member Organization for Economic Co-operation and Development, with the exception of Italy. In 1980, the total Canadian tax burden represented 31.6 percent of GDP compared with an average of 36.6 percent for European members of the OECD. By 1991, Canadian taxes had climbed to 37 percent of GDP whereas the OECD average was 40 percent.

Our overall tax burden was still middle of the pack: we stood fourteenth among OECD countries. But our personal income taxes, 14.5 percent of the economy in 1992, were fifth highest among member nations, behind Denmark, Finland, Sweden, and New Zealand. The corporate taxation picture is less clear cut. It represented only 1.8 percent of GDP, below the OECD average of 2.5 percent, and slightly below the U.S. level of 2.1 percent. On the other hand, at 4 percent of GDP, Canadian property taxes, which are paid by both companies and individuals, were twice as high as the OECD average.

There are two other significant points that our social democrats seldom acknowledge when they attack corporate profits and taxation. First, Canadian rates must remain competitive with rates in the U.S. and other countries or we risk losing investments. As Perry told the Commons finance committee, "Although corporate income taxes could be modified, the extremely competitive situation in this area and the effect on our fragile recovery would make it difficult to raise large amounts of money from this source. Of all the tax sources available to governments, the corporate income tax is the only one that is inevitably designed with a view to the systems in competing jurisdictions. Individual comparisons are regularly made to see which jurisdiction provides the best after-tax rate of return for a specific project."

Second, the total take from corporate taxation has fallen as corporate income fell during the post-war period. In an article that appeared in January 1995, *Globe* editorial writer Andrew Coyne pointed out that corporate profits represented 13 to 14 percent of national income in the mid-1940s. By the 1990s, they had fallen to 5 percent. "Corporations are paying a smaller share of the taxes because they're earning a smaller share of the income," Coyne wrote. "It's as simple as that." He concluded his piece by noting, "The rich should pay a higher share of their income in taxes than the rest of us. They do. Corporate profits should be taxed just like personal income. They are. Reasonable people can differ over whether these groups should be taxed at higher rates. But it is a childish fantasy to pretend they are a piggybank we can crack open to pay off our debts."

The failure of commentators like McQuaig and Laxer to provide satisfactory explanations of our fiscal crisis, or to present realistic solutions, reveals much about what is wrong with the left in

Canada today. High interest rates do not explain the accumulation of our enormous public-sector debt. New taxes and higher taxes do not represent a solution. The only way out is to admit that spending is the problem and that spending cuts are the solution. But our social democrats can never bring themselves to make such admissions. Instead, they are relying on the inflammatory rhetoric of the desperate and the defeated.

The left likes to portray the debate in stark and simple terms: the rich versus the rest of us, to use the terminology of McQuaig, or the right-wing, corporate elite against working Canadians, to use Bob White's preferred terms. It is a battle between the powerful people with access to money, media, and politicians, and ordinary Canadians who are exposed, vulnerable, and increasingly marginalized. Under this scenario, left-wing labour leaders, feminists, and anti-poverty activists become the good guys in white hats who ride to the rescue of beleaguered and defenceless working Canadians. It's a classic story line, with heroes and villains, Davids and Goliaths. Unfortunately, it is a crude caricature of reality that reduces a crucial national issue to the level of clichés and stereotypes.

If McQuaig, White, and other prominent voices on the left are to be believed, average working Canadians who believe in fiscal prudence have been duped by the rich or the right-wing corporate elites. The arguments from the left imply that ordinary Canadians would never conclude on their own that deficits and debts threaten their well-being. The hidden message in the left's arguments is that the general public has been misled and manipulated, a position that demeans the very people that the left ostensibly represents.

In fact, public opinion polls conducted over the past three years have consistently shown that Canadians are deeply concerned with our level of government indebtedness. An April 1993 Gallup poll revealed that 70 percent of Canadians thought that the government should cut spending to reduce the deficit rather than increase spending to stimulate the economy. In December 1993, after the Liberals were elected on a job creation platform, 33 percent of those polled by Gallup still thought that the government should concentrate on reducing the deficit rather than unemployment. Janet Brown, a senior associate with Toronto-based Environics Research Group, adds, "We always ask people what their top-of-mind issue is. Unemployment, the economy and the deficit eclipse all the others. We've seen the deficit come out of nowhere in the last three or four years. A large majority of Canadians are now really concerned about the deficit."

It is altogether likely that ordinary working Canadians have concluded on their own that chronic overspending, mounting deficits, and crushing debt loads are unsustainable. Canadians have long valued fiscal prudence. We have historically had higher rates of personal savings than Americans and have been less inclined to use credit than our neighbours to the south. We are a nation of savers who have stowed away billions of dollars in RRSPs. Most Canadians have a gut-level, inherent fear of too much debt for the very simple reason that they know it can sink them. Most Canadians strive for a balanced budget in their personal lives. In this egalitarian age and this equality-minded society, they know that there cannot be one set of rules for the individual and another for the state. Individuals cannot live beyond their means in perpetuity, and nor can governments.

Canada's corporate elite is undeniably concerned about government deficits and debts. But so are main-street merchants and middle-class homeowners, and for very good reasons. They understand, as the left does not, that their personal well-being and the future of the country are at stake. Today, they have children in the public school system and parents who are pensioners. They know that ten or twenty years from now they will need Old Age Security and the Canada Pension Plan to supplement their retirement savings. They know that as they age they will require more, not less, health care. They know that the children they are raising today will be taxpayers tomorrow, and as compassionate parents they are deeply disturbed by the tax burden being imposed on their children.

There are millions of ordinary working Canadians, people with mortgages, car payments, and kids to put through college, who recognize that deficits must be eliminated and our debts drastically reduced because they have a huge vested interest in preserving our social programs. Those same Canadians know that, conversely, we are jeopardizing our prosperity and gambling with our standard of living if we allow the country's debt crisis to become a catastrophe.

8

THE SHENANIGANS
IN ONTARIO

As Mike Harris and his rejuvenated Progressive Conservatives took over the management and administration of the province of Ontario in the latter half of 1995, the public, the press, and advocacy groups of every hue discussed, debated, and in some cases denounced the new government's program, the Common Sense Revolution. The CSR, as party insiders called it, was the bold and sweeping plan to slash spending, reduce taxes, and balance the budget. The talk in the papers and on the street was all about cutbacks and cancellations and layoffs, the nuts and bolts of a government shake-up. Those practised in the art of protest politics — labour unions, child care advocates, and anti-poverty activists — wrote fresh slogans for their picket signs, organized demonstrations, and even tried to crash the doors at Queen's Park in their efforts to "Embarrass Harris." On the opposite side of the divide, Bay Street brokers and bond raters applauded, and a well-financed group known as Ontarians for Responsible Government erected a billboard at the corner of Bay and Gerrard streets in downtown Toronto featuring a photo of Harris and the message, "Good Luck Mike! (We're watching.)"

All of this was perfectly understandable. There was, after all, plenty in the Tory program to get excited or upset about. The CSR, outlined in a twenty-one-page booklet which the Conservatives distributed to more than two million people prior to their June 1995 election victory, is a clear, detailed, and radical plan to reform government and revitalize the economy. The Conservatives have put a simple proposition to the citizens of Ontario. They plan to cut personal income taxes by $4 billion, slash nonessential spending by $6 billion or 20 percent, balance the budget, and create 725,000 jobs during their first term in office. Health care, classroom education, and justice are supposed to be the only untouchables. But everything else is on the table, including the credibility of the Tories should they fail or lose their nerve. "Our commitment is carved in stone — we will cut 20 percent of all non-priority spending in three years," they say toward the end of their Common Sense Revolution booklet. "We are unconditionally committed to reaching our goals."

Political platforms of this nature, which offer major change and carved-in-granite guarantees, are a rarity. And there is a good reason for that: it is tough to deliver on a multitude of detailed promises. In fact, the last time that Ontarians voted for a program as comprehensive as the Common Sense Revolution was in August 1943, when George Drew and his provincial Conservatives ran on a twenty-two-point platform for post-war reconstruction. Drew, a World War One veteran and a more outward-looking, forward-thinking leader than most provincial politicians, was already anticipating an allied victory and the immense challenges peace would bring: demobilization, rapid urbanization, and the conversion of the economy from military to civil purposes.

In response, he developed his twenty-two reforms with the help of a few close advisers. He did not consult his caucus or party, and he shocked some traditional Conservatives, still rooted in Ontario's

British, Protestant past, when he announced the program in a radio broadcast on July 8, 1943. Drew promised, among other things, universal medical and dental care, more generous pensions and mothers' allowances, the creation of a crown corporation to build and manage public housing, "the fairest and most advanced" labour legislation in the country, and an overhaul of the school system to ensure that the province's children were properly educated — "no matter where they live or what the financial circumstances of their parents may be."

The program was a striking departure from the norm. The next day's *Globe and Mail* observed that "There was no parallel for the speech in Ontario politics of the last generation." Even the staunchly liberal *Toronto Star*, whose reaction to Conservatives and conservatism has swerved over the years from critical to hostile to hysterical, was forced to concede that "The platform contains some admirable proposals which any government, irrespective of party, should find worthy of adoption." It made Drew's Conservatives more progressive than either federal or provincial Liberals, cut off a surging CCF, and, more importantly, contributed to a minority Tory victory.

Drew implemented parts of the platform but let the most progressive elements fall by the wayside. Nevertheless, the Tory premier, his twenty-two-point platform, and the election of August 1943 spawned something lasting in Ontario politics: a Tory dynasty that would remain in power for forty-two years, until David Peterson's NDP-backed Liberals finally ousted a tired, lacklustre Conservative government in June 1985. Drew led Ontario through war and into peace before leaving provincial politics in October 1948 to take over the leadership of the national party. His successors, Leslie Frost, John Robarts, and William Davis, guided the province through an era of massive expansion, symbolized by the proliferation of suburbs, shopping centres, and expressways. Under their tenure, Ontario was the stablest and, some would say, sleepiest of provinces, a gentle giant with a humming economy that produced hundreds of thousands of jobs for its citizens and, through Canada's system of equalization and transfer payments, wealth for the nation.

But after nearly half a century of steady growth and predictable government, Ontarians have experienced a decade of economic upheaval, political turbulence, and mediocre leadership. They watched the Tory dynasty expire under the colourful but confused Frank Miller. They handed David Peterson's profligate Liberals a landslide victory in 1987 and three years later, in a surly mood, they took a chance on Bob Rae's mixed up New Democrats. The economy went from red hot to ice cold. Government spending soared. Unemployment rose sharply. The welfare rolls exploded. Branch-plant manufacturing withered. Ontario wound up with a debt load — almost $100 billion — that would sink many of the world's smaller nations, and earned the dishonour of being the world's largest nonsovereign borrower.

Harris's Common Sense Revolution, with its welter of detail and specific promises, addressed all these issues. And rightly so, since many average Ontarians were clearly irritated by rising taxes and the apparent excesses of the welfare system. But the program also responded to a broader and deeper set of concerns among the working men and women of Canada's most populous province — fears that a floundering economy and an ever-expanding state were eroding their prosperity and threatening their aspirations.

Finally, the Tory platform spoke to the major issue of our day: it acknowledged that Ontario must change because the world has changed. Just as George Drew realized in 1943 that the province needed a blueprint to deal with the return of peace and all its challenges, Harris and his Tories recognized that Ontario's government required a plan to cope with the globalization of commerce, the advent of the information age, and the triumph of the market over the state. Their solution, they say, is pure common sense: the province's government must be fiscally fit and its industries competitive.

But an election victory, even one that gave the Conservatives 82 of 130 seats in the legislature, is no guarantee of political success or longevity. Harris *could* launch another Tory dynasty. Alternatively, the province's voters may decide that he belongs on a list that already includes the names Miller, Peterson, and Rae. In Ontario, a successful premier must have more than sound policies. He must have the right persona. He must be smooth in public and tough in private. He must be self-assured without being arrogant. He must have the grace of a diplomat and the confidence of a corporate chief executive. An Ontario premier must have the aura of a leader.

The first modern politician who possessed these qualities, and left them indelibly stamped on the office, was Leslie Frost, the affable, small-town lawyer from Lindsay, Ontario, who ruled the province from 1949 to 1961 and was the most popular premier of the post-war era. Robarts and Davis, who kept the Tories in power through the 1960s, the 1970s, and into the 1980s, fit the mould established by Frost. And Ontarians thought that this elusive persona had resurfaced in Peterson, who was youthful, dynamic, and successful.

The Liberal leader had a look, the deep blue suits, white shirts, and red ties of the polished professional, and a stance, hands on his hips, collar unbuttoned, and tie loosened, which implied that he was a hard-working, caring, and concerned politician. And initially, his actions matched his image. He confronted the province's doctors over extra billing and forced them to back down. He protected the interests of average Ontarians, and they rewarded him with 95 of 130 seats in the September 1987 election, the fourth-largest legislative majority since Confederation.

But Peterson turned out to be a Mr. Fizz rather than an Old Man Ontario, as Frost was called toward the end of his career. Peterson was undone by overconfidence and poor judgement. In the summer of 1990, a time when Ontarians were steamed at politicians in general and their premier in particular, Peterson went to the polls a year before an election would normally be called. He started with a huge lead in the public opinion polls, but it melted like butter in a southern Ontario heat wave. The Meech Lake fiasco and his role in it, especially the offer to relinquish eight Ontario Senate seats to appease the West's demands for more power in Ottawa, were fresh in the minds of many voters.

And Mike Harris reminded people of something else they did not like about the Peterson government: its record of reckless spending and relentless taxation. The Tory leader cleverly ran a campaign that was narrowly focused on spending and taxation, because he realized he had no hope of winning. He did not do himself or his party a lot of good; they won twenty seats, up from sixteen in 1987, but retained their third-party status in the legislature. However, he did a lot of damage to Peterson. Harris tapped into the voter resentment that was simmering just beneath the surface, and made an angry electorate even angrier. Peterson recognized the threat posed by the Harris campaign and reacted by promising to lower the provincial sales tax by one percentage point. But that was too little too late to reverse the impact of the six bloated budgets of provincial treasurer Robert Nixon.

Nixon was the senior member of the Liberal caucus that took over from the Miller Tories in June 1985, with the support of Bob Rae's New Democrats. He was a former party leader, he was first elected as the member for Brant in January 1962, and he succeeded his father, Harry, who had represented the constituency since 1919 and was the last Liberal premier of Ontario prior to Peterson. Nixon was a rural politician who looked right at home whether he was attending a corn roast or chairing a committee meeting. As provincial treasurer, he liked being referred to as "a parsimonious old farmer." Yet, his budgets contained a bewildering array of new and increased spending that was totally incompatible with thrift or parsimony.

His first budget, unveiled on October 25, 1985, was typical. There would be a $75-million increase in funding for existing youth employment and training programs, and an extra $100 million the following year. The Liberals would provide farmers with

$50 million worth of assistance to lower the interest rates paid on loans. They allotted funding for 10,000 new social housing units over three years and subsidies for 10,000 new childcare spaces. They created a new Northern Development Fund with $100 million to spend over five years and gave the Small Business Development Corporation an extra $30 million. They bumped up transfer payments to colleges and universities, school boards, municipalities, and hospitals by anywhere from 4 to 8 percent. And even though Ontario's booming economy was generating windfall revenues for the government, Nixon increased the personal income tax rate from 48 to 50 percent of the federal rate and introduced a surtax on provincial income tax exceeding $5,000.

In almost every budget, the Liberal treasurer declared that his revenue and spending projections were "fiscally responsible," or fit the government's "fiscal framework." These terms were virtually meaningless, however, since they were never defined. The real mentality that prevailed among the Peterson Liberals was evident from Nixon's personal comments about credit ratings in his first budget. "Credit ratings serve as a valuable guide for investors unfamiliar with . . . the many thousands of corporations and governments that issue or guarantee securities," he told the Legislature. "In practical terms, the triple-A credit rating has little significance. Having a triple-A credit rating does not provide needed jobs for young people, nor improve access to affordable housing, nor improve the quality of and availability of health care." In response to the Liberals' cavalier attitude, New York–based Standard & Poor's lowered Ontario's credit rating to Double-A from Triple-A.

◄o►

Such were the fiscal starting points of the Peterson years, in numbers and words. And in that regard, it is worth considering the ideas that prevailed among Drew's Conservatives when they arrived in office full of ambition and short on experience. In the first of many budgets during the Tory dynasty, Drew's treasurer

Leslie Frost told the legislature on March 16, 1944, that the government should live by "the principle of surplus, namely that we should adhere to the policy of pay-as-you-go except in cases of great emergency." He also spoke of "the principle of mandate," meaning that "The electors should understand that additional services cost additional money which, in the final analysis, can only be obtained by additional taxes." Frost concluded that portion of his budget speech with these words about borrowing: "I am not opposed to the proper use of our credit. Credit, however, should be soundly used. Our credit is a great asset which we should protect and conserve at all times for use in times of emergency."

Where Drew and Frost recognized the need for caution and frugality in government, Peterson and Nixon and their Liberal colleagues were not constrained by such sentiments. And as long as the freewheeling, highrolling 1980s lasted, it did not seem to matter. In fact, Nixon's last budget, presented to the legislature on April 24, 1990, showed that the government's spending and the province's debt as a proportion of GDP, as well as the ratio of interest charges to total revenues, had all declined under the Liberals. Moreover, Nixon wound up with an unanticipated $35-million surplus in fiscal 1989–90 and budgeted for a small surplus in 1990–91.

The Liberal treasurer was immensely proud of these accomplishments. Nobody had balanced the provincial budget since 1969–70, when Charles McNaughton was the Tory treasurer, John Robarts was premier, and Nixon himself was leader of the provincial Liberals. Nixon reminisced fondly about McNaughton and spoke glowingly of his budget when he addressed a joint meeting of the Empire and Canadian clubs at Toronto's Royal York Hotel on May 14, 1990. "Charlie McNaughton — I used to accuse him of being nothing more than an alfalfa merchant from Exeter," Nixon said, "and if he were here he would be able to say that I am nothing more than a corn grower from Brant County."

As for the budget, Nixon casually observed that the province would spend about $44.5 billion in the upcoming year, or $140 million a day. "The fiscal position is one of balance," he said. "I certainly don't believe it is a precarious balance because we ended last year with about a $35-million surplus. It may be higher by the time all the accounts are paid and all the revenue is accounted for . . . but there is a solid surplus, not just on our operating account . . . but with all of our capital requirements as well. As we approached the budget this time, there was some concern that because the rate of growth has been reduced substantially we would not be able to present another balanced budget. The economists at treasury are predicting a reduction in real growth but with a levelling out at about 1.7 percent. On that basis, we still feel that we will pay all our bills, including our capital account, and we are projecting a surplus of about $30 million."

In the same speech, Nixon told his blue-chip luncheon crowd that "the provincial tax base has been expanded, deepened, and strengthened!" That was a polite way of saying that the Liberals had found numerous ways to raise taxes, although the treasurer wisely chose not to elaborate on the twenty-eight tax hikes contained in his six budgets. On four occasions, Nixon increased the personal income tax rate, boosting it to 53 percent of the federal rate from 48 percent. As well, he followed the practice of the Mulroney Tories and imposed surtaxes on high income earners. He broadened the retail sales tax, making it applicable to new goods and services, and in his 1988 budget he increased the rate from 7 to 8 percent.

Like treasurers of every political persuasion, Nixon realized that he could raise taxes on gasoline, alcohol, and tobacco with impunity — and did. But he also demonstrated a flair for innovative new taxes. In the 1989 budget, he slapped a $5 tax on every new tire sold in the province. He introduced a gas-guzzler tax on big, inefficient automobiles. And he imposed a commercial concentration tax of $1 per square foot on buildings and parking lots over 200,000 square feet in size in the greater Toronto area.

The Liberal tax measures, combined with those levied by the Mulroney government, put a discernible dent in the disposable income of most Ontarians. The impact was tangible and lasting. But events would prove that Nixon's celebrated surpluses, especially the second one, were little more than political chicanery. Within six months of his address to the Empire and Canadian clubs, the Grits had been swept from power by a wave of voter wrath, and the incoming NDP treasurer, Floyd Laughren, announced that his predecessor's surplus was destined to become a multi-billion-dollar deficit. And when the final figures were in, the government had posted a deficit of $3.029 billion, the second-highest budgetary shortfall up to that time. The problem was that during the opulent 1980s, Peterson and Nixon had built the government to such a size and raised entitlements to such a level that they could only be sustained by an extraordinary economic boom. The Liberals achieved one small surplus, not through thrift or prudence, but simply because they couldn't spend all the revenues generated by a sizzling economy and their own tax grabs.

They certainly tried, though. Nixon's budgets were peppered with boasts about how much he had increased spending, and 1984–85, the final year of the Tory era, was always the benchmark for comparison. In his 1987 budget, the "parsimonious old farmer" trumpeted the fact that he had boosted funding for the ministry of agriculture by 72 percent in a scant twenty-four months, and a year later the ministry's funding was up 86 percent. By 1988, the environment ministry's budget was up 51 percent, and by 1989 it had grown 70 percent from 1984–85. Funding for the Ontario Student Awards program was up 55 percent, Nixon noted, while spending on roads, highways, and rapid transit had grown by a relatively modest 30 percent. Health care spending rose, on average, more than 10 percent a year, for a whopping total increase of 84 percent. And in a mere five years, while Ontario enjoyed higher rates of growth than any other OECD nation and the provincial economy was generating new jobs at a blistering pace, the Liberals raised spending on social assistance by an astronomical 92 percent.

In the 1989 budget, as the Liberals began implementing some of the recommendations of their social assistance review committee, Nixon took stock of the changes that had occurred in welfare benefits primarily under the Peterson government. He noted that there had been a general rate increase, effective January 1, in each of the last seven years. Accordingly, benefits would be bumped up by an average of 6 percent on January 1, 1990. Overall social assistance spending had risen, on average, 12.6 percent annually since 1984–85, and benefit levels in all categories were up by an average of 37.9 percent. The Liberals had improved the financial resources available to children in poor families, enriched the shelter benefits, and put more money into employment support programs. "Ontario provides the highest level of benefits for single parents and disabled individuals," Nixon told the legislature. "The government is committed to helping recipients attain greater economic self-sufficiency and, therefore, has decided to strengthen social assistance."

The Liberal treasurer clearly took delight in reviewing these measures, and understandably so. At the time, Ontario had to pay for only half of the cost of the yearly increases. Ottawa covered the balance under the provisions of the Canada Assistance Plan (CAP). The advantage of this system, for the Ontario government, was that it could spend fifty cents on welfare and deliver a dollar's worth of benefits. By increasing those benefits, as they did every year, the Peterson Liberals reaped a handsome political dividend because they appeared to be generous, compassionate, and concerned about the plight of the poor. For the Mulroney Tories, who were making their own feeble attempts to control spending, this arrangement was nothing more than a headache. They automatically got stuck with half the bill, reaped none of the political rewards, and wound up with a larger deficit each year.

After several unsuccessful attempts to put a leash on his Liberal counterpart, Tory finance minister Wilson announced in his 1990 budget that he was unilaterally putting a cap on CAP: henceforth, funding for Ontario, Alberta, and B.C. — the three wealthiest provinces — would increase by no more than 5 percent a year. To put that figure in perspective, note that Ontario had already decided to increase its overall social assistance spending by 19 percent for the year.

In retrospect, some observers now contend that the Peterson Liberals single-handedly wrecked CAP. At the very least, they left the province with obligations that were unsustainable in the long run. Prior to the cutbacks imposed by the Harris government in July 1995, Ontario's welfare rates were substantially higher than those of other provinces for every category of recipient. According to a report published in 1995 by the Ottawa-based National Council of Welfare, based on 1993 rates, single employable males in Ontario were entitled to $8,036 per year, almost three times as much as they would get in New Brunswick, and 29 percent more than they would receive in B.C., where the cost of living is roughly comparable to Ontario. A single parent with one child was eligible for $15,061 a year in Ontario, 77 percent more than the same parent would receive in New Brunswick, 35 to 45 percent more than that person would get elsewhere in the Maritimes, and 50 percent more than any of the Prairie provinces pay. In a report dealing with cutbacks in federal transfer payments, the Dominion Bond Rating Service of Toronto arrived at this conclusion about Ontario's social assistance programs: "Ontario is presently locked into one of the most liberal welfare schemes in North America, far ahead of any other province and, with recently announced federal cutbacks, is largely on its own to finance welfare."

During their brief stint in power, the Peterson Liberals seemed to believe that to govern effectively they had to spend generously and to govern benevolently they had to spend lavishly. They may have been misguided but they were consistent. Their successors, Bob Rae's New Democrats, were terminally afflicted by inconsistency and uncertainty. Labour leaders and party loyalists attributed this lack of resolve to a vacillating leader and the devastating recession which descended upon Ontario just as the NDP took power. In fact, the party's problems went much deeper. It had spent years in opposition pandering to advocacy groups and special interests rather than developing a progressive and coherent set of policies aimed at the general public.

Ultimately, the Ontario NDP became a haven for single-issue organizations and for individuals whose ideas were too radical for the more centrist Conservatives and Liberals. The *Toronto Star*'s provincial affairs columnist Thomas Walkom captured this weakness in the character of the party in his 1994 book, *Rae Days: The Rise and Follies of the NDP*. "Anyone with any beef against government could be sure to have a friend in the NDP," Walkom wrote. "It supported residents east of Toronto who didn't want a second international airport built in their region. It supported residents west of Toronto who didn't want the existing international airport expanded. And it supported aircraft workers who wanted anything built that would increase demands for airplanes.

"It supported environmentalists who wanted the province rid of pop in cans. And it supported Hamilton steelworkers who made, and wanted to keep making, those cans. It supported anti-nuclear activists, determined to shut down the province's atomic generating stations, and it supported the unions whose workers were employed at these stations. It supported small business, while at the same time calling for a steep hike in the minimum wage, the policy that small business owners hated most. As the NDP accelerated its drive to attract interest groups, its vinyl-covered policy binder — the pride and joy of members who believed their party alone had a real program — became a bewildering array of contradictory resolutions."

As an opposition party, accustomed to criticizing rather than making decisions, New Democrats never bothered resolving such contradictions and inconsistencies. Hence their 1990 campaign platform, the People's Agenda, was littered with conflicting positions.

Rae and a few of his close advisers knew that most of these policies, which so appealed to party members, would be as impractical in Ontario as toques and parkas in Florida. Alternately, initiatives that found favour with ordinary voters were often anathema to the NDP faithful. This created numerous dilemmas for the NDP caucus, which continually had to choose between the hard ideological positions of its supporters and the more pragmatic demands of the wider public. And in most cases, the Rae government chose the latter, shedding toques and parkas for more appropriate attire in an attempt to broaden the party's appeal.

They abandoned their long-standing commitment to public auto insurance — which infuriated many of their supporters — when it became apparent that the public had no interest in a costly and contentious government takeover of the private auto insurance business. They allowed Sunday shopping, to accommodate the lifestyles of two-income couples, but angered labour leaders who maintained that retail workers should be guaranteed one day off per week with their families. They introduced casino gambling to Ontario, a move that appalled some party loyalists but caused little or no trouble with the public. On such issues, the Rae government deftly stickhandled through the competing demands of its backers and the public. But these matters were of secondary importance.

In order to overcome public skepticism and enhance their credibility, the New Democrats had to demonstrate that they were capable of managing the province's finances and its economy. And here the NDP failed miserably. Shortly after their surprise election victory, Rae and his caucus received some advice from former Saskatchewan NDP premier Allan Blakeney. He told them that they could run Ontario for a generation provided they were fiscally conservative and socially progressive. But on April 29, 1991, the day that Floyd Laughren delivered the first NDP budget in Ontario history, it became apparent that the Rae government had not heeded the counsel of the fiscally prudent Blakeney. Laughren stood in the legislature, like a soldier armed with pike and shield, and issued his famous battle cry: "We had a choice to make this year — to fight the deficit or fight the recession. We are proud to be fighting the recession."

For Ontario New Democrats, who were still savouring their first taste of political power, those were stirring words. They also found plenty to applaud in the government's plans. Spending would rise 13.4 percent and the deficit would be allowed to triple to $9.7 billion, levels that were supposed to create or preserve 70,000 jobs. This was social democracy in action. The New Democrats would show that government could act as a brake when the economy went into freefall. Bob White called it "a reasonable and compassionate budget." And Gord Wilson, president of the Ontario Federation of Labour, was positively exuberant. "I give it an A-plus," he told reporters. "We have a terrible mess on our hands. At least one government has the courage to act like the Lone Ranger, get on the horse and gallop out there to defend the people."

But outside of party loyalists, not many people were impressed by the NDP's heroic gesture. Media coverage was heavily focused on the soaring deficit rather than the war on the recession. The next day's *Ottawa Citizen* carried a large front-page headline that simply said, "Spend, spend, spend." And an accompanying column was headed, "Colossal deficit unmatched by big ideas." Less than three weeks later, on May 16, Moody's Investors Service cut the province's credit rating from Triple-A to Double-A2, putting Ontario a notch below Alberta and B.C. That same day, 1,500 protestors, most of them from the Toronto business community, marched on Queen's Park and screamed "Out, out, out" when Laughren tried to address them.

Even more damaging for the government, the public did not like the budget. A Gallup Canada poll released May 29, 1991, revealed that 75 percent of those questioned were aware of the budget, and 63 percent said that it would not do anything to strengthen the province's economy. An unpopular budget was the last thing the NDP needed. They had started the year at 60 percent in the polls. By late May, they had plummeted to 41 percent, and they continued falling. One month later, Gallup checked Ontario's political pulse again, and reached this conclusion: "In the past six months, the ruling NDP has witnessed the evaporation of a commanding 37-point lead in public opinion, and today finds itself trailing the opposition Liberal party."

The budget was only one factor behind the government's precipitous slide. Rae and Laughren and a few colleagues realized, however, that they could not ignore the combined opposition of the media, the business community, and the public. Stunned and chastened, they began to talk about the merits of fiscal responsibility. But their conversion to a concept they had spent years denouncing was a slow process, which occurred over a two-year period and did nothing to reverse Ontario's fall into a financial hole.

The NDP's second budget, introduced on April 30, 1992, called for a 5.2 percent increase in spending and a $9.9-billion deficit and set these priorities: "The first is jobs. The second is human services, such as health care and education. The third is keeping the deficit in check."

Twelve months later, in the 1993–94 budget, the Rae government's priorities had changed. Deficit reduction "at a responsible pace" had moved to the top of the agenda. Preliminary estimates put the deficit for the previous year at almost $12 billion, more than $2 billion higher than originally anticipated, and it was in danger of hitting $17 billion in the coming year unless something was done. In his budget speech, Laughren summarized the magnitude of the province's financial woes: "Excluding sovereign countries, Ontario has become the largest borrower in the world. On average, we borrow more than $1 billion a month. We spend more on interest costs than we spend on our schools. About two-thirds of our borrowing comes from outside Canada, which means that most of the interest we pay on this borrowing goes to foreign bankers, investors, and economies."

The budget contained tax hikes and spending cuts that would allegedly save the government $8.7 billion in 1993–94. But more than half of these savings, $5.1 billion worth, were similar to those achieved by the Mulroney Tories. They were largely cuts in antici-pated spending increases. The bottom line was that the Ontario government was still planning to spend $53.1 billion, down 1.1 percent from $53.8 billion the previous year.

The New Democrats did, however, impose some real restraint on public-sector wages through their so-called social contract. They froze the wages of 900,000 workers, including provincial civil ser-vants, nurses, teachers, academics, and others, for three years and forced them to take several days of unpaid leave per year. Their goals were to save $2 billion annually, which amounted to less than 5 percent of the total annual public-sector compensation of $43 billion, and to avoid laying off up to 40,000 workers.

But rather than winning broad public support for the NDP, these measures alienated many hard-core supporters, and failed to satisfy the skeptics among the business community, investors, and the gen-eral public. The New Democrats had been impaled by a fiscal crisis that they had helped to create. The party could not stickhandle past the competing positions and produce a solution that was satisfac-tory to both supporters and outsiders. Public-sector union leaders, who were in no mood to compromise, viewed the social contract as an excessive, unfair, and totally unacceptable violation of collective bargaining rights.

The government's decision to legislate the cutbacks, after nego-tiations failed to produce an agreement, led to a deep and ragged rift between the NDP and some sectors of the labour movement. At the annual convention of the Ontario Federation of Labour in November 1993, delegates voted in favour of a resolution with-holding their support for the NDP unless the government withdrew the social contract prior to the next election. Private-sector unions, however, with the exception of the CAW, stuck with the govern-ment and walked out of the convention to protest the resolution.

Within the business community, the displeasure with the NDP's efforts to control the deficit was nearly universal. And that sentiment was shared by the province's international lenders, particularly in Japan. "The Ontario government asked Nomura to organize an information tour of the Far East after they had released one of their budgets and we had to plead with our clients to meet with Laughren," recalls deBever, who was involved in putting together the event for the big Japanese securities firm. "The next year, they asked another Japanese company to do the same thing, with the same result. Laughren would go over there and in Japan they would be very polite and make sure they didn't say anything confrontational to him. The meetings would be over and Floyd would be happy because he thought he'd really explained what was going on. The feedback we'd get from Laughren was that it had been a successful mission. In fact, they were shaking their heads and saying, 'This guy is totally off the planet.'"

Labour leaders can rant, businessmen can fume, and international investors can sputter in disbelief, but only the voters can defeat a government. And in June 1995, Ontarians decisively rejected Bob Rae's administration, one of the major reasons being that it had proved incapable of managing the province's finances or resuscitating its economy. The NDP did not create the recession of the early 1990s, but the party's responses to it — increased government spending and a tripling of the deficit — did nothing to alleviate unemployment or avert factory closures. Instead, they led to a deterioration of Ontario's already dubious finances. Under the New Democrats, the provincial debt nearly doubled to hit $90 billion. To put that figure in context, the debt was equivalent to almost one-third of the provincial economy at the end of their administration versus one-fifth in 1991 when they took over. Debt per capita rose 62 percent. Interest charges shot up to 17.6 percent of provincial revenues from 10.3 percent, a change of 71 percent. Those are the type of numbers that give businesspeople and bond raters heartburn.

But a fiscal crisis also has a direct and very detrimental effect on the average citizen, which quickly becomes evident by looking at what has happened to taxes and disposable income in Ontario since the late 1980s. When it came to taxing the public, Laughren was just as proficient as his Liberal predecessor, though less imaginative. He brought in twenty tax increases in his four budgets. But rather than looking for new goods and services to tax, he tended to concentrate on personal income taxes, surtaxes, gas taxes, and the so-called sin taxes — levies on tobacco and alcohol. For example, the tax rate on personal income went from 53 percent of the federal rate to 54.5 percent, then 55 percent, and finally 58 percent. Laughren also increased surtaxes on personal income four times.

Like most governments, the Rae New Democrats took every opportunity to boast about the benefits of their spending programs. They were much more reticent about the cost of their taxation measures. And no wonder. Tax changes in the 1992–93 budget, introduced on April 30, 1992, cost the public $771 million in the remaining eight months of the year, and $1.1 billion in 1993, when they were in effect for the full year. The bill for Laughren's 1993–94 tax hikes was even steeper: $1.6 billion the first year and $2.0 billion the following year.

Furthermore, the New Democrats chose the worst possible time for such massive tax grabs. For one thing, the Ontario public was suffering from a severe case of tax fatigue after absorbing all the levies and tolls imposed by the tax-happy Peterson Liberals and Mulroney Tories, not to mention the municipalities and school boards. Second, in the early 1990s, wages and salaries were generally not growing fast enough to outrun both inflation and cash-starved governments. The net effect was that the average citizen wound up poorer, a fact confirmed by a StatsCan study on disposable income published in mid-1995. The federal agency reported that between 1989 and 1993, average family income across the country fell 6.5 percent to $43,225 per year from $46,250.

Rising taxes, falling incomes, and deteriorating public finances can have profound and lasting consequences for any community.

They gradually erode the standard of living. They undermine public confidence. And unchecked, they threaten the prospects of the next generation. Ontarians intuitively understood this when they went to the polls on June 8, 1995. Most New Democrats never grasped these underlying realities, a fact which was evident when Rae's caucus and cabinet met at Queen's Park one last time following the election. On his way out of that meeting, NDP Transport Minister Mike Farnan charged that "There were undercurrents of meanness, of bigotry and racism that permeated this election." Fellow cabinet minister Marilyn Churley chipped in with the observation that "Harris picked up on the fear and resentment that come out of a recession."

These comments reflected the tenor of much of the commentary as the Conservatives took office. There was no possibility, according to defeated NDPers and other critics, that the electorate had chosen wisely. Instead, what brought voters and Tories together were some of the basest of human sentiments: meanness and resentment, bigotry and racism. And the quality of the criticism did not improve after the Harris government began implementing its program. In late July, 1995, provincial treasurer Ernie Eves announced $1.9 billion in spending cuts, including a 21.6 percent reduction in welfare rates, a move aimed at saving $1.4 billion over two years and ensuring that Ontario's benefits were no more than 10 percent higher than the average of the other nine provinces.

The welfare cuts attracted far more strident criticism than any other part of the package. Judy Darcy, president of the Canadian Union of Public Employees, which represents thousands of welfare case workers, predicted that lower social assistance rates would lead to "greater social inequities . . . greater social unrest, more and more people falling through the cracks, more and more people ending up in the criminal justice system." The *Star*'s Walkom was even harsher in his assessment. "Mike Harris' Tories are keeping their word," he wrote. "They are savaging the poor today in order to reward the rich tomorrow."

There was one gaping omission in both of these typically grim assessments. Neither took any account of the middle-class men and women who do most of Ontario's work, produce most of its wealth, and pay most of its taxes. For too long, policy makers in Ontario overlooked these wage earners, too, and this was a mistake. A government that neglects their needs and interests threatens the well-being of the entire community, since they are the cornerstone of a healthy economy and the foundation of a vibrant province. Hence, when average family incomes decline over a prolonged period of time, sound public policy should take account of this, and welfare benefits should fall accordingly.

Other cutbacks led to equally vehement denunciations of the government and more dire warnings of dark days ahead. The cancellation of a Toronto subway line that was already under construction was said to be a disaster. A 5 percent reduction in funding for hundreds of social agencies that assist abused women and children, and needy seniors, among others, was described as totally irrational. The mere prospect that the provincial government would trim its transfer payments to municipalities had some Metro Toronto councillors sounding like prophets of doom. They foresaw less police protection, deteriorating transit, unsafe roads, weed-filled parks, and, as one elected official put it, a "really, really mean city."

The public, however, wasn't buying any of this. A record 7,000 *Star* readers called the paper's StarPhone survey line on a single day to respond to a question about whether the July 1995 cuts were fair and necessary. Only about 4,000 were able to leave recorded messages before the system became jammed. Seventy percent supported the government's actions. As well, Gallup polls revealed that during their first few months in office the Conservatives enjoyed higher levels of public support than they received in the election. The public was unswayed by the criticism coming from union leaders and local politicians because much of it was nonsense.

For example, the notion that budget cuts would transform "Toronto the good" into "Toronto the mean" was simply not credible. The city's reputation for goodness, which it has enjoyed for the better part of this century, is based on a civic culture that values clean streets, safe neighbourhoods, hard work, and adherence to the law. Furthermore, because that culture is rooted in the attitudes and beliefs of the populace, it is capable of surviving budget cuts and service reductions.

But there were other, more basic reasons why the pleas and prognostications went unheeded. Ontarians were no longer buying into the idea that more government meant a better society. In fact, many had concluded that the opposite is true. Nor were they sold on the notion that collective activity, funded or organized by government, was the only sound basis of a strong community. Instead, they had come to believe that a strong community is based on strong individuals, and that governments ought to be in the business of encouraging self-reliance rather than fostering dependence.

In this, Ontarians were merely catching up to voters elsewhere in Canada, and indeed the entire Western world, who had already made the same sharp shift to the right, according to Reginald Stackhouse, a Mulroney-era Tory MP. "What is the idea that has elected right-wing governments all the way from France to New Zealand," he asked rhetorically in a *Globe* op-ed piece that appeared shortly after the Ontario vote. "It's a sea change of an idea, a total turnaround in the way people look at not only politics but everything else. Mike Harris is premier of Canada's largest province because he was the leader most aware of this earthquake of a social upheaval. He made an impact in this election with the most powerful charisma there is: putting into words the hopes men and women are feeling.

"For the first time in more than half a century, those hopes do not involve new government programs. All over the democratic world, men and women are giving up on thinking governments can solve their problems for them. Even more important, they are giving up the notion that society as a whole can make things right for the individual. The shift is now to individuals coping with life on their own. What they want from government most of all is to be left alone."

Several commentators, including the *Globe*'s national affairs columnist Jeffrey Simpson, have argued persuasively that suburban middle-class voters led this swing to the right in Ontario. They noted that the so-called Metro belt, the ring of ridings around Metro Toronto, went solidly Tory, and voters in the heavily urbanized region stretching from Hamilton to the Niagara Peninsula also voted overwhelmingly Conservative. Simpson explained the Tory sweep through suburbia this way: "Unlike folks who can afford expensive houses and condominiums downtown, or even older suburbs, many new suburbanites earn middle-class incomes, often because both husband and wife must work. They have mortgages on recently purchased homes, pay large property taxes and worry about security of employment for themselves and their children. When analysts note the decline in real incomes of Ontarians in the past five years, they are talking, above all, of suburbanites.

"The Conservatives understood the suburbs brilliantly, and were accordingly rewarded. Their call for lower taxes resonated with suburbanites, as did the determination to scale back the size of government. Similarly, the anti-welfare message worked brilliantly in suburbia whose identity is of hard-working families. Policies perceived to benefit particularistic groups based on ethnicity, race or gender are political death in suburbia. Its whole ethos is of homogeneity."

Suburban Ontarians were unquestionably driven by self-interest when they went to the polls in June 1995, and they were harshly criticized for it. They were accused of meanness and resentment or, worse still, bigotry and racism. In fact, by pursuing their own interests, they were attempting to preserve something of vital importance to the economic well-being of all Canadians. That is because the suburbs represent upward mobility in Canadian society. They have proliferated over the past half-century because Canada has been a growing and prosperous country. And the cornerstone of the suburbs, and the most potent symbol of Canada's growth and prosperity, is the single-family home.

For millions of Ontarians who now reside in suburbs, their large, sturdy, comfortable homes represent a move up the economic ladder. The two-storey, four-bedroom brick house with the attached two-car garage out front — the standard suburban home of the 1980s — is really just a larger version of the three-bedroom bungalow — the ideal home of the 1950s and 1960s — or the split-level and ranch-style homes that middle-class Ontarians aspired to own in the 1970s. Furthermore, the family that moved from an apartment to a starter home and, finally, to a two-storey, four-bedroom dwelling in the 1980s was experiencing the same type of economic success that Ontarians have enjoyed since the early nineteenth century when a pioneer family could move from a log cabin to a wood-frame home to a brick dwelling within a lifetime.

Harris and his Tories won their huge majority because they understood that a shaky economy, sprawling governments, and deteriorating public finances had led to a decline in disposable income and threatened the financial security of millions of hard-working couples with young families and big mortgages. The Conservatives recognized that after half a century of growth and prosperity, Ontario faced the prospect of stagnation and decline. And they drafted a platform, the Common Sense Revolution, that addressed the public interest in the broadest possible sense, because citizens of all sorts, even the weak and the vulnerable, are better off in a province that is growing and prosperous than in one that is stagnating and in decline.

9

RALPH'S REVOLUTION

Since the day in August 1980 when he announced that he was running for mayor of Calgary, Ralph Klein has built his career by surpassing expectations and defying political conventions. With his loopy grin, his wandering waistline, and his friendly façade, the former television reporter could pass for a life insurance salesman who coaches peewee hockey in his spare time. In fact, Klein is one of the most successful Canadian politicians of this generation. His only rival is the prime minister. Klein's electoral record stands at six wins, zero losses. He won three Calgary mayoralty races, the last two by collecting over 90 percent of the votes cast. In 1989, he was elected to the Alberta legislature as a Tory MLA. Three years later, in December 1992, he captured the party leadership. Six months after that, he performed what became known as "the miracle on the Prairies" by resurrecting the moribund Alberta Conservatives and leading them to a majority government.

Fresh from that triumph, he embarked on the biggest gamble of his political career — a four-year plan to cut government spending by 20 percent and balance the provincial budget, without raising taxes. By Canadian standards, the pace and scope of the changes in Alberta have been nothing short of breathtaking. Three months after being elected, Klein's government began selling off the province's 202 publicly owned liquor stores, and threw the business of alcohol retailing wide open to private operators. Since then, he and his ministers have dismantled dozens of school boards, closed hundreds of hospital beds, cut the provincial welfare rolls in half, and laid off thousands of civil servants.

Klein was the first political leader in Canada to conclude that the only way out of a deficit-debt mess was to slash expenditures. He was the first to rule out tax increases altogether. But there is another, much more significant difference to his approach. Klein recognized that the changes must be permanent. Governments must deliver less and citizens must expect less. What the Alberta premier has launched is far more sweeping than an exercise in deficit reduction. His program is a wholesale attempt to change public values and expectations. And for that reason, it has been widely described as a revolution.

The Klein initiatives have attracted high praise and harsh criticism. Influential publications such as the *New York Times* and the *Times* of London carried favourable reports on Klein and his government in early 1995. *Barron's* called him "Canada's Newt," a reference to U.S. congressional leader Newt Gingrich, and the *Wall Street Journal* described him as "Canada's Reagan." After visiting the province, *Journal* writer John Fund concluded that "Alberta is home to North America's most radical revolution in budget downsizing."

The Klein government has also been celebrated at home. In November 1994, the Toronto-based National Citizen's Coalition awarded the Alberta premier its Colin M. Brown Freedom Medal, which is presented annually to individuals judged to have encouraged "more freedom through less government." Two months later, the Vancouver-based Fraser Institute honoured Klein again by bestowing upon him its first annual Fiscal Performance Award. The award was based on an assessment of tax and spending policies which showed that Alberta had done more in the previous year to clean up its books than the nine other provinces, as well as thirty-four American states.

"The changes in Alberta are exciting and remarkable in modern Canadian history," institute analyst Fazil Mihlar concluded in a mid-term report card prepared to coincide with the award. "Alberta's program could become a model of fiscal responsibility and small government in Canada, if not North America. Alberta gives Canadians the ideas needed to revamp the social contract between the government and its citizenry. In short, it provides a framework to move away from dependency on government to self-sufficiency."

But the kudos on the right have been matched by denunciations and dire warnings from the left. Linda Karpowich, a former president of the Alberta Federation of Labour, has accused the Klein government of "lies and deceptions," and of inflicting "the worst cutbacks since the 1930s." She sees the entire program as a "noxious disease" that is in danger of becoming an epidemic by spreading to other parts of Canada. In March 1995, in one of his rare appearances in Alberta, the CLC's White told a gathering of labour leaders and union members that "If the so-called Klein experiment comes to be widely seen as a success, if it comes to be seen as the best way to deal with the deficit and debt issue, then the future we face as a country is grim indeed."

For Klein and his Conservative colleagues, neither the praise nor the criticism matters very much. There is only one audience they need to worry about, and that is the Alberta electorate. And in the first half of their mandate, when they inflicted the deepest cuts, they enjoyed higher public approval ratings than any other government in Canada except perhaps the Chrétien Liberals. A December 1994 poll conducted by Toronto-based Environics Research Group showed that 68 percent of Albertans supported the government while 63 percent approved of the premier's performance. An Angus Reid survey two months later, commissioned by the *Edmonton Journal, Calgary Herald,* and CBC Alberta, found that Klein's approval rating had climbed to a stratospheric 73 percent. Furthermore, the support was equally strong in rural and urban areas, including Edmonton, the provincial capital, which did not elect a single Tory in the June 1993 election. The Angus Reid poll produced two other startling results: half of those surveyed said that the cutbacks had had no effect on the quality of their lives, while another quarter said that their lives had actually improved under the Klein government.

The survey numbers, which were bad news for Klein's opponents both inside and outside the provincial legislature, reflected three things. First, the dearth of negative effects from sharp spending cuts revealed that the province previously had far too much government. Second, Klein's personal approval ratings demonstrated his ability to succeed through unconventional means: he is probably the first Canadian politician to see his personal popularity soar even while pursuing a policy of fiscal austerity. Finally, the poll numbers revealed Klein's uncanny ability to sense the mood of the public. He insists that his government has merely met the electorate's desire for change. "I think we bought into a program that Albertans wanted for a number of years," Klein says. "They had been telling us, at least this is my reading of it, 'Get your financial house in order. We don't need a lot of rules, a lot of regulations. We can manage our own affairs so get out of our lives. Make sure we pay reasonable taxes and get good value for our money. But get out of the business of being in business.' We're simply catching up with the people."

The government's mid-term surge in popularity also revealed how much distance the Klein Tories had been able to create between themselves and the fiascoes of the Don Getty era. Getty captured the Conservative leadership in the fall of 1985 following the resignation of Peter Lougheed, one of the most effective and admired premiers in the history of the province. By the time Getty relinquished the position in September 1992, amid the referendum campaign on the Charlottetown Accord, Albertans were ready to throw his party out of office. And changing governments is something Albertans rarely do.

Social Credit ran the province from 1935 until 1971, when they were displaced by Lougheed's Conservatives, who all but wiped the opposition parties off the political map. This preference for what amounts to one-party rule is often interpreted, particularly among the Eastern Canadian media, as a sign of a docile, acquiescent electorate. In fact, the two dominant figures of this period, Socred premier Ernest Manning and Tory leader Lougheed, provided Albertans with competent, scandal-free government. They earned their long stays in office by managing the province's resource wealth wisely and by defending Alberta's oil and gas industry against the federal government's occasionally predatory moves.

Getty, on the other hand, had an unerring knack for walking into economic debacles and political blunders. The first of these was the collapse in the summer of 1987 of an Edmonton-based financial services company called the Principal Group. On the day that the story broke, reporters anxious to question Getty caught up with him on a local golf course. Meanwhile, hundreds of distraught investors were lined up outside Principal Group offices hoping to get their money back. A provincial inquiry later revealed that lax government regulations were partly to blame for Principal's demise, and the province had to cough up $100 million in compensation.

Then there was a series of misguided investments and loan guarantees — in an Edmonton meat packing plant, a Vancouver port facility, and a magnesium smelter in High River, Alberta — that cost the taxpayers of Alberta an estimated $1.5 billion. The worst of these ventures was a company called NovAtel, a manufacturer of cellular telephones that came to epitomize the incompetence of the government. A perennial money loser, NovAtel was a joint venture originally involving the provincially owned Alberta

199

Government Telephones and NovaCorp, a gas transmission and petrochemical company. Through a series of corporate shuffles, the government ended up as sole owner of NovAtel and sold it in 1992. The provincial auditor-general later determined that this foray into high tech had cost the public $566 million.

The Getty government was equally inept at managing its own fiscal affairs. Getty had the misfortune of becoming premier at a time when world oil prices were collapsing. In 1986–87, provincial revenues from oil and gas royalties plummeted by $3 billion, or nearly one-third, and never fully recovered. The government compounded its problems by allowing spending to continue growing at an average annual rate of 5.1 percent and by basing budgetary revenue forecasts on unrealistic assumptions about petroleum prices. A former financial adviser recalls that in one of his administration's early budgets Getty insisted that the revenue projection be based on $23 per barrel of oil, despite the objections of treasury department officials. In fact, oil prices that year averaged around $9 a barrel.

Although the government ostensibly had a multi-year plan to balance the budget, it consistently ran deficits, and never came close to breaking even. On budget day in the spring of 1991, then treasurer Dick Johnston stood in the legislature and told the assembled members that he was introducing a blueprint to balance the books that year. Twelve months later, he had to concede that there would be a deficit of $2.3 billion. And in 1992–93, Getty's final year in office, his government ran a $2.7-billion deficit.

Despite this miserable performance, MLAs ensured that they were well compensated for their efforts. Shortly after the 1989 election, they voted themselves a 30 percent pay increase. They had earlier approved annual living allowances of up to $22,300 for MLAs who represented ridings outside Edmonton. This perk came to the attention of the public in April 1992 and caused an uproar that lasted six weeks. Alberta voters were outraged when flagrant abuses were exposed. For example, several members whose constituencies were adjacent to the capital city, and whose homes were a half-hour drive or less from the legislature, were claiming the full allowance.

Klein served as Getty's environment minister for over three years yet emerged untarnished by the gaffes and miscues. But in winning the party leadership in December 1992, he inherited a government that was unpopular and widely seen as incompetent. Albertans had turned their backs on the Tories, which was evident from the party's approval rating of 17 percent in the polls. At the same time, public opinion in the province had coalesced around the idea of more fiscally responsible government. Surveys revealed that over 90 percent of Albertans wanted the deficit cut sharply and a similar number were prepared to accept spending reductions.

In some respects, those numbers were hardly surprising. Albertans have a knack, unmatched elsewhere in the country except perhaps in Quebec, for speaking with one voice. This is most evident in provincial elections, when they consistently elect governments by huge majorities. Second, since the days of Bible Bill Aberhart, Albertans have been receptive to conservative ideas and agendas. Finally, the Reform Party and the Edmonton-based Canadian Taxpayers Association had aroused the public's latent antipathy toward government waste, excess, and mismanagement.

"We established ourselves in 1991 at the height of the Getty profligacy and irresponsibility," says Jason Kenney, the youthful, articulate rabble-rouser who founded the taxpayers' association. "We just relentlessly hammered the government on issue after issue: openness in government, handouts to big business, fiscal irresponsibility, bloated MLA pensions, and perks. We achieved a significant prominence here and, together with the Reform Party, galvanized the small-c conservative segments of the populace. We gave voice to a constituency that demanded tough fiscal action. It quickly became evident that the old political bromides and the conventional wisdom had changed dramatically."

As an astute and experienced politician, Klein undoubtedly knew how the public viewed his government and where the voters stood on fiscal issues. But seasoned observers of the new premier had serious doubts about whether he was capable of delivering the tough measures that Albertans apparently wanted. He had largely avoided the issue of deficit reduction during the leadership campaign, whereas some of his rivals had made it a central part of their platforms. And he certainly hadn't arrived in provincial politics with a reputation as a fiscal conservative. In fact, he was known as a spender. Calgary had an accumulated debt of $1.6 billion by the time Klein quit as mayor, which was the second-highest municipal debt in the country, on a per capita basis, next to Montreal's.

"If you look at his record as mayor of Calgary," says Kenney, "a lot of people were very skeptical, when he became premier, that he would be able to get this situation under control. As a fiscal manager, he was deplorable. They wracked up a massive debt trying to finance the 1988 winter Olympics. They raised taxes over and over again. He was pretty much an interventionist environment minister who was not known for dissenting against some of the Getty regime's more grandiose industrial megaprojects. So there was no reason to believe that Ralph Klein would be a different kind of leader."

But Klein has been different. He has led Alberta through a period of radical change. He has reduced the size of government and he is attempting to change the behaviour and character of the provincial bureaucracy, as well as the broader public service that includes municipalities, universities, schools, and hospitals. He is trying, among other things, to re-establish the principle that governments should live within their means rather than spending in good times and bad and banking on economic bonanzas, and the tax windfalls they produce, to bail them out.

This is a different Klein than the one who ran the city of Calgary for nine years, the mayor who promoted the Olympics, pushed for construction of a rapid transit line, and liked to have a drink at one of his favourite watering holes, the tavern at the St. Louis Hotel, after a day's work. And Klein's wildly successful stint as a mayor represented a sharp break from his career before entering politics.

There was nothing in his personal or professional experience to suggest that he was destined for high office. He had not served a political apprenticeship as an aide, adviser, or party worker. He did not have a distinguished academic record. Nor did he come from a family that was wealthy, prominent, or given to public service. Klein was born in 1942. His parents split up before his tenth birthday, sending him and his younger brother to live with their maternal grandparents in a working-class section of Calgary. Klein quit high school at age seventeen, enlisted in the Royal Canadian Air Force, and was stationed in Portage la Prairie, Manitoba.

By 1961, when he was nineteen, Klein had returned to Calgary, married his first wife, Hilda Hepner, with whom he had two children, and enrolled at the Calgary Business College. After completing his courses, he became an instructor and three years later had been elevated to principal. Next, Klein took a public relations job with the Red Cross in Calgary, later jumping to the United Way. In 1969, he made another career move, this time becoming a reporter and newsreader with the Calgary radio station CFCN. He worked briefly in radio before moving to CFCN's television station as a general assignment reporter. But while his career was taking off, his first marriage was falling apart, and in 1971 he was divorced. A year later, he married his second wife, Colleen, who had two children of her own, and they subsequently had one child together.

As a reporter, Klein had a reputation for being industrious, inquisitive, and frequently unconventional. He covered city hall for several years and developed street-level contacts among municipal workers, prostitutes, and bikers, who could provide their own unique perspectives on stories. Among his colleagues he was known for his late-night drinking and dining at the city's Chinese restaurants and for his chronic inability to make it to work for the daily 10:30 a.m. story meeting. And fellow workers were extremely skeptical when he announced in the fall of 1980 that he was running for mayor. "A lot of us laughed at the whole thing," recalls radio reporter Murray Dale, who worked alongside Klein. "During that first campaign, a lot of his co-workers, including me, wouldn't donate any money to him. We said, 'He hasn't got a chance.' We really underestimated his likability and trustworthiness."

At every stage of his career, Klein's opponents have underestimated him as well, partly because he seems so ordinary. He appears to be no more sophisticated or complicated than the average voter. Nor is there anything distant or formal about him. Calgarians called him Ralph when he was mayor of their city, and Albertans call him Ralph now that he is premier. But he possesses intuitive political skills. "He is unique," says University of Alberta sociologist Trevor Harrison, author of a book about the Reform Party and editor of a collection of essays about the Klein government. "There's no getting around that. He knows who the power brokers are and he manages to get close to them. He has a real gift with the media. Having come up through television, he knows what makes a good sound bite. People trust him. A lot of people would feel comfortable sitting down with Ralph and having a beer. He really represents them. One of the interesting aspects of his administration is that he is closely tied to big business yet successfully portrays himself as a populist, a man of the people. That is a rare political talent."

◄o►

Klein's ability to establish a personal bond with the public goes a long way toward explaining his success as a mayor and his remarkable resurrection of the Alberta Tories. Prior to the June 1993 provincial election, most pundits and pollsters considered the party near death. The Conservatives won by making Klein the centrepiece of their campaign. Tory candidates downplayed their party affiliation and billed themselves in campaign literature as members of "Ralph's team." With their attention focused on Klein, the voters forgot about the sins of the Getty gang, and passed on the opposition.

Klein's political persona — likeable, trustworthy Ralph — is the basis of his appeal and his biggest political asset. Because his relationship with the electorate is inherently personal, he has the freedom to embrace or abandon ideas and policies without damaging his credibility. Hence the Alberta public readily accepted his belated conversion to fiscal conservatism, which occurred only after he became premier. Initially, he was undoubtedly being more pragmatic than principled. Public opinion polls showed that Albertans wanted something done about the fiscal mess left behind by the Getty government. And an independent commission, appointed by Klein's government in January 1993 to review the province's books, concluded within two months that something had to be done. Klein, a good listener and a skillful politician unencumbered with ideological baggage, got the message and shifted directions.

But like many converts, Klein quickly became zealous about his newfound cause. It was not only a good approach to take because of the potential political benefits. It was the right way to go, fiscally and ethically. Klein emerged as his government's most effective salesperson when eliminating the deficit and paying down the provincial debt became matters of personal conviction for him. And no matter what the polls showed, the government had to sell its program, given the scale of the cutbacks, the speed with which they were introduced, and the opposition of students, doctors, nurses, teachers, and others who were affected.

The Conservatives' blueprint for the remaking of government in Alberta was contained in their spring 1993 budget and became a central part of their message to the voters in the election that followed. The Tories reintroduced the budget, entitled "A Fiscal Plan for Alberta," in September 1993 and quickly began implementing it. Subsequent budgets in February 1994 and 1995 added detail to the fiscal plan. It stipulated that the $2.7-billion deficit that the Klein Tories inherited from the Getty Tories would be eliminated within a four-year period ending on March 31, 1997.

The government set declining annual deficit targets and gave them the weight of law by incorporating them into its Deficit Elimination Act. Klein and his colleagues planned to achieve their

205

objective through a 20 percent reduction in program spending. They also promised that they would not introduce a sales tax or increase existing taxes, although they have raised medicare premiums and dozens of user fees. And this is where they parted company with their peers in other provinces, most of whom have also devised plans to balance their budgets. A majority of the others were prepared to raise taxes. The Alberta Tories were committed to erasing their deficit solely through spending cuts.

They launched what has come to be called the Klein revolution by slashing their own salaries 5 percent, getting rid of pensions for incoming MLAs, and cutting the cabinet to seventeen members from twenty-six. These measures had next to no impact on the province's multi-billion-dollar problem, but they allowed Klein and his colleagues to occupy the moral high ground at the outset of a fight over how to distribute diminishing resources. No matter what their opponents said, members of the government could always claim that they had taken a hit.

In year one of the plan, they eliminated 2,800 civil service positions, which was part of a larger goal of reducing the provincial bureaucracy to 27,500 from 34,000, a decrease of 20 percent. They announced plans to slash public-sector salaries, including the wages of teachers and health care workers, by 5 percent and froze their compensation for two years after reducing it. They took the province out of the retail booze business by selling the government's liquor stores to private operators. They also sold the government's registry services, that is, the recording of property transactions, births, deaths, marriages, and other vital statistics, to private companies.

Amid these specific measures, the Conservatives began laying the foundation for a disciplined and prudent approach to governing. For example, they adopted a policy of using unexpected revenue windfalls, or the profits from the sale of government assets, to reduce the deficit and the debt, whereas in the past such funds likely would have been spent elsewhere. They also decreed that forecasts of government revenue from oil and gas royalties must be based on the province's average annual take for the previous five years.

The February 1994 budget, entitled "Securing Alberta's Fiscal Future," ventured well beyond provincial finances and spoke of the values and attitudes that should shape Alberta society. The government said that it expected individual Albertans to be productive and self-reliant, and to be responsible for meeting their basic needs. More importantly, Klein and his party provided the terms of a new relationship between the government and the populace. "Significant changes will take place in Alberta," the 1994 budget stated. "The role of government in people's lives will be smaller. The province will have a government that lives within the taxpayers' means. The province will be well managed and free from unnecessary bureaucracy."

The Klein government demonstrated its determination to bring about fundamental change, as opposed to merely nibbling at the edges of government spending, by reducing the budgets of every department, some by as much as 30 percent. They also went after the three big-ticket items, health care, education, and social assistance, which account for 70 percent of program spending and most directly affect the public. The fiscal plan calls for funding in these areas to fall to $7.7 billion by March 31, 1997, from $9.2 billion four years earlier, a decrease of $1.5 billion, or 16 percent. Primary and secondary education are losing $255 million, or 12 percent of their funding, while family and social services lose $328 million, a 19 percent reduction. Health care spending is slated to fall $749 million, or 18 percent. And by the end of 1994, the government had closed three hospitals in Edmonton and Calgary. In early 1995, Klein's Tories began closing and scaling back operations at some of the province's 120 rural hospitals.

But shrinking budgets are just one of a series of changes. Klein's government has rewritten the rules for both the professionals who deliver these health care, education, and social assistance services and the public that relies on them. The province's 147 health facility boards, which ran hospitals and health units, have been scrapped in favour of seventeen regional health authorities that will manage all the hospitals within set geographical areas. Among other things, the new bodies are responsible for determining the mix of services available and which hospitals will deliver them. They are also supposed to eliminate duplication, reduce the public's reliance on hospital care, and use the money saved "to enhance community-based services that allow Albertans to remain in their homes," according to the 1994 budget.

The government is making equally profound changes to primary and secondary education. Perhaps the most controversial and widely discussed move was a reduction in the funding for kindergarten. For years, the government had funded 400 hours per year, the equivalent of five half-days per week from September to June. In 1994–95, funding was provided for 200 hours of kindergarten. But in response to public pressure, the Tories agreed to fund 240 hours in 1995–96. Local school boards can offer additional kindergarten time but they must cover the cost themselves, either by charging parents admission fees or by diverting money from other programs in their budgets. This has led to dozens of different kindergarten programs across the province, with fees ranging from a few hundred dollars annually up to more than $1,000, and what some observers see as virtual chaos.

Other innovations, though less contentious, will ultimately have a greater impact on education in Alberta than the reduction in kindergarten funding. The Conservatives have attempted to reduce the power of school boards and administrators, while increasing the role and influence of parents and the general public. They eliminated almost 125 school boards, leaving the province with just under 60. The Tories stripped the boards of their powers of taxation in part because they were unable to control their spending or curb the salary demands of the Alberta Teachers' Association. Municipalities now collect school taxes, then remit them to the province, which distributes the money to the boards on a per student basis. As well, the Conservatives have stipulated that administrative costs cannot exceed 4 percent of total spending on education.

Klein's Tories have moved to enhance public involvement in education by passing legislation requiring each of the province's 1,800 schools to set up a council comprising teachers, parents with children in the system, and other members of the local community. The councils, which were to be in place by February 1996, are supposed to be consultative as opposed to decision-making bodies. They can work with the principal and the school board to determine what programs their school offers and how the budget is spent. Councils may also have a say in the selection of principals, the hiring of staff, and the drafting of codes of discipline.

The Tories are also attempting to make the educational establishment more accountable to the public. During the 1994–95 academic year, they introduced performance reports for school boards in which administrators assessed the schools in their districts according to a number of criteria and objectives. The first reports were due to be submitted to the minister of education in November 1995. Administrators were required to compile data showing how their students performed on provincial achievement tests and high school diploma exams. The local results were then compared with the provincial averages. Administrators must set objectives for the coming school year, and include financial data on spending per student as well as the ratio of spending on instruction versus administration. Beginning in the 1996–97 academic year, principals and vice-principals will have to prepare similar reports for their schools. Both the board and the school reports will be available to the public. The government wants to give parents the tools necessary to see how their children's schools stack up against others in the community or across the province. Ultimately, parents should be able to use the information to select a school for their children or to demand a better performance from teachers.

The provincial welfare program has been overhauled faster and more thoroughly than either health care or education. Benefits were among the lowest in Canada to begin with, in some cases exceeding only those for Newfoundland and New Brunswick. They have remained low, or been cut. In 1995, single employable males were entitled to benefits totalling $5,748 annually. On a monthly basis, they received a $165 shelter allowance, $85.30 for medical expenses, and $229 to cover other expenses. A single employable parent with one child over the age of six could get $380 a month for shelter and $386 to cover the remaining living expenses.

Along with cuts in benefits, the number of people collecting social assistance fell sharply during Klein's first two years in office. By February 1995, the caseload had been cut to 52,285 from 94,650 in December 1992, a drop of 45 percent. But here, as with health care and education, the numbers were only part of the story. "We are trying to change attitudes," says family and social services minister Mike Cardinal, the first aboriginal Canadian to serve as an Alberta cabinet minister. "We have to get away from passive welfare and get into providing money for training or encouraging people to get back into the workforce. More welfare is not the answer to ending poverty. More job training and active employment are the ways to end poverty."

And this government has put those ideas into practice. Welfare recipients, particularly employable males, are encouraged to think of the benefits as temporary. They are not eligible for welfare unless they have first looked for work through a Canada Employment Centre and followed up any leads. They must also meet with a family and social services career counsellor to develop a plan for finding employment. If they are illiterate, or have no marketable skills, the government encourages them to enroll in a literacy course or an upgrading program. In the new Alberta, a person becomes eligible for welfare only after taking a number of steps to ensure that he or she doesn't become wedded to welfare.

The Tories are providing work experience for those on social assistance through their Alberta Community Employment program, which is very close to the concept of workfare.

Municipalities and nonprofit organizations can come up with a variety of community projects such as planting trees, cleaning up parks and river banks, and maintaining or repairing buildings. The province provides these organizations with $6 per hour to hire welfare recipients to perform the work. Between July 1993, when the program was started, and December 1994, the government approved over 1,800 projects and put more than 2,800 people to work. For those who will not accept such work, or any of the other options available, the Alberta government has another solution, one that has been widely publicized and attacked as harsh and insensitive. If a recalcitrant recipient is from out of province, the government will buy him or her a one-way bus ticket home.

Cardinal makes no apology for the one-way bus tickets, or for any of the other reforms he has introduced. He dislikes what social assistance has become in Canada, and he came to that position through personal experience on an Indian reserve in northern Alberta: "I grew up in the 1950s when there was no welfare and the native communities were completely self-sufficient. We survived very well. After welfare was introduced, the whole community became dependent. People lost their culture, alcoholism increased, and we suffered a total community breakdown. I spent nineteen years in government trying to make changes. It took me a long time but I'm doing it."

Even though a substantial majority of the electorate supports the substance and intent of the reforms, according to public opinion polls conducted midway through the Klein government's first mandate, it would be a mistake to assume that imposing fiscal austerity has been easy or risk-free. Initially, the budget cuts aroused the wrath of thousands of Albertans. High school students demonstrated against changes to education funding. Senior citizens marched on the legislature to oppose reductions in their benefits and subsidies. Parents in the provincial capital objected to the cutbacks in kindergarten funding. And in April 1994, an estimated 15,000 people converged on Edmonton's Grey Nuns Hospital, which serves the community of Millwoods, to protest government plans to convert the institution to a psychiatric facility. Klein likes to observe that "When we started, my day wasn't complete without a protest."

Those days are behind him and his government. Public displays of discontent fizzled quickly when it became apparent that the Conservatives would stand their ground. But opposition to the Tory program certainly has not evaporated. Even the most favourable mid-term opinion polls showed that 30 percent of the public did not support the government or approve of its reforms. And the changes have created resentment, as well as lasting hostility, among many public-sector workers and their union leaders.

"There's a tremendous amount of uncertainty, stress, and disillusionment among employees in the health care system, up to and including physicians," observes Linda Sloan, former president of the Staff Nurses Associations of Alberta, a small union with 2,500 members. "All that uncertainty and pressure is occurring in an environment in which people normally have to deal with a high level of stress because they are caring for human beings who are sick. I don't think that people feel a high degree of loyalty today. I know many of them feel compromised in their ability to provide safe and adequate care for their patients. When they raise concerns about it, the standard response from management seems to be, 'Well, our hands are tied. The government has taken away the money and we don't have the authority to hire people.' There were a lot of things about the status quo that were efficient and cost-effective and didn't need to be subjected to this kind of radical cost-reduction."

Some labour leaders have accepted the need to deal with the deficit but vehemently dislike how the combination of budget cuts and restructuring have transformed the professions they represent. "Nobody has a problem with eliminating the deficit," says Bauni Mackay, president of the 30,000-member Alberta Teachers' Association. "But the deficit is simply an excuse for restructuring the province in a way that nobody ever guessed at and certainly this government does not have a mandate to do. We see the government as being obsessed with accountability, choice, and competition in education. They want schools competing with one another. They want parents having all this choice over which schools they send their kids to. The government's approach is to let people look after themselves. This is the me generation at its worst because it's looking after me and mine and making sure things are okay here. It negates what public education is all about. Public education exists, not for the individual parent and not for the teachers, but for society. We pay tax money for public education so that we perpetuate the values and ideas that society deems necessary to perpetuate."

The most persistent criticism of the government has appeared in the pages of the province's two largest newspapers, the *Edmonton Journal* and the *Calgary Herald*. They have vigorously pursued stories linking program or funding cutbacks to hardship, suffering, and tragedy. The *Journal* published so many hardship articles that members of the government accused the paper of looking for a victim of the week. As well, both papers have relentlessly attacked the government from their editorial pages.

Journal editorial writer Satya Das, who has written some of the most vitriolic pieces, says that he and his colleagues agree that the provincial finances had to be cleaned up. They just think that the Tories have gone too far, too fast. "A lot of this stuff isn't planned," says Das. "It's done ad hoc. It's the whole chaos theory of management. You make quantum leaps, not in one area at a time, but in every single department, watch the fallout and take corrective measures. That's the way these guys are operating. If they were writing a book, they wouldn't understand that having the words in the right order is as important as having words in the book.

"For example, health care funding was cut before the regional health authorities were established. The authorities think they have a mandate to do certain things but the minister says, 'No, they don't,' and it's back and forth. The hospitals are caught in the middle. So we've got a situation where every hospital is desperately trying to hang on to what it has and to provide core services. You have low staff morale because of layoffs. And because of the stupid union seniority system, you're getting junior nurses, who are trained in, say, intensive care, bumped by nurses who don't have the right training. You have senior nurses going on stress leave because they can't take their new responsibilities. All of this could have been avoided by taking some time to plan the changes."

The Tories did hold brief but extensive roundtable discussions with the public on health care, education, and other provincial responsibilities before they began to implement their reforms. But they avoided the standard procedures governments rely on when making major changes — the internal reviews, legislative committee hearings, consultants' reports, or royal commissions, which are invariably costly and time-consuming. Instead, Klein and his colleagues have set out to reform in four years a government, a bureaucracy, and myriad programs and services that evolved over four to five decades. In doing so, they recognized that to engage in prolonged discussions or a protracted argument with civil servants, special interests, or the recipients of government largesse would lead to a stalemate and produce minimal results.

Hence, speed has been an integral part of the government's strategy. Both the premier and his treasurer, Jim Dinning, have spoken publicly on why they believed it was necessary to move quickly. In an April 1994 speech at Queen's University, Dinning put it this way: "You can't cross a chasm in small leaps. Some Albertans are saying, 'You're going too fast. Why can't we move more slowly?' We simply cannot afford to go slow. Spreading the difficult process over more years and more studies will not make the job easier. In fact, it will make it more difficult. Going slow may be comforting to some, but it's a house of cards built on false hopes."

Moving fast and cutting all departments simultaneously proved to be very effective political tactics, as Klein revealed in a speech to the Vancouver Board of Trade in the spring of 1994. "We're attacking everyone from different fronts," he said. "So what happens is that if the seniors are mad, then the schoolteachers will say, 'We're getting it too, and they're better off than we are.' And the nurses won't support the teachers because they say, 'Well, my gosh, we're getting hit harder than the teachers, so what are they complaining about? They get paid more than we do.' It's perhaps because we have hit everyone — I mean no one has been excluded — that the unions have been unable to sustain an all-out co-operative attack."

But even though there were advantages to cutting quickly, there were also inherent dangers. Klein and his cabinet have had to plan many of their reforms on the run. They have announced their objectives in broad terms and, in most cases, filled in the details later. There is, in this approach, a huge potential for mistakes, miscues, and accidents.

In fact, a series of health care horror stories occurred in 1994 and the provincial press attributed them to the cutbacks. There was the northern Alberta resident who died when an air ambulance was forced to fly to Calgary because there were no beds available in Edmonton. There was the case of an Edmonton man who severed three fingers, and had to wait seventeen hours for surgery, by which time doctors were unable to reattach them. And there was the retired Medicine Hat resident who flew from Calgary to Edmonton for a liver transplant, and took a taxi to hospital only to discover that the organ had been given to another recipient. Each of these incidents caused a considerable stir but none turned into lasting or major controversies.

Through perseverance, and perhaps luck, Klein and his caucus have managed to keep the public on their side. Their most serious brush with political trouble occurred in mid-November, 1995, when 120 low-paid laundry workers at a Calgary hospital walked off the job illegally to protest wage cuts. Some 2,500 other hospital workers and nursing-home support staff also joined the strike. Calgary hospitals were reduced to offering emergency and intensive care, and the protest threatened to spread to other parts of the province.

Klein sensed, however, that public opinion had swung in favour of the strikers and, eight days after the disruption began, he announced the cancellation of $53 million in planned spending cuts.

Despite that setback, it is highly unlikely that this group of Tories will lose its commitment to fiscal reform. There are enough hardline conservatives in the caucus and around the cabinet table to prevent that from happening. They also have a leader who is determined to make a lasting difference in how the province is governed. "As long as I'm the premier of Alberta, no longer will this government be looking for new programs and new ways to spend money," Klein says.

"We're putting in place legislative safeguards to make sure we remain fiscally frugal and responsible. One is the Deficit Elimination Act, which says we must, by law, balance our budget each and every year. Another piece of legislation is the Taxpayers' Protection Act, which stipulates that we can't introduce a sales tax unless it goes to a referendum. Another is the Debt Retirement Act, which says we must dedicate a certain amount each year to paying down the debt for a period of twenty-five years. We're making it as difficult as possible for another administration, whether it's Conservative or Liberal, to change our reforms."

Klein has often compared his program to a home renovation. It is dusty and messy, not to mention noisy and disruptive. He has assured the electorate that, if they put up with a little inconvenience and upheaval, they will be rewarded with what he calls the Alberta Advantage — the lowest taxes in the country, sustainable public services, and affordable government. His blueprint contains specific goals. But he has never said that the renovations would be complete when the targets are reached. Being a clever politician, Klein has kept his options open. The four-year plan to balance the budget has become a twenty-five-year plan to eliminate the provincial debt. Fiscal reform has grown to encompass a complete overhaul of public education, health care, and social assistance.

With their home renovation well under way, Klein and his colleagues have signalled their intent to redesign the neighbourhood, or at least certain aspects of it. They have challenged federal control over medicare and conventional thinking about who can deliver health care services. Alberta is the first province to attempt to break Canada's public health monopoly. For several years, the Klein government has allowed the operation of privately owned, profit-producing clinics that provide specialized medical services such as eye surgery.

In 1994, the Tories gave the Cardston General Hospital permission to recruit American patients and charge them $10,000 (U.S.) for a type of stomach surgery that leads to weight loss. The Cardston facility, which is located a few miles north of the Alberta-Montana border, promoted the service through newspaper and television advertisements that ran in nine western states in the fall of 1994. The campaign generated inquiries from 600 to 700 people, of which close to 100 were selected as prospective patients, according to the hospital's former executive-director, Roger Walker.

The February 1995 federal budget, which announced cuts of several billion dollars in transfer payments and the creation of a block grant called the Canada Health and Social Transfer, gave the Alberta Tories another opening for an attack on Ottawa. Provincial health minister Shirley McClellan declared that universality is dead. Klein demanded that the federal government make a distinction between essential and nonessential medical services and allow the provinces to charge people for nonessential care. "I just don't think we can support the system as we now know it," he says. "In this province alone, health care costs went up 219 percent over the past fourteen years. The cost of living only went up 83 percent in the same period. The population only grew by 5 percent. It's out of whack."

While Klein modestly refers to his program as a renovation, others see it as a revolution. It has entailed swift, top-to-bottom change and brought radical restructuring to the public sector. It has become one of the most highly publicized and closely watched experiments in North America. Klein's revolution has become the standard by which other governments, particularly the NDP administrations in neighbouring Saskatchewan and British Columbia, have differentiated their own programs. It has prompted plenty of speculation about the Alberta premier's future and the prospect that he might run nationally. He has consistently denied having any interest in federal politics, however, and in all likelihood he is being truthful. His wife, Colleen, has reportedly told him that he can visit her in Calgary if he goes to Ottawa. As well, the federal Tories seem destined for a long stay in opposition after their 1993 election debacle. And, having his entire political career conducted the orchestra as a mayor, a provincial cabinet minister, and now a premier, Klein hardly seems cut out for opposition.

But more to the point, there is no need for Klein to leave Alberta. He has emerged as a potent and high-profile symbol of a new era of fiscally prudent leadership. Klein represents decisive change after two decades in which our leaders took a cavalier attitude toward deficits, debts, and the state of their treasuries. He stands for principled leadership after an era in which politicians of every stripe tried to meet the public interest by appeasing special interests, an era when issuing press releases, handing out cheques, and arranging photo opportunities was often confused with governing. He has proven that a politician in Canada can do what good leaders have always done — make tough decisions about the allocation of scarce resources — and still remain popular.

10

IF
WE FAIL

ach generation of Canadians has faced a major challenge that shaped it, the nation, and our culture. Canadians of the Confederation era had to build a transcontinental railway. Turn-of-the-century Canadians had to populate the West. Two generations of twentieth-century Canadians had to fight in European wars. Many of those same Canadians had to struggle to survive the Depression. In the post-war years, the Canadian people and their leaders transformed the economy from military to civilian purposes and created some of the most generous social programs in the world.

The offspring of those post-war Canadians, the baby boomers, have been blessed with unprecedented affluence and a surplus of social harmony. Watch the nightly news or read a daily newspaper and the world often resembles a smorgasbord of horrors. The stories come from any number of small, normally obscure nations and would-be nations: Rwanda, Bosnia, Haiti, Chechnya, Sri Lanka. Sorry sagas of coups and rebellions, wars and invasions, rooted in disputes over race or religion, language or ethnicity. And the plot is almost always the same: violence and bloodshed, death and sorrow.

By comparison, our lives have been distinguished by peace and prosperity. For Canadians, the latter half of the twentieth century will undoubtedly come to be seen as an age of growth, opportunity, and the accumulation of wealth, a time when our standard of living rose sharply, when life expectancies increased dramatically and when a good education, generous social programs, and excellent health care were considered rights rather than privileges. But the status quo in Canada is no longer sustainable.

Our economy is on a skid, our governments are wallowing in debt, and the unity of the nation is in jeopardy. We are living in a period of high unemployment and widespread underemployment, a time when the skilled and the unskilled can face prolonged or permanent joblessness, and record numbers of people — 10 percent of the population of some provinces — are collecting social assistance. We have witnessed the devastation of an historic resource, the Atlantic fishery, and the decline of one of the country's economic engines, central Canada's manufacturing sector. Our governments have overspent, we are overtaxed, and for two decades the national debt has grown faster than the economy.

The economic and psychological costs have been enormous. Interest payments on the debt have become the largest single item in the federal budget. They keep growing while spending on programs declines. Debt is undermining the level and quality of public services, and there are other repercussions. Taxes go up and user fees are introduced but most of the new revenue goes to servicing our debts. This represents a transfer of wealth from middle-class Canadians to the wealthy individuals and large institutions who finance our deficits and collect the interest.

To allow this state of affairs to continue is a recipe for disaster. It undermines public confidence in and support for government. It creates resentment and breeds discontent. To tax relentlessly, as most of our governments have done over the past decade, reduces the disposable income of every wage earner, leaves each of us poorer, and erodes one of the central beliefs upon which this country was built: that Canada is a place where individuals can prosper, and dream of a better life for themselves and their children.

As we contemplate the future and the beginning of a new century, our choices and challenges are clear: we can allow the country to suffer a crushing and calamitous slide into bankruptcy; or we can embark on a long march back to solvency. We are stuck with these alternatives because other approaches have been tried and proved ineffective. Trudeau and his followers took a laissez-faire attitude toward exploding deficits, thinking that economic conditions would naturally right themselves and the nation's finances. Mulroney understood the problem but lacked the courage to solve it. He followed the path of least resistance, hoping that tax increases, economic growth, and moderate restraint — mere decreases in the rate of growth in spending — would lead the government back to a balanced budget.

Furthermore, over the past twenty to twenty-five years, prime ministers and premiers were afflicted by a pervasive psychology of expedience. Initially, it was a time of easy credit and unlimited expectations. So why upset anyone by trying to mediate between competing interests or allocating scarce resources? Borrowing billions and raising taxes were easier than cutting expenditures, so our leaders chose the former alternatives. Appeasing special interests was more rewarding than safeguarding the public interest, so again they opted for the former. Better to hand out a cheque and pose for a photo than confront a gaggle of angry demonstrators on Parliament Hill or the lawn of the legislature.

Belatedly, most of our leaders have begun to understand the folly of their ways and have accepted the limited choices they face. One by one, beginning in the early 1990s, the leaders of the eight smaller provinces began to steer their governments onto fiscally sustainable paths. They wisely chose the long march rather than the calamitous slide. In most cases, they were simply returning to the values and

221

practices that prevailed in the provincial capitals prior to the era of easy credit and unlimited expectations. They have restored fiscal prudence to its rightful place at the heart of budget making.

Nor should this be regarded as mere political gimmickry or opportunism. The governments of the four Western provinces have all drafted or passed so-called balanced-budget laws, which, ideally, entrench a sound approach to taxation and spending. Alberta led the way with its 1993 Deficit Elimination Act. In March 1995, B.C. Finance Minister Elizabeth Cull announced that her government would accept the recommendation of a joint business-labour panel calling for a legislated ceiling on the amount of debt the province can accumulate. The panel suggested a cap of 15 percent of provincial gross domestic product, whereas B.C.'s debt at the time stood at 20 percent of GDP.

Saskatchewan's NDP government introduced its legislation, the Balanced Budget Act in April 1995, and passed it before adjourning the legislature for a June election. The law stipulates that following each provincial election, the minister of finance will prepare a four-year fiscal and debt management plan that includes forecasts of revenues and expenditures for each year. Total expenses over the life of the plan must be equal to or less than revenues. The legislation gives the party in power an escape hatch in the case of a "major, identifiable, unanticipated" economic catastrophe like a crop failure or collapse in commodity prices that causes a sudden drop in provincial revenues.

The approaches taken by B.C., Alberta, and Saskatchewan appeared tame next to Manitoba's Balanced Budget, Debt Repayment, and Taxpayer Protection Act. Premier Gary Filmon's Conservative government unveiled the legislation in March 1995, prior to a provincial election, and passed it in early November after being returned to office. Under this law, the government would be required to hold a referendum before raising the provincial income tax, the retail sales tax, or payroll taxes used to finance health care and post-secondary education. The government must balance the budget every year or cabinet ministers lose 20 percent of their salaries. Ministers would forfeit 40 percent of their pay if they failed to balance the budget a second time. The law does allow for exceptions when natural disasters or other unforeseen events lead to a decrease of 5 percent or more in provincial revenues.

While the budgetary and legislative steps taken in Atlantic Canada and the West are both necessary and welcome, we should remember that legislators in Charlottetown or Fredericton or Regina, and their counterparts in the other small provinces, cannot resuscitate the nation's finances on their own. Their combined spending represents only one-third of total provincial expenditures. Ontario and Quebec account for the other 65 percent and their deficits, a combined $13 billion to $15 billion in fiscal 1995–96, more than nullify the progress made elsewhere.

Throughout the first half of the 1990s, Ontario's New Democrats and Quebec's Liberals conducted their financial affairs with a cavalier disregard for what was happening elsewhere in the country. They ran big deficits and added wantonly to their debts while political leaders and voters in other provinces accepted the service cuts, program reductions, and financial burdens that come with balancing a budget. Others paid the price while the governments of the two largest provinces dithered.

With the election of a new Conservative government, Ontario has begun marching to the same tune as the rest of the country. However, the province remains one of the largest nonsovereign borrowers in the world, it is still years away from a balanced budget, and there are no guarantees that the Tory plan to eliminate the deficit will work. And then there is Quebec, whose separatist government was in its own lonely orbit in 1995, pursuing its goal of independence, with no plans to balance the provincial budget and no stomach for eliminating its deficit. So, Ontario and Quebec give tax-weary voters every reason for remaining skeptical and vigilant.

The same reservations must be applied to the Chrétien government. There is no question that the February 1995 federal budget was a landmark. For the first time since 1951, federal program spending actually shrank as a proportion of the economy. But it would be a mistake to think that one budget can undo the damage caused by two and a half decades of excessive spending, taxing, and borrowing. Thus far, the Liberals have managed to get the patient, the federal treasury, out of the ambulance and into the emergency department. It will take years before the country's finances can be considered healthy again. They are attempting to reduce the deficit to 3 percent of GDP, they have declared their intention to cut it to 2 percent, but the real goal should be a balanced budget. That objective, however, remains somewhere over the horizon, perhaps two years or four years or six years away, depending on how much credence we put in Martin's rolling two-year targets for reducing and then eliminating the deficit.

In the aftermath of the 1995 budget, a number of well-informed observers cautioned Canadians to prepare for a long, tough battle. "While Paul Martin's recent budget seems to have marked a turning point in Ottawa's war on debt, the length of this struggle is likely to be measured in decades rather than years," John McCallum, senior vice-president and chief economist of the Royal Bank, wrote in an April 1995 analysis of the country's long-term debt outlook. He concluded that with the right interest rates, the right rates of economic growth, and substantial federal operating surpluses, the debt-to-GDP ratio could fall from 74 percent in 1995 to 67 percent at the turn of the century, 49 percent in 2010, and 24 percent in 2020. In other words, it will take twenty-five years to get the debt back down to a level even remotely close to where it was in the early 1970s, when our current difficulties began.

Deputy Finance Minister David Dodge, speaking at a conference of business economists in Ottawa in May 1995, warned that if we hope to be deficit-free by the end of the century then we should prepare ourselves for new tax hikes and more spending cuts. "Even if we're very clever and a major social consensus emerges as to what we ought to do, it doesn't get us all the way to eliminating the structural deficit," Dodge said. "It's going to be addressed one way or another. Either the revenue hole will have to be filled in or expenditures will have to be reduced even further."

And while attending the same event, Vincent Truglia, a vice-president at Moody's Investors Service, predicted that the country is in for a decade of drudgery, despite the progress made to date. "Canadians have barely seen the beginning of what these cuts mean," he said. "This is going to go on for ten years, year after year of austere budgets. When there is rising unemployment, will the Canadian electorate be quite as amenable to austerity? Political will recedes suddenly. Canada will be very vulnerable to this in future years."

In fact, an erosion of will is almost certain to occur. The 1995 budget was set in an atmosphere of near crisis. Our lenders and their watchdogs, the credit rating agencies, forced the government's hand and virtually dictated the major thrusts of the budget — namely, big spending cuts and minimal tax increases. We have a prime minister who is a most reluctant reformer, who has no real enthusiasm for restructuring and retrenchment. Chrétien eschews grand plans, big designs, and lofty visions, and he has failed to present any coherent blueprint for the future.

Chrétien and many members of his caucus will be tempted to ease up and either increase spending or cut taxes, either in the run-up to an election or to offset the impact of a recession. Voters will undoubtedly grow weary of making sacrifices and begin to demand their due, particularly if the Liberals ever manage to eliminate the deficit and the sense of urgency surrounding our national finances begins to fade. And regardless of what happens, the advocates of the status quo — left-wing Liberals, New Democrats who have never been in government, public-sector union leaders, and the special interests who owe their existence to big government — will always be poised to reassert themselves. Many of them continue to believe that all the talk about deficits, debts, and insolvency is part of a corporate conspiracy or a neoconservative plot. They have dismissed any proposed solutions as part of a right-wing agenda and have refused to participate. Our whole noisy, wiser-than-thou crowd will keep right on telling us that Canada's fiscal crisis has been manufactured, that the risks have been exaggerated, and that countries can't go broke.

—◄o►—

But history and common sense tell us that countries *can* go broke. And the consequences, for a country and its citizens, are infinitely more dreadful than any business bankruptcy. To think otherwise is human folly right out of the book that says empires never fall and *Titanics* don't sink. When a company goes broke, a lot of people get stung. The president and the senior managers wind up with tarnished reputations. The employees generally lose their jobs and a few weeks' or months' wages. The shareholders lose their investments. The creditors usually receive a few cents on the dollar from the sale of the assets. Everyone limps away dazed, hurt, and a little disillusioned. Everyone can say they are a little wiser and won't let it happen again. The crucial thing to remember is that for everyone involved, there is usually a new job, a new venture, another investment. Everyone starts over

But a country is different. The leaders and the populace cannot disperse and start over elsewhere. They cannot sell off the national assets and allow some other enterprising people to put them to use. To understand the implications of going broke as a country, we should consider the case of New Zealand, the small South Pacific nation of three and a half million people which enjoyed one of the highest standards of living in the world in the 1950s and 1960s. But in July 1984, near the end of a national election in which the left-wing Labour Party defeated the conservative National Party, New Zealand experienced a severe currency crisis. Over a decade later, it was still recovering from the aftershocks.

The crisis itself was a short but traumatic event that shocked the electorate and changed the course of the country's history. Trouble began brewing when Labour promised during the election campaign to devalue the country's dollar and then it became apparent that the party was heading for victory. International speculators started dumping the currency, while wealthy New Zealanders began converting their money to other currencies and moving it out of the country.

In response, the New Zealand Reserve Bank, the equivalent of the Bank of Canada, used its foreign currency holdings to buy up the unwanted dollars in a futile bid to defend their value. The bank nearly ran out of foreign reserves and was forced to suspend foreign-exchange transactions for an indefinite period. All of this occurred within a few days before and after the election of July 14, 1984. When trading resumed four days after the election, the value of the currency immediately fell 20 percent. In effect, every New Zealander lost one-fifth of his or her salary overnight, and everything from apples to automobiles was worth 20 percent more than it had been before.

The New Zealand experience has attracted considerable interest, and provoked some intense debate in Canada. The Klein government reportedly adopted some of the Labour Party's tactics for radical restructuring: specifically, hitting everyone at once and doing it fast. Ontario's Bob Rae apparently decided his government had to do something about the province's exploding deficits and debt after watching a February 1993 edition of CTV's *W5* dealing with the New Zealand crisis and its aftermath. Commentators on the left, like journalists Murray Dobbin and Linda McQuaig, have taken a look and declared the whole thing a disaster.

What is beyond dispute, however, is that the crisis occurred after a long-term deterioration in the country's economy and finances. New Zealand had an overregulated economy that was protected from international competition. A decade or more of high inflation and low productivity growth had eroded the country's prosperity. By the time of the currency crisis, New Zealand's standard of living was ranked twenty-second in the world, whereas the country had once been rated third, behind only the United States and Canada. Accompanying this slide were big deficits and a rising debt. The deficit stood at around 9 percent of GDP at the time of the crisis, slightly higher than Canada's combined federal-provincial shortfalls in the early 1990s. And New Zealand's total government debt stood at 62 percent of the GDP, whereas Ottawa and the provinces are well beyond that level.

The newly elected Labour government of David Lange responded to the emergency with one of the most radical reform programs ever introduced in a developed and democratic country. "We came in appealing to the hearts and minds but after the boom dropped, we went for their bowels," former prime minister Lange told CTV's Eric Malling in an interview for W5's special on New Zealand. "Can you imagine a Labour Party, with a tradition of being the heart of working class people, that arose out of the trade union movement, suddenly being forced to behave as if it were to the right of Genghis Khan? Making Margaret Thatcher look like Joan of Arc? Ronald Reagan look like a Jesuit brother? We were tougher than any of them."

When New Zealand hit the wall, the government was forced to make real cuts in spending and services. Here are a few examples of what happened. The postmaster-general closed 732 postal stations in one day. The labour force at the state railway company was cut to 6,000 employees from 22,000. The staff at TV New Zealand, their equivalent to the CBC, was cut in half and a law was passed stipulating that the network had to make a profit. Agricultural subsidies and price supports were eliminated. Business subsidies and export incentives were cancelled. Government monopolies in bus, truck, and train transport were removed. The government privatized over two dozen crown corporations, including the national steel company, the national railway, the national airline, and a state insurance firm.

"What we did was traumatic for our rural sector," Lange told Regina-based journalist Dobbin, who reported on the New Zealand experiment for the CBC program *Ideas* in October 1994. "Farmers were dispossessed of their land. Interest rates went up. It was an enormous revolution. In about three years, we changed from being a country run like a Polish shipyard into one that could be internationally competitive. Costs were big; people with privileges were dispossessed of them. They crashed. It was rough."

Despite the hardship and dislocation the program caused, Lange's government was re-elected to a second three-year term in 1987 before losing to the National Party in 1990. After six years in office, the Labour Party managed to cut the deficit to 2.1 percent of GDP from almost 9 percent through a combination of public-sector layoffs, sales of government assets, and the elimination of farm and business subsidies. But government spending, particularly on health, education, and welfare, continued to increase under Labour, and by the time the party was defeated, the country was facing another potential crisis.

The National Party completed the reform process, and prevented a recurrence of the 1984 crisis by cutting personal entitlements to health, education, and welfare — the riskiest and most painful changes any government can make. For example, anyone with an income above the national average must pay $50 a day to stay in hospital, up to a maximum of $500 a year. Anyone on unemployment benefits who rejects two job offers gets cut off. Single mothers on social assistance must seek employment once their youngest child reaches age seven. People under twenty-five are entitled to only $100 a month in welfare benefits and must reside with their families. The eligibility age for public pensions was raised to sixty-five from sixty, and the wealthy are no longer entitled to the benefit at all.

These reforms have aroused anger and anxiety among many New Zealanders, yet most citizens have clearly accepted them. And for good reason. The changes have produced tangible benefits. The country has a balanced budget and one of the fastest growing economies in the developed world. In a March 1995 report, the Toronto-based brokerage firm Midland Walwyn concluded that

New Zealand had found itself in "a virtuous circle." It has paid down some of its debt, therefore interest charges are falling, which makes it easier to keep the budget balanced or produce a surplus.

"The vast majority of New Zealanders are convinced that the world they have now is far better than the one they had ten years ago," says Neil Quigley, an economics professor at Victoria University of Wellington who spent five years teaching in Canada before returning to his native New Zealand in 1994. "A lot of the attacks on our model have come from people, like your middle-class Canadian left-wing types, who feel really threatened by what's happened here. The social safety net still exists for the genuinely disadvantaged. What's really at stake is whether the spouse of someone who earns $60,000 a year is eligible to draw unemployment benefits. Or whether people who earn $65,000 a year, and probably go to their doctor far more than working-class people would ever imagine going, should have to pay for a portion of the health care costs that they incur."

◄○►

Down under in New Zealand, they have had a debate about the size and scope of the contemporary welfare state, and they have resolved that it must be smaller, and less costly. We haven't reached a consensus on this issue. In fact, the debate has just begun. The Chrétien Liberals launched it in the February 1995 budget by announcing that, commencing April 1, 1996, they will begin withdrawing billions of dollars in transfers to the provinces for such services as health, post-secondary education, and social assistance. The provinces, which administer these programs, cannot afford to tax or borrow to make up the lost funding. For Canadians in every province, this can only mean that hard and basic questions — how many hospitals can we afford, how many universities, how much welfare — must be raised and debated.

We will also be confronted with some basic choices about the generosity of our government-run pension plans. "There are some very important issues that we have to struggle with," Dodge said in his April 1995 address to the conference of business economists. "The first is the reform of the public pension system. It's quite clear we are going to have to do something to reduce the cost of Old Age Security to ensure that it's there on a sustainable basis for future generations. The second component of the public pension system is the Canada Pension Plan, which is not in very good shape financially. It will be extraordinarily important that we come to grips with that."

There are alternatives, of course. But none are viable or realistic. We could make some minor reforms, by tinkering with funding formulas or looking for new efficiencies in the design and delivery of services, only to see one or more of our social programs collapse when the costs become utterly exorbitant. Or we could continue to fiddle with our national finances, rather than acting decisively, and run the risk of a New Zealand–style crash.

By almost any measure, Canada's debt problem is as bad as or worse than New Zealand's at the time of its crisis. And over the past two years, there have been plenty of signs that we are headed for trouble. Credit rating agencies have downgraded the debt of the federal government and most of the provinces, in some cases more than once. We had the currency crisis of January and February 1995, and the sharp rise in interest rates over the second half of 1994, both directly attributable to our debt problems. There have also been periodic warnings in the financial pages of the country's newspapers.

The *Globe's Report on Business* carried a story in late June, 1994, quoting a currency trader named Norm Duncan, of C. M. Oliver and Co., as saying, "I want my money, as much as I can, out of this country for the next few months." In the same article, financial analyst Katherine Beattie, of MMS International, said, "First, they [investors] sell the Canadian dollar, then they sell Canadian bonds." A few days later, the *Report on Business* included a piece in which a German bond fund manager stated, "It's a nightmare,

Canada. With all this Quebec stuff, the high budget deficit and the ever weakening currency against the U.S., it's a disaster."

The cost of such uncertainty is obvious. It raises doubts and creates fears. A falling dollar and rising interest rates pose real threats to the country's economic growth and prosperity. Mortgages, car loans, and consumer credit of every sort become more expensive. Furthermore, financial turbulence due to our indebtedness and dependence upon foreign lenders means stability is out and volatility is in. Buying a home or renewing a mortgage is like rolling dice. Make a deal today, and your lender has a five-year mortgage for 9.5 percent. Wait six months and the same money may be available for 7.5 or 8 percent. Or it may cost 10.25 percent.

It is unnerving when purchasing something as fundamental as shelter comes to resemble a game of chance. It means that some people wind up paying thousands of dollars more than their friends and neighbours for a mortgage, or other form of credit, simply because of the timing of their purchase. Such debt-induced volatility, if allowed to continue, can only have a debilitating effect on public morale.

Despite such clearly defined threats, several powerful constituencies remain committed to defending the status quo and are determined to resist any attempt to shrink our governments, overhaul our social programs, or clean up our finances. Senior citizens are not going to surrender any part of their pensions or other benefits quietly. Seasonal workers, whether they are fishermen, loggers, or tourism industry employees, are not about to meekly accept a two-tiered unemployment insurance plan that would charge them higher premiums and pay lower benefits. Welfare workers, health care employees, and a whole range of helping professions are always ready to attack any proposed changes to existing programs, services, and institutions. The arts community can be equally zealous in protecting its turf, as the federal Liberals learned in mid-1995 when they attempted to terminate funding for Toronto's Harbourfront Centre. And Liberal Members of Parliament, who should be prepared to lead by example, put self-interest ahead of the national interest when they rejected any meaningful reform of their own gold-plated pension plan in early 1995.

Defenders of the status quo rely on numerous tactics to sway public opinion and the politicians who control the flow of public money. They circulate petitions and stage protests. They organize letter-writing, lobbying, and advertising campaigns. But language is their most potent tool. Language is used to define the debate and to disparage their opponents. It is effective because of the nature of our financial difficulties. After two decades of political delay and public denial, we are at a crossroads: a fiscal problem has turned into a crisis and threatens to become a catastrophe.

As we straddle the line between crisis and catastrophe, we have begun an urgent and anxious debate. Points are made and positions defended on the basis of statistics and studies. There are arguments about whether we should raise taxes or cut spending, and whether lower interest rates and higher inflation would solve our problems. But we are really discussing our values, and what hangs in the balance is the type of country we live in. Those who support the status quo claim to believe in a caring, compassionate society. They would have us believe that anyone who advocates balanced budgets or smaller government is selfish and mean spirited. They have succeeded in controlling the debate by using language to cast aspersions and demean the motives of their fellow citizens.

A fine example of this approach appeared on the op-ed page of the *Globe and Mail* in mid-April, 1995. A Dr. Paul Steinhauer, a physician at Toronto's Hospital for Sick Children and chairman of the Coalition for Children, Families and Communities, had written a letter to members of the Metro Toronto Council during their annual budget debate, and the *Globe* published an excerpt: "It is profoundly worrisome that, in this time of hardship, so many of our fellow citizens, and our politicians, are behaving according to the African proverb: When the water hole shrinks, the animals get meaner. We, as a community, have but two choices. We can all decide to look after Number One, in which case we will face a continuing erosion of our social capital and become less and less civic as a society. Or we can agree to shoulder our fair share of the burden and, by doing so, preserve the humanity and the equity of our society."

At a more fundamental level, we are often told, directly or indirectly, that to rationalize or downsize or eliminate government programs would be tantamount to dismembering the country itself. This was the starting point for a special two-hour edition of CBC Radio's *Morningside* broadcast one day in late January, 1995. "Can we afford to be Canadian?" host Peter Gzowski asked his guests and his listeners. The program was ostensibly an objective discussion about the difficulties we face in funding many government programs. But Gzowski was really asking a loaded question. The underlying assumption was that to be Canadian is to spend money on health care or unemployment insurance or welfare or regional development or any number of other programs. According to this line of reasoning, if we spend less we will be less Canadian, because our social safety net binds us together. It is the essence of the country. In other words, Canada *is* a welfare state.

This is a narrow, one-dimensional idea about what it means to be Canadian, because Canada has always been a work in progress rather than a finished product. And the evolution of this country has never been linear or straightforward. Over the past century, for instance, Canada has experienced a number of profound transformations. The rural society of the nineteenth century has become the urban society of the twentieth century. Towns and villages have become cities and suburbs. The deeply religious populace of pre–World War Two Canada has become the stridently secular populace of the post-war era. The French-English biculturalism that dominated our national consciousness for 200 years, from the mid-eighteenth to the mid-twentieth century, has been permanently altered by the multicultural potpourri of immigrants who have arrived from every corner of the globe.

Fundamental change has occurred intermittently, because no racial, ethnic, linguistic, or religious group has ever been able to impose its values, ideas, or beliefs permanently and say, "This is Canada. This is what it means to be Canadian." The country is simply too big and too diverse for that to happen. And so the definition of Canadian is always open to interpretation, and the status quo is periodically under review. We are now faced with the difficult and unavoidably painful task of making one of these major transitions. Our enormous national debt, and the oppressive annual carrying charges that come with it, have left us no choice but to reconsider and reduce our generous and comprehensive social safety net. And this change should be seen in its historical context.

The federal government acquired the powers and attitudes necessary to create a welfare state during World War Two, according to University of Toronto historian Michael Bliss. "The most lasting changes sparked by the war involved the intrusion of government in our lives," Bliss wrote in the May 1995 issue of *Saturday Night* magazine. "From 1939 to 1945, Ottawa ran a command economy. It intervened in the marketplace as often and as forcefully as seemed necessary to get the job done. It slapped on foreign-exchange controls; it put the whole country under wage and price controls. The government of Canada financed the war effort on terms it dictated — setting interest rates, confiscating private wealth when necessary, running up the national debt in a good cause.

"The state would never shrink to anything like its pre-war role. If Ottawa could spend without restraint to make war against the Nazis, if it could compel citizens to work for a greater good, if it could supersede the marketplace in the national interest, why couldn't it be just as vigorous in waging war against poverty, inequalities and ill health after the war? Collectivist ideas, collectivist methods were given a new legitimacy during the Second World War."

Along with legitimacy came confidence, ambition, and assertiveness. It was not enough to put the state to work eliminating poverty, hunger, and disease. There were all sorts of problems to be solved, needs to be met, and groups to be helped. Rather than controlling or deterring demand, governments encouraged demands. This process, the unchecked expansion of the welfare state, is the real reason why we are faced with the prospect of scaling back so many government programs.

A few astute observers of the welfare state have been making this point for years. One of them is John McKnight, director of the community studies program at Northwestern University in suburban Chicago and the subject of a three-part series on the CBC Radio program *Ideas* in January 1995. Over the past twenty years, he has written close to two dozen essays and academic papers assessing the impact of the relentless growth of social services. One of the central dilemmas facing developed societies is that services have become the fastest growing sector of their economies, and governments deliver more services than any other organization. Social services, McKnight argues, have proliferated because they are usually an expression of care and concern for the well-being of others. And there is no limit to how much care people need, or desire.

"Every modernised society, whether socialist or capitalist, is marked by the growing percentage of service in its gross domestic product, not only of services such as postal deliveries, catering, car repairs, etc., but social services such as marriage guidance, birth control counselling, care of the young, the adult and the old, and all that falls under the general heading of social help. This stage of economic development is distinguished by its unlimited potential since service production has none of the limits imposed by goods production — limits such as natural resources, capital and land. Therefore, the social service business has endless possibilities for expansion as there seems to be no end to the needs for which services can be manufactured.

"The politics of serviced societies are gradually being clarified. Public budgets are becoming strained under the service load. Many national and local governments find themselves in the unprecedented politics of deciding between competing services — should we give more to education and less to medicine. These choices create an impossible politics in traditional terms. Indeed, the allocation of services is so immune to political debate that many governments resolve the dilemma by deciding that we will have less wheat and more education, less steel and more medicine."

In Canada, the task of making such choices has become all the more difficult because of the mythology that has grown up around public services and programs. They have been elevated to the status of the single most important defining characteristic of the country. Hence, anyone who proposes significant cuts to, say, the budget of the CBC or to our myriad cultural organizations, cuts to health care budgets, cuts in social assistance benefits, or meaningful reform to unemployment insurance, is accused of attempting to destroy the fabric of the nation.

But it is an exaggeration to insist, as many people do, that social programs are the heart and soul of the nation. To suggest that we will go from compassionate to uncompassionate, or from tolerant to intolerant, simply because we spend less money, run fewer programs, and balance our budgets, is incorrect. To assert that we would be returning to the bleak and mean-spirited society of the past is to insult previous generations of Canadians. The Canada of our predecessors, a Canada without a cradle-to-grave social safety net, was undoubtedly a leaner society where hardship and injustice were more prevalent than they are today. But those shortcomings were always balanced by our predecessors' strengths, among them incredible resilience and resourcefulness, a capacity for compromise, a desire for consensus, and a preference for the peaceful solution.

As we confront a period of restructuring and retrenchment, those who preach generosity and compassion should have some faith in the basic decency and civility of the Canadian public. They should recognize that the pursuit of compromise and consensus led this country through difficult times in the past, and can help us resolve our current financial problems. They should understand that

Canada can remain a civilized, equitable nation even if the size and role of government is reduced, our budgets balanced, and our debt controlled. They should acknowledge that our social programs are privileges rather than rights. Lastly, they should accept the fact that the health of a nation depends upon the wealth of a nation.

If we are truly an enlightened society, we will all agree that we need to produce more wheat and steel and dozens of other products in order to maintain universal health care, good public education, and various essential public services. There is no way around the simple fact that a growing and dynamic economy is the basis for providing a strong and comprehensive social safety net. The creation of wealth is the only way to ensure the well-being of the citizen. If we hope to continue producing the wealth required to sustain our social programs, then we should recognize that freedom and opportunity are the heart and soul of this nation. They are powerful ideals that are capable of unleashing the initiative and enterprise of the individual citizen. Canada has become a dynamic, prosperous, and generous nation because of individual initiative and private enterprise rather than the comfort and security provided by social programs. Yet, initiative and enterprise are seriously threatened by a sprawling, overgrown public sector, by rising and increasingly onerous levels of taxation, and by our mammoth, uncontrolled government debt.

◄o►

Should our lenders ever officially declare this country bankrupt, every Canadian — man, woman, and child — will be forced to live with the consequences. There will be no great escape, no fresh start. We will pay for years, maybe for generations. The blizzard of spending and subsidization that created yearly deficits and mountains of debt will stop. The redistribution of wealth will stop because there will be no more wealth to redistribute. The foreign bondholders, the American, Japanese, and European institutions to whom we have surrendered our sovereignty, will not accept nickels and dimes on the dollar. They will insist upon being repaid in full, even if we merely pay off the interest on the interest and our children or grandchildren finally pay down the principal.

We will be a poorer nation economically. But the true price will be spiritual impoverishment. We will have failed where our predecessors succeeded. Previous generations of Canadians accepted the challenges that confronted them, and each of those challenges tested their character. Confederation-era Canadians displayed daring and vision when they built their railways. The men who marched off to war to defend democracy and the mother country possessed remarkable courage. Canadians of the 1930s had the tenacity to survive the Great Depression. Those of the post-war years possessed the ingenuity and enterprise to convert a military economy to a consumer one.

And what of us? What will we be remembered for? If we fail to solve the debt crisis, and it is far from certain that we will, then this generation will be known for its profligacy. We will have evaded the central challenge of our day and damaged one of the most blessed nations on earth. We will have a blemish on our record and we will leave a blight on our nation.

If we fail, the final quarter of the twentieth century will be remembered as an era of dubious leadership. It will come to be known as the era of Canada's financial decline, and the plot is as simple as the tale of the three little pigs and the big bad wolf. With a twist. The children's story begins with a house of straw and ends with a house of bricks, and a clever little pig safe and sound inside. Our prime ministers have written their own version of this kiddie's classic, but it does not end happily. Pierre Trudeau inherited a federal treasury made of bricks and turned it to sticks. Brian Mulroney reduced sticks to straw. And who knows where Jean Chrétien will leave us? But one thing is certain: there is a storm at our door.

Epilogue

SELLING
SACRIFICE

A s the end of the century draws closer, we will inevitably find ourselves immersed in reflection and contemplation about the past 100 years. We will relive our triumphs, celebrate our accomplishments, and lament our failures. As we embark on this exercise, we would do well to remember Sir Wilfrid Laurier's famous words to the Canadian Club of Ottawa in January 1904. The twentieth century, he boldly declared, would belong to Canada. For decades, teachers of Canadian history and their students have scoffed at this prediction because the United States has greatly overshadowed Canada on the world stage in terms of political power, military might, and economic clout. But in many ways, Laurier was right.

The twentieth century has been ours, because we have enjoyed most of its benefits and been spared most of its horrors. We have maintained peaceful relations with our neighbour to the south and lived free from fear of invasion. We have developed a stable

240

democracy, and reaped immeasurable rewards: national unity and political freedom, economic opportunity, social harmony, and cultural diversity. We have been blessed with tangible and quantifiable benefits: a rising standard of living and longer life spans, universal health care, free public education, and high rates of literacy. In short, we have attained a level of financial, territorial, and spiritual security unknown to previous generations of Canadians and almost unparalleled in the world today.

Looking back, we have much to be proud of. Looking ahead, we have much to be apprehensive about. The bonds that unite our federation have become worn and frayed after two Quebec referendums and three rounds of constitutional negotiations in fifteen years. The separatist movement in Quebec threatens the diversity, harmony, and opportunity which many of us have long taken for granted. We have compromised our financial security by the lavish and excessive demands we have placed on our governments over the past three to four decades. We have turned a low-debt, low-tax country into a high-debt, high-tax country. Fiscal pressures, much more than political or economic problems, are pushing us into a period of profound transition. We have no choice but to examine the scope and the costs of the welfare state. We are being forced to reassess the role of the state and the responsibilities of the citizen.

These are formidable undertakings. From many quarters we hear that such changes will benefit the wealthy and the powerful at the expense of the poor and the vulnerable. We are told that turmoil and adversity are inevitable. Yet Canadians in every part of the country have decided that we must confront our fiscal crisis at whatever cost, because there is a growing recognition that the price of evasion is disaster. That is the message voters have delivered in the 1990s by electing or re-electing governments in Alberta, Saskatchewan, Manitoba, Ontario, New Brunswick, and the other Atlantic provinces when all of those governments are committed to balancing the books. Even the federal Liberals, who campaigned on a job-creation platform, have made the same sensible choice, due largely to the influence of Paul Martin. This emerging consensus is a manifestation of the collective wisdom of the Canadian people and a legitimate reason for optimism about the future.

But it is only a beginning. We will require bold and forceful national leadership to maintain public support for the hard realities of fiscal reform: program cancellations, service reductions, and higher costs. We will need articulate and persuasive voices to convince the public to accept changes that will shift many costs and burdens from government departments and agencies to local communities, families, and even individuals. There is no escaping the fact that our leaders must sell sacrifice to a generation of Canadians that has been nurtured and schooled in a culture of growth.

This may seem like a thankless, even impossible task. But it needn't be, not if there are political leaders among us who can persuade ordinary Canadians that fiscal reform is the only morally responsible approach open to us. Our leaders must be able to offer hope rather than simply inflict hardship, and they must be capable of convincing skeptical voters that these changes will lead to a healthier government and a more robust economy. The transition from a comprehensive to a more modest welfare state should be seen as a source of renewal rather than turbulence, as the road to opportunity rather than adversity. It should be accompanied by a change in attitudes and priorities. We should focus our collective energy and initiative on the creation of wealth rather than the redistribution of wealth. And we should have faith in our resourcefulness, our resilience, and our capacity for self-reliance, as individuals and as a people, because these are the qualities that will make this exercise successful and ensure the well-being of the country.

The transition to a less comprehensive but more affordable welfare state should also be seen as a search for balance between the parsimony that characterized the first half of the century and the profligacy that distinguished the latter half. Prior to World War Two, our governments lacked the will and, in most cases, the resources to provide anything more than rudimentary care for the poor, the unemployed, the sick, and the elderly. Individuals were responsible for their own well-being. In the post-war era, what began as a noble attempt to mitigate the debilitating effects of poverty, joblessness, and sickness has turned into a free-for-all in which governments have tried to help anyone who showed up at the door or walked up to the counter. Our politicians gradually gave up on controlling the demands of the populace and devoted their energies and resources to meeting needs, however marginal or dubious.

The lesson that we should all learn from the experience of the past half-century is that the demands are infinite. They come from the wealthy as well as the poor, the strong as well as the weak, the young as well as the old, prosperous regions as well as disadvantaged ones. We acquired our gargantuan national debt by attempting to satisfy unlimited needs with limited resources. We did this during a period of unprecedented prosperity, a period free from war, famine, plague, and drought — all the curses that have afflicted human societies since time immemorial. As a result, the debt will loom in our national consciousness for decades as a symbol of the excesses of our era, just as the bread lines and work camps of the Dirty Thirties came to symbolize the deficiencies of pre–World War Two Canada. As we redefine the roles of the state and the citizen, we should keep in mind that we are looking for a politically sensible and fiscally sustainable approach to government.

We should not be distracted by the alarmists who allege that we are shredding the social safety net, destroying our governments, and undermining our communities. In fact, the opposite is true. Fiscal reform will help restore public confidence in our institutions and our leaders and will help save our social programs. It will impose a discipline on our governments and our political elites that has been missing for years. Our leaders will be forced to devote their efforts and resources to problems that need to be solved and can be solved.

If they are wise, they will establish national goals and objectives to guide us into the twenty-first century. They could begin by pledging to preserve those programs — health care, public education, and public pensions, along with less costly unemployment insurance and social assistance — that are essential to the good of every citizen. They should set a deadline for balancing the federal budget. They should work with their provincial counterparts to reduce our reliance on foreign borrowing and to develop a consensus on an acceptable level of debt. They should strive to lower taxes. They should draw upon the energy of all Canadians to create a dynamic economy. Above all, they should set out to restore hope and instill optimism so that Canadians can begin the next century with the confidence that it, too, will belong to them.

Index

Alberta, budget cuts under Klein,
    195–98, 202, 205–218
Alberta Community Employment pro-
    gram, 210–11
"Alternative Federal Budget, 1995,"
    152–53
Angus Reid surveys, 23, 198
Atlantic Canada Opportunities Agency
    (ACOA), 17, 65, 102, 119
Axworthy, Lloyd, 12, 90–92, 94

Baker, George, 17
Balanced Budget Act (Saskatchewan),
    222
Balanced Budget, Debt Repayment,
    and Taxpayer Protection Act
    (Manitoba), 222–23
Bank of Canada, 125, 131, 152
Barlow, Maude, 133–34, 147, 161
Battle, Ken, 93
Blakeney, Allan, 157, 184
Blenkarn, Don, 56, 63, 65
Bliss, Michael, 27–28, 235
bond rating agencies, 86, 129–30, 131,
    182, 185, 231
bonds. See government bonds
Brown, Janet, 169
Browne, Paul, 147
Bryden, John, 15–17
budgets of the federal government
    12, 37, 39–40, 44–48, 54, 60–61,
    63–65, 67–72, 81–83, 86–87,
117–18, 121, 130–32, 148, 217,
    223–24, 225, 230
business subsidies, 117–19

cabinet ministers, empire-building by,
    63–64, 67
Cameron, Duncan, 148
Camp, Dalton, 127, 128
Campbell, Kim, 80
Canada Assistance Plan (CAP), 72, 92,
    93, 181–82
Canada Health and Social Transfer
    (CHST), 92–94, 217
Canada Pension Plan (CPP), 169, 231
Canadian Auto Workers (CAW),
    151–52
Canadian Broadcasting Corporation
    (CBC), 53, 55, 108–109
Canadian Forum, The, 146, 148
Canadian Labour Congress (CLC), 16,
    153
Canadian Labour Market and
    Productivity Centre, 120
Canadian Luge Association, 109–110
Canadian Taxpayers Association, 201
Canadian Team Handball Federation,
    109
Cardinal, Mike, 210, 211
Carmichael, Ted, 32
changing times, 1–2, 148–49, 220,
    232, 234–35
Child Tax Credit, 54

Chrétien, Jean, 8, 12, 23, 107, 126
  and campaign deficit-reduction
    plan, 79–81, 85
  as finance minister, 45–46, 47
  government changes social
    programs, 92–95, 96–97
  leadership of to control debt, 78–
    79, 95–98, 225, 242–44
  responsiveness of to the public
    mood, 77–78, 86
  skilful public performance of,
    75–77, 78
civil service
  administration of social programs,
    158–59
  advise gradualism to Mulroney, 62
  busy approving grants, 99
  empire-building in, 8–9, 36
  employment steady under
    Mulroney, 55–56
  growth of in 1970s, 34–36
  job cuts, 90
"Common Sense Revolution" in
  Ontario, 171, 172, 174, 194
Commons finance committee, 82–84,
  86, 88, 92, 94, 165, 167
Compas Inc., 23
Cooper, Sherry, 125
Council on Canadian Unity, 110
Council of Canadians, 133–34
Courchene, Thomas, 119–20, 120–21
Coyne, Andrew, 167
credit rating agencies, 86, 129–30,
  131, 177, 182, 185, 231
Cross, Philip, 33–34, 39, 43–44,
  133–34
Crow, John, 147, 164
cultural life, public funding for, 15,
  118
currency crises, 124–26, 128, 131,
  231
  Mexican peso crisis, 86, 125
  in New Zealand, 226–28

Darcy, Judy, 190
Das, Satya, 213–14
de Cotret, Robert, 60, 64
deBever, Leo, 143–45, 188
debt of governments (accumulated
  deficits)
  growth of, 4–5, 137–39
  provincial debt in Ontario, 188

size of, 3–4, 6–7
Debt Retirement Act (Alberta), 216
debt-to-GDP ratio, 138
Decima Research polls, 23, 59
Deficit Elimination Act (Alberta), 205,
  216, 222
deficits (annual)
  eliminating, and reducing debt, 88
  Liberal plans to reduce, 79–81,
    83–95, 224–25
  under Mulroney, 56–74, 111, 221
  under Trudeau, 32–33, 50
deregulation of financial services in
  1980s, 140
Dinning, Jim, 214
Dodge, David, 224–25, 231
Dominion Bond Rating Service, 70,
  129, 182
"double-dipping" for government
  funds, 16, 101–102
Drainie, Bronwyn, 14–15, 18
Drew, George, 172–73, 174, 177–78
dumping of Canadian dollars, 1,
  124–25, 128, 131

economic boom of the 1980s, 70–71
Economic Council of Canada, 40–41
Economist, The, 150–51
education, changes in Alberta, 207,
  208–209, 211–12, 212–13
Eggleton, Art, 90
Ekos Research associates, 24
Environics Research Group, 197–98
Ernst & Young, 73
Established Programs Financing (EPF),
  92
Eves, Ernie, 190
expenditure control plan (1990), 68
expenditure review committee (1988),
  66

Family Allowance, 72
  indexation of payments, 39
  replaced by Child Tax Credit, 54
Federal Office of Regional
  Development – Quebec, 119–20
finance committee hearings, 21–22
finance ministers
  Michael Wilson, 60, 61–62, 64, 65
  of Trudeau years, 36–37, 44–46,
    47, 48–49
  See also Martin, Paul; Turner, John

financial markets of world, 6–7, 13, 31–32, 123–33, 134–37, 139–45, 238–39
    concerns about Canada, 83, 86, 142, 231–32
    major changes in 1980s, 140
    Ontario as borrower from, 185, 186
Foreign Investment Review Agency, 143
Fraser Institute, 2, 3, 196–97
free trade, 143, 160–61
Friedman, Thomas L., 134–35
Frost, Leslie, 175, 178

Galbraith, John Kenneth, 42
Getty, Don, 198, 199–200
globalization of trade and commerce, 1, 18–19
Goods and Services Tax (GST), 71, 72, 73
government
    core roles and responsibilities of, 112–13
    growth of under Trudeau, 34–36
    new powers of during and after Second World War, 235–36
    See also welfare state
government bonds, 13, 31–32, 125, 128, 129–30, 131, 140
    foreign investment in, 142–45
    trading of, 141, 142
    See also financial markets of world
"gradualist policy" of deficit reduction, 61, 62
grain subsidies, 64–65, 121
grants and subsidies, 99–106
    lead to dependence, 111
    obtaining government funding, 115–17
Guaranteed Income Supplement (GIS), 39, 94
Gwyn, Richard, 13, 46–47, 58
Gzowski, Peter, 96, 234

Harbourfront Centre (Toronto), 121, 232
Harris, Mike, 10, 171–72, 174, 176
    public support for, 190–94
Harrison, Trevor, 204
health care, 92–94, 96–97
    changes in Alberta, 207–208,

212, 213–14, 215–16, 217
    cuts in New Zealand, 229, 230
historic implications of fiscal crisis, 135–36, 239
human resources committee, public hearings of, 20–21
human rights law, 113–14

incomes, declining, 189, 194
indexation, 38–40, 45, 48
    deindexation of personal tax system, 71
    of OAS, 39, 63
    of personal exemptions and tax brackets, 39–40
    of transfer payments to individuals, 39
inflation, 47
    in 1970s, 38, 39–40
    "inflation dividend," elimination of, 39–40
information technologies, 18, 19
"infrastructure program" of Chrétien government, 11
interest groups. *See* special interest groups
interest on public debt, 160
    compound interest, 84–85
    growth of, 5, 6, 220
interest rates, 47, 82–83, 124, 125, 131, 134, 164, 168
    cost of to taxpayers, 23
    record levels in early 1980s, 28
International Monetary Fund (IMF), 22–23, 95
investment dealers, 128–29, 130

Jeffrey, Brooke, 53

Karpowich, Linda, 197
Kenney, Jason, 201, 202
Keynes, John Maynard, 42
Keynesian economics, 42, 43, 50
Klein, Ralph, 195–98, 201–218, 227
    education, health care, welfare programs changed by, 207–211
    praise and criticism for, 196–97, 211–16
Kroeger, Arthur, 93–94, 95

labour movement and NDP, 157, 187
Lalonde, Marc, 48–49

Langdon, Steven, 148
Lange, David, 228–29
Laughren, Floyd, 180, 184–85, 186, 188, 189
Laxer, James, 164–65
Lazar, Fred, 44
leadership, need for, 19, 24, 25, 78, 98, 242, 243–44
"left-wing" advocates, 20–21, 146–68, 225–26
  debt issue transcends "left against right," 10
  faith of in state action, 152–53
  See also New Democratic Party
Lindbeck, Assar, 106
lobbying of interest groups, 48, 51–52, 111, 115–16, 233
Lorje, Pat, 115, 117, 158–59
Lougheed, Peter, 198–99

McCallum, John, 224
McCrossan, Paul, 59–60
Macdonald, Donald, 44–45
McDonough, Alexa, 153–55
MacEachen, Allan, 47, 48, 69
Mackasey, Bryce, 38
Mackay, Bauni, 212–13
Mackness, William, 62
McKnight, John, 236–37
McLaughlin, David, 66–67, 69
McMillan, Charles, 61–62, 63–64
McQuaig, Linda, 147, 162–64, 168
Manley, John, 12
Manning, Preston, 80
Martin, Paul, 4, 6–7, 12, 106, 242
  comments of to Commons finance committee, 82–84
  converted to goal of deficit reduction, 83–95
  and cuts in Feb. 1995 budget, 87
  and failure of first budget (Feb. 1994), 81–83
  Jackson Hole speech of (Sept. 1995), 88, 89, 96
Massé, Marcel, 90, 107, 108
Maxwell, Judith, 43, 49
Mazankowski, Don, 66, 67, 68–69, 119
medicare, 96–97
Mexican peso crisis, 86, 125
Midland Walwyn, 229–30
Mimoto, Hideo, 33–34, 39, 43–44, 133–34, 163

Moody's Investors Service, 86, 129, 131, 135, 185, 225
Moscovitch, Allan, 91
Mulroney, Brian, 8, 9, 26, 29
  ambivalence of, 58–59, 60, 61, 62, 63
  and attack on fiscal restraint attempts, 51–53
  failure of to reduce deficits, 56–74, 111, 221
  and preoccupation with constitutional issues, 68, 69
  restraint promises of, 56–57, 60–61
  spending under, 54–55, 64–69
  tax increases under, 70–73
multiculturalism grants, 104–105, 113–15
mutual funds, 123, 141–42

Nash, Knowlton, 53
National Action Committee on the Status of Women (NAC), 110, 153
National Energy Program, 44, 48, 143
Neufeld, Edward, 129–30, 135–36
New Democratic Party (NDP)
  drop in public support for, 160
  federal, 148, 149, 150, 153–59, 160
  and mistaken view of deficit problem, 161–67
  and organized labour, 157, 187
  Rae's government in Ontario, 174, 182–90
  in Saskatchewan, 157–58, 159
  selection of new federal leader of, 153–55
New Zealand
  currency crisis in, 226–28
  reforms in, 228–30
Newell, Edward, 4, 118
Nicholson, Peter, 84–85
Nielsen, Erik, 60
Nixon, Robert, 176–77, 178–81
NovAtel, 199–200

Old Age Security (OAS), 54, 72, 94–95, 169, 231
  indexation of payments, 39, 63
Ontario
  "Common Sense Revolution" in, 171, 172, 174, 194, 223

economic upheaval in, 174
and growth of deficits and debt,
188
postwar growth in, 173–74
and spending under Peterson government, 176–82
operations committee of Mulroney
government, 66–67
Osbaldeston, Gordon, 34, 35, 112–13,
114–15, 121
"*Other* Red Book, The," 151, 153

Parizeau, Jacques, 10
parliamentary committee hearings
(1994), 20–22
pension reform, 94–95, 230–31
Perry, David, 165, 167
personal exemptions, indexation of,
39–40
Peterson, David, 175–77, 178
Pickersgill, Jack, 30–31, 49
Plaut, Peter, 128–29
Prince, Michael, 52–53, 54
"productivity collapse," 43
provincial governments, 138–39
in Quebec, 10, 223
in Saskatchewan, 157–58, 159
and small provinces' debt reduction, 10, 221–22
See also Alberta; Ontario
Public Accounts of Canada, 100–101
public opinion polls, 59
on deficits and debt, 168–69
and fall of Ontario's NDP government, 185–86
on Harris's government in Ontario,
191
on Klein's government in Alberta,
197–98, 211
on social programs, 23

Quebec, deficits in, 10, 223
Quigley, Neil, 230

Rae, Bob, 126–27, 174, 182–90, 227
Rai, Satish, 141
Rauhala, Ann, 149
recession
of early 1980s, 5, 47, 139
of early 1990s, 6, 68, 139, 182–83
"Red Book" of Liberal campaign
promises, 12, 77, 79

Reform Party, 74, 148, 201
regional development programs, 17,
65, 102–103
cut by Chrétien government,
117–18
ineffectiveness of, 120–21
political nature of, 119–20
Rice, James, 52–53, 54
Richards, John, 156–58
Robertson, Gordon, 31
Romanow, Roy, 157–58

Salomon Brothers Inc., 128–29
Salutin, Rick, 11
Saskatchewan, effective government in,
157–58, 159
Savoie, Donald, 64, 66, 119
Simeon, Richard, 14, 18–19, 24–25,
138
Simpson, Jeffrey, 193
Slater, David, 36, 41
Sloan, Linda, 212
social contract in Ontario, 187
"social justice versus economic success," 19–22
social policy review under Axworthy,
90–92
social programs
changes in Alberta, 207, 209–211
changes by Chrétien government,
92–95, 107–108
cuts in New Zealand, 229, 230
cuts in Ontario (1995), 190
expansion under Trudeau, 38
as factor in national debt, 133–34
growth of, 163–64, 235–37
increases in Ontario under
Peterson, 180–82
indexation of, 39
universality of, 158, 159
social values, 25, 233–35, 237–38,
239, 242–44
special interest groups, 61, 63, 157
alternate sources of funding of,
109–110, 122
as defenders of status quo, 232–34
demands of on government, 19–21,
159, 243
and funding review by Chrétien
government, 107–112, 117
grants and subsidies for, 99–106,
115–17

lobbying by, 48, 51–52, 111, 115–16, 233
and Ontario NDP, 183
report on funding of (1994), 15–17
spending by government
cuts in 1995 budget, 87–88, 117–18, 223–24, 230
cuts in Alberta under Klein, 195–98, 202, 205–218
cuts necessary, 74, 165, 168, 241, 242
excesses under Peterson in Ontario, 176–82
grants and subsidies, 99–106
growth of from 1960s to 1990s, 163–64
under Mulroney, 54–55, 64–69
under Trudeau, 12–13, 31, 33–34, 44–48, 50
Stackhouse, Reginald, 192–93
Standard & Poor's, 177
Statistics Canada studies, 72–73, 133–34
Steinhauer, Dr. Paul, 233–34
suburbanites' support of Harris government, 193–94

tax shelters, 41, 134, 165
Taxation Statistics, 166
taxes, 166–67
increases under Mulroney govern-ments, 2–3, 13, 70–73
policy under Trudeau, 39–44, 45, 48
public resentment of, 13, 73, 166, 189, 220–21
raises in Ontario, 177, 179–80, 189
Taxpayers' Protection Act (Alberta), 216
Taylor, Gary, 105
Toronto, effects of cuts on, 191–92
trade associations, government support of, 102, 118
trading floors, 140–41
transfer payments
definition of, 100
to individuals and organizations, 99–112, 115–19, 160
to provinces, 72, 92–94, 160, 230
Transport Canada, 90

Trudeau, Pierre, 8, 9, 26–29
announcement of spending cuts by (1978), 46–47
changing image of, 27
deficits under, 32–33, 50
growth of government under, 34–36
as poor economic manager, 9, 13, 28, 31–50, 221
spending under, 12–13, 31, 33–34, 44–48, 50
tax policies under, 39–44, 45, 48
Turner, John, 36–37, 39–40, 42, 44, 58, 60, 80, 139

unemployment insurance (UI), 38, 39, 72, 91, 94
changes in New Zealand, 229, 230

Via Rail, 54, 58–59

wage and price controls, 59–60
Walkom, Thomas, 183, 190
Wall Street Journal, 23, 126–28
welfare
changes in Ontario (1995), 190
cuts in New Zealand, 229
high rates in Ontario before Harris, 181–82
reforms in Alberta (1993–1995), 209–211
welfare state, 13–14, 24–25, 106, 230, 234, 235–36
checking growth of, 241, 242
See also social programs
Wente, Margaret, 115–17
Western Economic Diversification Fund, 65, 102, 119
White, Bob, 16, 147–48, 168, 185, 197
White, Randy, 17
Williams, Rick, 154
Wilson, Michael, 60, 61–62, 64, 65, 71–72, 181
workfare, 23
world economic situation. See financial markets of world

Young, Doug, 90